Empedocles' Shoe

Brecht's Plays, Poetry and Prose
Series Editors: John Willett, Ralph Manheim and Tom Kuhn

BRECHT COLLECTED PLAYS: ONE
Baal, Drums in the Night, In the Jungle of Cities, The Life of Edward II of England;
A Respectable Wedding; The Beggar or The Dead Dog; Driving Out a Devil; Lux in
Tenebris; The Catch

BRECHT COLLECTED PLAYS: TWO
Man Equals Man; The Elephant Calf; The Threepenny Opera; The Rise and Fall of the
City of Mahagonny; The Seven Deadly Sins

BRECHT COLLECTED PLAYS: THREE
Lindbergh's Flight; The Baden-Baden Lesson on Consent; He Said Yes / He Said No; The
Decision; The Mother; The Exception and the Rule; The Horatians and the Curiatians;
St Joan of the Stockyards

BRECHT COLLECTED PLAYS: FOUR
Round Heads and Pointed Heads; Fear and Misery of the Third Reich; Señora Carrar's
Rifles; Dansen: How Much is Your Iron?; The Trial of Lucullus

BRECHT COLLECTED PLAYS: FIVE
Life of Galileo; Mother Courage and Her Children

BRECHT COLLECTED PLAYS: SIX
The Good Person of Szechwan; The Resistable Rise of Arturo Ui; Mr Puntila and his
Man Matti

BRECHT COLLECTED PLAYS: SEVEN
The Visions of Simone Machard; Schweyk in the Second World War; The Caucasian
Chalk Circle; The Duchess of Malfi

BRECHT COLLECTED PLAYS: EIGHT *
The Days of the Commune; Antigone; Turandot

Poetry
POEMS 1913–1956
POEMS AND SONGS FROM THE PLAYS
BAD TIME FOR POETRY: 152 POEMS AND SONGS
FURTHER POEMS *

Prose
BRECHT ON THEATRE, VOL. 1
BRECHT ON THEATRE, VOL. 2
DIARIES 1920–1922
JOURNALS 1934–1955
LETTERS 1913–1956
SHORT STORIES 1921–1946
BRECHT ON ART AND POLITICS *
BRECHT ON FILM AND RADIO *(edited by Marc Silberman)*

* in preparation

Empedocles' Shoe

Essays on Brecht's poetry

edited by

Tom Kuhn and Karen Leeder

Methuen

1 3 5 7 9 10 8 6 4 2

This edition published by Methuen Publishing Limited
215 Vauxhall Bridge Road, London, SW1V 1EJ

Methuen Publishing Limited Reg. No. 3543167

© Tom Kuhn, Ronald Speirs, Hans-Harald Müller, Hilda M. Brown,
David Midgley, Elizabeth Boa, Anthony Phelan, David Constantine,
Ray Ockenden, Ermut Wizisla, Karen Leeder

The editors have asserted their moral rights

A CIP catalogue record for this book is available from the British Library

ISBN 0 413 75730 7

Designed by Bryony Newhouse

Printed and bound in Great Britain by
Creative Print and Design (Wales), Ebbw Vale

CONTENTS

POEMS AND TEXTS

ILLUSTRATIONS

ACKNOWLEDGEMENTS

The list of those we have to thank coincides closely with the list of names appearing on the contents page. We are grateful to our colleagues in German at Oxford University: for supporting the original seminar on which this book draws, for inspiring us with their contributions and for helping with the preparation of the essays. Perhaps we may single out David Constantine, who has contributed a scholarly essay on Brecht's sonnets, a foreword and several new translations, and who has been an inspiration throughout. We are grateful also to friends from Birmingham, Cambridge, Nottingham, Hamburg and Berlin. Erdmut Wizisla, at the Brecht Archive, has been, in particular, a constant source of information, wisdom and encouragement.

We should also like to apologise to the friends and colleagues whom we omitted to approach for contributions. These are many; but the book can only be so long. Some absent friends are at least represented by translations and poems: Michael Morley, Darko Suvin and Antony Tatlow by just one poem each, John Willett on almost every page. Without John's contribution, we would be nowhere.

Finally, thanks are due to the Warden and Fellows of New College, to the Faculty of Medieval and Modern Languages at Oxford, to Ruth Owen and Laura Bradley for help with editorial matters, and to Max Eilenberg and Elizabeth Ingrams at Methuen.

The editors and publishers record their gratitude to the following in relation to the use of copyright material:

Anvil Press for 'The Big Deal' and 'Two photographs' by Michael Hamburger from *Collected Poems 1941–1944*. Stefan S. Brecht for permission to translate a number of previously untranslated poems or parts of poems by Brecht, or to do new translations. The copyright in all such translations resides with Stefan Brecht. Andy Croft for 'Desert Island Discs' and 'After the Deluge' from *Nowhere Special*. Faber & Faber for an extract from 'Clearances' by Seamus Heaney from *The Haw Lantern* and 'A singing prayer' from *Selected Poems* by Christopher Logue. The Gallery Press for 'Brecht in Svendborg' by Derek Mahon from *Selected Poems*. Libris for 'Ophelia' by Georg Heym translated by Antony Hasler, which will appear in a forthcoming Libris volume, Georg Heym, *Poems* (Spring 2002), and for the illustrations and text of 'Here are the cities...' translated by John Willett from the *War Primer* (1998). Jamie McKendrick for 'When I'd brought the pair'. Methuen Publishing Ltd for 'Bad time for poetry',

ABBREVIATIONS

BBA the Bertolt-Brecht-Archiv in Berlin

BFA Bertolt Brecht, *Große kommentierte Berliner und Frankfurter Ausgabe*, 30 vols, edited by Werner Hecht, Jan Knopf, Werner Mittenzwei, Klaus-Detlef Müller and others (Berlin, Weimar, Frankfurt am Main, 1988–2000)

Plays Bertolt Brecht, *Collected Plays*, vols 1–7, translated by various hands, edited by John Willett, Ralph Manheim and Tom Kuhn (London, 1970–2001)

Poems Bertolt Brecht, *Poems 1913–1956*, translated by various hands, edited by John Willett and Ralph Manheim (London, New York, 1976, 1979)

Poems and Songs Bertolt Brecht, *Poems and Songs from the Plays*, edited and mainly translated by John Willett (London, 1992)

Brecht on Theatre *Brecht on Theatre: The Development of an Aesthetic*, edited and translated by John Willett (London, 1964)

Journals Bertolt Brecht, *Journals 1934–1955*, translated by Hugh Rorrison, edited by John Willett (London, 1993)

Letters Bertolt Brecht, *Letters 1913–1956*, translated by Ralph Manheim, edited by John Willett (London, 1990)

This is not just a volume of critical essays and commentaries, but also a book full of poems. Mindful of a readership who may not know German, we have taken care to provide quotations in English translation. However, it is essential to get a flavour of the original German, as far as this is at all possible, and of course in some cases a particular point is being made about the poetic language which requires illustration in German as well as English. So many of the poems are presented in parallel translation.

The translations perform several functions and are of several sorts. Some of the versions of shorter quotations embedded in the essays are relatively simple, literal translations, designed only to give the meaning of the words. The translations of whole poems, on the other hand, are intended to be readable as poems in their own right, whether with reference to a parallel German text or not. Finally, there are also poems in this volume which are departures from a Brechtian base, versions of and variations on his own poems or attempts to capture a poetic moment by means other than what is normally understood as translation. Such, for example, are the poems on pages 154, 225 and 222–4 by Jamie McKendrick, Tom Paulin and Derek Mahon. Theorists of translation tend to exploit the metaphorical potential of the term and tell us that all acts of communication involve a 'carrying over' or trans-lation. But it is easy enough to appreciate that some of these movements from one language to another, and from one poetic imagination to another, involve a more vigorous appropriation than others. One can make too much of the metaphor. As one can also insist too much upon the converse: the untranslatability of poetry. If we were not convinced that – difficult as it may be – something of the essential gesture of Brecht's poems could be conveyed in English, we would have never embarked on this project.

A great many of the translations of Brecht's own poems are derived from the magisterial volume edited by John Willett and Ralph Manheim, *Poems 1913–1956* (first published by Methuen in 1976) and its companion volume, *Poems and Songs from the Plays* (Methuen, 1990). In some cases, however, we have provided new translations. The work of detailed commentary on a poem sometimes revealed aspects which we felt a new translation could better capture (for example, the gestures towards hexameters and classical forms in our title poem). Besides, this book is, in part, about the life Brecht's poetry can have in English: there could be no more appropriate sign of lively engagement than the new versions supplied for this project and for this volume by poets such as David Constantine, Jamie McKendrick and Tom Paulin.

In quotations of whole poems we have, wherever possible, credited the translator by name; translations of fragments are either taken from the Willett/Manheim volumes, or are the work of the editors or the author of the essay in which they appear. References are given both to the English versions in the Methuen edition and to the five volumes of poems in the now standard German edition of Brecht's works, the *Große kommentierte Berliner und Frankfurter Ausgabe* (Aufbau and Suhrkamp, 1988–93, for volumes 11–15).

Finally, the book also contains several whole poems and quotations from poems which are not, in any sense, originally by Brecht. Some of these, such as the poems by Rimbaud, Heym and Benn quoted at the beginning of Hilda Brown's piece, or the Mehring poem quoted in the essay by David Midgley, are examples of texts which inspired and provide a context for Brecht's own lyric voice. However, we have also permitted ourselves to gesture in the other direction, and have included poems which, in their turn, are inspired and informed by Brecht's own verse. This is the subject of Karen Leeder's essay at the end of the volume. So we have the voices, not just of Constantine, McKendrick and Paulin, but also of Derek Mahon, Bernhard O'Donoghue, Ken Smith and others. Some of these were amongst those who participated in the Oxford celebrations of the Brecht centenary in 1998; others have subsequently allowed us to include their work in the book, sensitive to the possibility of a new use, and a new readership.

FOREWORD

The political poet

David Constantine

1. Poetry may come from and work upon any kind and context of human life. The language of poetry must be free to shape itself accordingly.

2. This may seem self-evident, but there have been times when restrictions were laid upon both the subjects and the language of poetry. Some subjects, some words, were held to be unpoetic. (Others – and this misapprehension is just as bad – were held to be intrinsically poetic.)

3. Generally it is modernity, the very conditions of present reality, the actual modern used language, that have been held unfit for poetry. But any poet who restricts himself thus goes into exile in never-never land.

4. Brecht, a great dramatist and an even greater poet, was determined in both genres to address the reality he lived in. What was that reality? The First World War, the German Revolution and its bloody suppression, the Kapp Putsch, hyper-inflation, Weimar, the Wall Street Crash, the Depression, Hitler, exile, the Second World War, East Germany, the Berlin uprising crushed by Russian tanks in 1953. Things like that. And among them, he lived out his life as a writer, an individualist and a hedonist.

5. Therefore his poetics were comprehensive. He discerned with regret a split in German poetry after Goethe into two lines: the pontifical and the profane. The pontifical, clearly, in its detested chief exponents George and Rilke, was quite unwilling and unable to treat the violent discrepancies of real life in the twentieth century. But Brecht did not simply opt for the profane. In that

line, too, poetry degenerates ('verlottert'), which is to say, it gets less fit. Instead, Brecht sought and achieved what he thought had been lost: the beautiful contradictory unity of poetic language. Which is to say, he restored to German poetry the power to say anything, to mix the languages and the tones, to range through the registers, in one and the same poem if appropriate, from the highest to the lowest. Because real life is like that: discrepant contiguities, contradictory coexistent possibilities.

6. The situation for English poets in the early twentieth century was perhaps rather better than for the Germans. I mean, in the question of the language at their disposal. After Wordsworth with his polemical insistence on the poetic resources of 'the real language of men' – and Hardy, his abundant invention and exploration of shapes, metres and diction – perhaps English was readier for whizz-bangs, duckboards, dugouts and poison gas. All the greater then, if that is the case, was Brecht's achievement.

7. Brecht is a good model for living poets in three particular ways:

   – First, because he shows you that modernity – its facts and its language, your real life in it – is your material and responsibility.

   – Second, because he shows you that the old forms – the sonnet, the epigram, elegy, psalm, chorale, blank verse, hexameter – are usable still and must be at your disposal, in the craft of poetry, as much as new forms of your own devising.

   – And thirdly, because he understood and if you study him you will understand it also: that in the struggle for a humane politics the responsibilities and the means of lyric poetry are quite peculiar, and by writer and reader they have to be attended to. He knew in practice as a poet that the poem itself, in its total working, its rhythm, the play of the language, the shifts of its appeal, must fetch the contradictions of our existence home to us, so that we know and feel the worst and want to alter and live better.

Frühling 1938

Heute, Ostersonntag früh
Ging ein plötzlicher Schneesturm über die Insel.
Zwischen den grünenden Hecken lag Schnee. Mein junger Sohn
Holte mich zu einem Aprikosenbäumchen an der Hausmauer
Von einem Vers weg, in dem ich auf diejenigen mit dem Finger deutete
Die einen Krieg vorbereiteten, der
Den Kontinent, diese Insel, mein Volk, meine Familie und mich
Vertilgen mag. Schweigend
Legten wir einen Sack
Über den frierenden Baum.[1]

Spring 1938

This morning early, Easter Sunday
There was a sudden snowstorm over the island.
Snow lay in between the greening hedges. My son
Fetched me out to a little apricot tree against the wall of the house
Fetched me from a line of verse in which
I was pointing the finger at men preparing a war in which
The continent, this island, my people, my family and I
May be erased. In silence
We laid a sack
Over the freezing tree.

Translated by David Constantine

INTRODUCTION

Empedocles' Shoe

1

When Empedocles of Agrigentum
Had garnered honour amongst his fellow citizens, along with
The infirmities of age
He decided to die. But since he
Loved some of them, by whom in turn he was loved
He didn't want to be wrecked before their eyes, but
Rather to be razed.
He invited them on an outing, not every one
This one or that he left out, so that in the choice
As in the whole undertaking
Chance might play its part.
They climbed Aetna.
The effort of the climb
Made for silence. No one missed
Wise words. At the top they
Caught their breath, their heartbeats steadied
They concerned themselves with the view, glad to have reached their goal.
Unnoticed, their teacher left them.
When they began to talk again, at first they noticed
Nothing, only later
Here or there a word was missing, and they cast about for him.
But he had long since walked off round the summit
In no great hurry. Once
He stopped and heard how
Way off beyond the summit
Their conversation started up again. The words themselves
Could no longer be made out: it was the onset of dying.
As he stood at the crater
His face averted now, not wanting to know any more of
What no longer concerned him, the old man bent down slowly
Carefully slipped from his foot the shoe and tossed it smiling
A few paces off, so that it shouldn't be
Found too soon, yet still in good time
Before it had rotted. Only then
Did he step to the crater. When his friends
Came home without him, looking out for him
Through the next weeks and months, bit by bit
So his dying began, as he had wished it. Still
Some held out, waiting for him, whereas others
Gave him up for dead. Still
Some stored up their questions for his return, whereas others
Sought the solution themselves. As slowly as the clouds
Drift from the sky, unchanging, diminishing merely

Ceding slowly when you're not looking, distant
When you seek them again, fused and confused now with others
So he receded from their ordinary ways, in an ordinary way.
Then a rumour started.
He had not died, he had not been mortal, they said.
Mystery enveloped him. People suggested
There was something beyond the earthly, the tide of human affairs
Might after all sometimes be altered: such was their chatter.
But at this time the shoe was found, the leather shoe
Tangible, worn, earthly! Left there for those who
When they can't see, turn at once to belief.
So the end of his days
Had after all been natural. He had died like anyone else.

2
Others however describe these events
Differently: in fact this Empedocles had
Sought to secure for himself honour as a god and
By his mysterious disappearance, his crafty
Leap, unwitnessed, into Aetna, to establish the myth that he was
Not merely human, not subject to
Mortal laws of decay. But that
His shoe had caught him out, falling into the hands of men
(Some go further, the crater itself, angered at
Such a beginning, simply spat
Out the degenerate's shoe). But we would rather believe:
If he didn't indeed untie the shoe, then it was just
He'd forgotten our foolishness, not thought how we'd hasten
To make what's obscure obscurer, and how we would rather believe
Some far-fetched story than seek a sufficient cause. As for the mountain
It wasn't outraged at anyone's carelessness, nor did it believe
Some mortal wanted to dupe us into honouring him as a god
(For the mountain has no beliefs and isn't concerned with us)
Rather, spitting fire as it always does, it threw out
The shoe for us, and so his pupils
Already busy scenting a mystery
All too busy spinning profound deep metaphysics!
Suddenly grasped in their hands, troubled, that tangible shoe
Worn, made of leather, earthly.

Translated by Tom Kuhn *and* Myfanwy Lloyd[1]

7

Introduction

Tom Kuhn

Empedocles' Shoe

Empedocles was one of the pre-Socratic philosophers. His dates are uncertain, probably approximately 494–434 BC. He came from Sicily. He was, it appears, politically active and he may also have worked as a doctor. There were fewer boundaries between the professions and the specialisms then; he felt free to engage with, and to write about, everything that moved him. He was a favourite subject for Hellenistic biographers, but not much of the evidence that comes from such sources is considered reliable. We do know that he wrote a number of works of both natural science and metaphysical speculation, all of them in verse. So he was a poet too. However, none of his works has survived – except in the substantial fragments and gists quoted by other authorities.[2] The intriguing, frustrating uncertainty about the mediation of Empedocles' writings calls to mind Brecht's own reflections on whether his works will survive, or indeed should survive. In his more youthful, culturally apocalyptic vein (in the poem 'Vom armen B.B.' / 'Of poor B.B.', for example) he held out little hope for any survivals from our 'provisional tenancy' of the cities. In later years he was more often sanguine: future generations ('An die Nachgeborenen' / 'To those born later') might have little use for a pre-revolutionary literature, conceived in dark times. None the less, like so many poets, he kept returning to ruminate on the prospects for his own poems and for his own immortality. One of his collaborators recorded that he asked her to remember his poems by heart, so that they would not be lost in the forthcoming war and the destruction of Europe.[3] And one of his poems, 'Besuch bei den verbannten Dichtern'/'Visit to the banished poets', envisages a trip with Dante down into the underworld, where he meets the great poets of the past – and also miraculously stumbles across those lost to the tradition. The poem ends:

> The laughter
> Was echoing still, when, from the darkest corner
> Came a cry: 'Hey you, do they know
> Your verses by heart? And those who know them
> Will they prevail and escape persecution?' – 'Those
> Are the forgotten ones', Dante said quietly
> 'In their case, not only their bodies, their works too were destroyed.'
> The laughter broke off. No one dared look over. The newcomer
> Had turned pale.[4]

This is one of many moments in Brecht's poetry that reflect on the problem of memory and of memorialisation. 'About the way to construct enduring works', 'I need no gravestone', 'Why should my name be mentioned?': these other titles make the matter clearer.

That is perhaps one tenuous reason to recall Empedocles when we remember Brecht. But why was Brecht interested in him? Why, in 1935, did he write a long poem about him and include it in the 'Chronicles' section of his great collection, *Svendborger Gedichte/ Svendborg Poems*? It seems unlikely that he knew all that much about Empedocles; he certainly didn't need to in order to write his poem. Brecht's knowledge of classical literature was good, but it was in the Latin canon above all that he knew his way about, and Empedocles is relatively obscure. He presumably picked up the conflicting legends of the Greek philosopher's death from later accounts by Latin authors (see p. 189). Maybe he knew that some scholars think it likely Empedocles died in exile in the Peloponnese. Although he was of a wealthy family, tradition presents him as a democrat and champion of the people, and his political activity may have won him enemies. A biography such as this would surely have appealed to Brecht, who, only a couple of years after 'Empedocles' shoe' and still in exile near Svendborg in Denmark – on the rim of the volcano that was pre-war Europe – wrote the poem 'Verjagt mit gutem Grund'/'Driven out with good reason'. Moreover, for Plutarch and Hippolytus, Empedocles is one of the first theorists of the state of exile. A main theme of his *Purifications* and *Physics* was the necessary fall of the thinking soul from an original state of blessedness: 'Among them am I too now, an exile from the gods and a wanderer'. 'And he calls birth by the gentlest of terms, a journey abroad' (Plutarch, *On Exile*).[5] To the modern reader, it smacks of some amalgamated pre-Christian and post-Freudian theory of the human condition. Another of Empedocles' subjects was the continual flux of being and matter. His *Physics* described a complex cyclical history of the universe, a sort of dialectic of the elements ruled by the overarching principles of Love and Strife: 'these things never cease their continual exchange of position, at one time all coming together into one through Love, at another again being borne away from each other by Strife's repulsion'.[6] Finally, he asserted a theory of metempsychosis, contending that the souls of the wise in the end become gods – a belief which provoked later commentators (Horace, Ovid, Brecht) to chide the philosopher and his followers, for his chutzpah and their foolishness.

Fun though it is to seek out resonances and to try to accommodate Empedocles in Brecht's pantheon of exiled intellectuals and theorists of historical change (Lao-Tsû, Lenin and the rest), none of this is what the poem 'Empedocles' Shoe' is about. It is a narrative poem in the characteristic irregular, unrhymed form of many of his exile poems, here given a rhetorical lift by the poised expressions and hexameter echoes; and, as Ray Ockenden demonstrates below, it is about a teacher and his pupils, or, better still, about the initiation of a pedagogy. For 'at first they noticed / Nothing'. It is only in their speculations about his death that his followers embark on their most important lesson, and begin to seek the solution themselves. You only prove yourself as a teacher by your absence. As in many other poems and remarks by Brecht on the subject of teaching, it is the contribution of the pupils which is crucial.

At the same time, this is a poem about the perils of installing gurus, and of leaping at every opportunity to 'make what's obscure obscurer'. In view of the later reception of Brecht this is pertinent. There have always been those who have sought to dismiss Brecht's literature because of his political sympathies. To some, it seems incomprehensible that a Communist should exercise himself in a medium so fragile as poetry; and Brecht has been accused of ungently ramming his opinions down his readers' throats (a glance at our title poem should dispel that notion). However, there have also always been disciples. On the left, there was a time when Brecht was hailed not simply as a good and brave poet but as some-one with a philosophy of the political life which we could all, uncritically, embrace. In their insistence on the sanctity of Brecht's messages, such friends may have been almost as harmful to a proper reception of the work as the detractors. Ronald Speirs, Elizabeth Boa and David Constantine give us very differing insights as to why we might wish to distance ourselves from at least some parts and aspects of the *œuvre*. We have moved on, in politics and gender politics, to such an extent that some of the poems may now appear quaint, historical, naïve, even offensive.

Use-value, characteristics of the legacy

It is not the purpose of this volume to win *uncritical* readers for Brecht. On the contrary, like Empedocles' sandal, his poems can be treated as a very tangible, earthly, concrete legacy. It is now up to us to work out what we want to do with them.

The insistence on 'use-value' is Brecht's own. In a famous early essay, he set out the principles by which he hoped to wrest poetry back into the realm of 'useful' communication, back into this world: the perfumed products of pure lyricism, he claimed, with a broad swipe at the traditional understanding of poetry, 'are too far distanced from the original gesture of the communication of a thought or of a feeling which might be of some advantage, even for a stranger. All great poems have the value of documents.'[7] There is another poem from the same collection as 'Empedocles' Shoe', 'Die Teppichweber von Kujan-Bulak ehren Lenin' / 'The carpet weavers of Kujan-Bulak honour Lenin'; it tells the story of poor Turkestani townsfolk who make a collection to honour Lenin and then decide to use the money to kill off the mosquitoes on the local swamp:

> So they helped themselves by honouring Lenin, and
> Honoured him by helping themselves, and thus
> Had understood him well.[8]

The best way to show your respect for someone is to do something *useful* with their legacy. Yet another (earlier) poem, 'Kohlen für Mike'/'Coal for Mike', describes how the brakemen on the trains of the Wheeling Railroad used to throw a lump of coal into the garden of Mike's widow as they thundered past: 'For Mike!', whose lungs had given up the struggle on the coal trains of Ohio, but who was not forgotten. A small, concrete gesture which illustrates memorably that the personal may also be political, and which invites us to reflect on the pragmatics of right living. The coal was surely useful, remembering Mike was useful, recalling how Mike was remembered (like recalling how the carpet weavers honoured Lenin) may now be useful to us too. Memorials such as these may even help us to live better – all the more because they don't take their normal forms of setting up busts and giving speeches.

In this volume, Erdmut Wizisla proposes the most concrete, immediate and political use for one Brecht poem, in a powerful argument for the adoption of Brecht's 'Kinderhymne'/'Children's Anthem' as a new German national anthem. But let us not lose sight of the other smaller gestures – more marginal, more dissident poems, more marginal, dissident readings – which may also be productive, as Ray Ockenden shows. David Constantine writes (pp. 158–60) about a poem which suggests how we may make practical use even of the legacy of our enemies, the 'Sonett vom Erbe'/'Sonnet concerning the legacy'.

It has not always been easy. At the end of the book, Karen Leeder considers the reception of the Brechtian inheritance by his successor-poets, and reflects on the usefulness of a poetics and a 'style'. Some have felt compelled to engage in poetic dialogue with the 'master', admired or resented, embraced or resisted. The danger, amongst the poets of post-war Germany, that Brecht be alternately 'honoured as a god' and denounced as a crafty myth-maker was not inconsiderable. Internationally, inevitably, the response has been more muted. The problems of translating a poetic *œuvre* adequately are almost overwhelming. And there are two characteristics, more particular to Brecht, which have inhibited the process of reception. Much of Brecht's poetry is, unsurprisingly and blatantly, political; and the political is often held, in the European traditions, to be at variance with the lyric. The problem of Brecht's outspoken political stance is confronted directly by Elizabeth Boa. In some poems his whole concept of 'use' was predicated on a specific political context and on a notion of Marxian historical progress. He wondered whether his poems would be read after the revolution; Elizabeth Boa wonders how we can read his poems after the collapse of a Communist alternative in Europe. Secondly, Brecht's poems, unlike much of his drama and his theory, have little of the experimental 'make-it-new' danger of high modernism; many of them are modest, more respectful of tradition than one might have expected. David Constantine has perhaps the most to say about that, in his discussion of Brecht's exploitation of the sonnet form; Ronald Speirs, Hans-Harald Müller and Hilda Brown, in commentaries on single poems, talk about a context in the traditions of certain motifs and tropes; David Midgley discusses the more contemporary context of a burgeoning fashion for cabaret and 'city culture'; and Anthony Phelan reflects not only on the relation of Brecht's 'Manifesto' to the *Communist Manifesto*, but also on its distant roots in the philosophical poems of classical antiquity. And all of the contributions to this book – whether close readings of individual poems in their historical and modern contexts, or overviews of a form, a mode, a method – are investigations and revelations of what we, twenty-first-century readers, can derive from reading, and rereading, this poetry.

Though we might sometimes wish to be sceptical about that notion of use, in his insistence on productive communication Brecht redefined the poetic, at least in German culture. Although he was never so experimental as the Surrealists, or the Dadaists, or the 'concrete poets' of the 1960s, he discovered, as all the essays demonstrate, new subjects for poetry, and new ways of speaking. Even in English: when the first great anthology of Brecht's poems came out in translation (in 1976, twenty years after the poet's death) it was greeted by Stephen Spender as 'one of the major poetic achievements of the present century', and George Steiner paid fulsome tribute: 'Brecht was that very rare phenomenon, a great poet for whom poetry is an almost everyday visitation and drawing of breath'.[9]

Only a fraction of Brecht's complete output was actually published in his lifetime. The new German edition, the *Große kommentierte Berliner und Frankfurter Ausgabe*, now contains over 2,300 poems, crammed into five fat volumes.[10] To this quantity we must add the quite exceptional variety of the work. Brecht wrote about almost everything, and in almost every poetic form. He wrote Shakespearean pentameters and rhyming couplets, rough *Knittelverse* (a traditional form of very irregular four-stressed rhyming lines) and classical hexameters (including the unfinished 'Manifesto' discussed below), closely rhymed songs and loosely skipping narratives, and he wrote page upon page in his own characteristic irregular, unrhymed forms (like the Empedocles poem). He wrote sonnets (*see* Constantine) and ballads and odes. He wrote long narrative poems and philosophical poems (*see* Phelan again), and he wrote epigrams and lapidary four-liners. He even wrote prose poems. He wrote children's jingles and alphabet poems, marching songs and political anthems (*see* Wizisla), graffiti and aphorisms, love poems of all varieties (*see* Constantine again, and Müller, Kindt and Habeck), laments for friends who had died in the struggle and hymns in praise of the Party and its principles (*see* Boa). He wrote elegiac reflections on the views from his various study windows, and he wrote calls to arms to the enemies of Fascism. His vision of the place of poetry was such that – like the poets of antiquity by whom he was inspired – he could engage with, and write poems about, everything that moved him. The range is staggering and unmatched by any German poet (perhaps by any poet in any language) since Goethe. Like Goethe, Brecht never stopped writing. There were times when the verses flowed from his pen at the rate of several a day, and times when they trickled, or meandered through revisions and redrafting, but they never dried up. Even the last half-year of his life, when he was ill and tired, saw the composition of some thirty new poems. In some quite astonishing way, it just came naturally to him. Every new observation, every reflection, every occasion seemed to call forth a poem.

It follows from this that it is very hard to write in general terms about Brecht's poetry. To every generalisation there are exceptions. It follows also that the contributions in this book, although they may offer a flavour of some of these many aspects, do not aspire to anything even approaching a comprehensive tribute.

And yet that very idea – that his poems were occasioned by events or observations of the outside world, that they were 'occasional' in the full sense of that word – may offer us one way into the mass and variety of his verse. For example, Brecht wrote a great many love poems, and in his hands it is an eminently pragmatic genre (as we see in the discussion of perhaps the most famous example of all, 'Erinnerung an die Marie A.' / 'Remembering Marie A.'. In later years, Brecht's love lyrics left behind this cynical and manipulative pose, and graduated, for example, into a remarkable dialogue in sonnets, both erotic and tender, with Margarete Steffin (*see* Constantine, and the example on pp. 152–3). Likewise, Brecht's children's poems were written as a part of a father's pedagogic relationship with his own children, above all with his son, Stefan, who was just ten when Brecht wrote 'Der Pflaumenbaum' / 'The plum tree', the famous rhyme which provoked Walter Benjamin's commentary on the part of nature in the work of the exiled political poet:[11]

> The plum tree in the yard's so small
> It's hardly like a tree at all.
> It's got a railing round
> To keep it safe and sound.

It is not inappropriate to imagine Brecht introducing his son to a tree in the garden of the home he made in anti-Fascist exile in Denmark, and discussing the nature of fruit trees, or the more abstract relationship between resources and productivity:

> The poor thing can't grow any more
> Though if it could it would for sure.
> There's nothing to be done
> It gets too little sun.[12]

A third example is provided by the great political songs of the later twenties and thirties. Many of these were direct responses to commissions and requests from comrades and associates, who *needed* such verses to carry the anti-Fascist fight into new contexts and new countries. The 'Einheitsfrontlied'/'United Front song' (1934) makes specific reference, even in its title, to the Communist International's new policy of cooperation between the forces of Communism and Social Democracy. Hanns Eisler, Brecht's most fruitful musical collaborator, immediately set the words to music, and the song went on to enjoy an almost legendary popularity in the German workers' movement and in the GDR.

> By the left, two, three! By the left, two, three!
> Comrade, there's a place for you!
> Take your stand in the workers' united front
> For you are a worker too.[13]

These are the easy examples. I shall go on to argue that the rest of Brecht's lyric output shares these characteristics: that it is, emphatically of *this* world (that word 'earthly' in the Empedocles poem is crucial), that it is, in some sense, occasional, that it strives, like the poems I have quoted, to be very directly communicative, and that it seeks always to unite the 'useful' with the pleasurable.

Short overview of a 'bad time for poetry', in three parts

All writers' lives and works get divided into three: early, middle and late. It is our misplaced desire for coherence, clarity, symmetry. The distortions are the greater when these categories are reinforced by loaded metaphors which may have little to do with the poetic imagination: immaturity, maturity, decline, or thesis, antithesis, synthesis. In Brecht's case, such schemata overlook all sorts of contradictory simultaneities and non-simultaneities; that there are *at least* two 'early' Brechts; that the 'middle' has hopelessly unclear limits; that Brecht did not live to old age (he died at fifty-eight), and so on. None the less, in what follows I reproduce the pattern, and remain very conscious of the dubious distinctions and gaps it entails. Brecht was born into the old German *Kaiserreich* and his writing took off after the First World War under another political system, the Weimar Republic; then he went into anti-Nazi exile and wandered for some sixteen years (broadly speaking, through Scandinavia and to California); and then he returned, to another system, that of the newly founded German Democratic Republic. Born in Augsburg in 1898, exiled in 1933, he returned to Germany in 1948–9, and died in Berlin in 1956.

(i) 1916–33

Brecht started his poetic career as a song writer. The first great collection, *Bertolt Brechts Hauspostille/Bertolt Brecht's Domestic Breviary* (1916–25), is packed with energetic, witty, romantic/anti-romantic verses and ballads, nearly all of them set to music: to Brecht's own strummed guitar chords, to the tunes of popular songs, and to the compositions of his schoolfriends. These are the poems discussed in the first three essays (by Speirs, Müller and Brown). They find their inspiration in the cabaret songs of Frank Wedekind, in the satirical ballads of François Villon and in the decadent romanticism of Arthur Rimbaud. Many of them seem to have been improvised spontaneously amongst a loose band of friends in Brecht's hometown of Augsburg.[14] An earlier notebook collection is entitled 'Lieder zur Klampfe von Bert Brecht und seinen Freunden'/'Songs to the Guitar by Bert Brecht and his friends', and in that collection 'Baals Lied'/'Baal's song', which now has the distinction of being the very first piece in the first volume of poems in the German edition, is expressly described as having been written, 'Together with Lud [i.e. Ludwig Prestel] on the 7 June 1918 at night by the river Lech':[15]

> If I find a well-stacked woman, then I take her in the hay,
> Air her knickers, skirts and so on, in the breeze – for that's my way.
>
> If she bites me in flagrante, then I wipe her down with hay,
> Mouth and teeth and crotch, gallantly: nice and clean – for that's my way.
>
> If the wench gets in a fever of excitement at our play,
> I salute and laugh and leave her, friendlily – for that's my way.

Translated by Tom Kuhn [16]

It was perhaps this shared life of the imagination, however ado-lescent it may appear, which encouraged Brecht to develop his later concept of readers of poetry, not as passive receivers, but as active participants in some poetic process. His first play, *Baal*, of which the language and the extreme subjectivist focus perhaps justify descrip-tion as a 'lyric' rather than 'epic' drama, was also conceived in this climate of unfettered productivity, collaboration and improvisa-tion. It presents us with an anti-heroic portrait of the 'genius' poet, all importantly as a profane social (and anti-social) performer, not as some lonely, muse-inspired dreamer.

The early poetry, up to the mid-1920s, is a poetry of many voices and many poses, few of which can be taken very seriously. There are more or less frivolous erotic and love poems (*see* Müller), icono-clastic revelling ballads of pirates and adventurers, songs of drunkards and drowning girls (*see* Brown), hymns to the special pleasures of nature and of life, and scurrilous rhymes dedicated to his friends. But there are also already works out of which a social conscience speaks directly and firmly. 'Von der Kindesmörderin Marie Farrar' / 'On the infanticide Marie Farrar' is a *Bänkelsang*-style ballad, a moral tale of a poor teenage abortionist. But with a differ-ence. The grinding attention to the awful detail of her fate over nine long verses and the pathos of the insistent refrain enable Brecht to turn around the moral message: it is not the girl we are invited to judge, as we might be by the kind of nineteenth-century ephemeral ballad on which Brecht's song is modelled; rather, we learn to question the social basis of the very morality of those who would pass such a judgement. The rage and the pity cry out from Brecht's confident lines.

> You who bear your sons in laundered linen sheets
> And call your pregnancies a 'blessed' state
> Should never damn the outcast and the weak:
> Her sin was heavy, but her suffering great.
> > *Therefore, I beg, make not your anger manifest*
> > *For all that lives needs help from all the rest*[17]

A still more important indicator of what was to come is provided by the 'Legende vom toten Soldaten' / 'Legend of the dead soldier' of 1918. The twenty-year-old poet pillories the German High Command for its exhortations to stand firm in the dying moments of the war and lambasts the pillars of the corrupt remnants of Imperial Germany. Nineteen limping, tripping, closely rhymed four-line stanzas relate the macabre tale of the soldier who has already died a hero's death and is now disinterred and sent out to fight once more. The song became a popular favourite in the cabarets and was the object of several press protests and court cases in the Weimar Republic. It was a potent irritant. Brecht gave it pride of place as the opening poem of his first exile collection, *Lieder Gedichte Chöre / Songs Poems Choruses*, published in Paris in 1934; and the Nazis responded by citing it in justification when they stripped Brecht of his citizenship the very next year.

The move to Berlin in the mid-1920s is an early watershed in Brecht's career, and towards the end of the decade, and especially in the years around 1930, there is an even more outspoken social engagement, even an explicit revolutionary purpose. Brecht has already come a long way in his reflections about the proper contexts and uses of poetry. From the outset he had been concerned to reach a different readership, to create a new readership for poetry, and to do that he was prepared to experiment with the medium. He was eager to exploit graffiti, posters and ephemeral forms; he was more willing to publish his work in cheap leaflets than in precious editions; and he was just as interested in performance as in publication. As well as gaining a reputation for himself as a reciter, he of course also included poems, songs and chants in cabaret programmes and wrote them into his own plays. He collaborated with a string of important composers, most notably Kurt Weill and Hanns Eisler. It is not for nothing that the works he composed with these men retain their place in the cabaret repertoire: 'Song of the inadequacy of human endeavour', 'Barbara Song', 'September Song', 'Pirate Jenny', not to mention the 'Mackie Messer Song', have been recorded by any number of modern performers. In the years 1927 to 1930, he also put together a further collection – *Aus einem Lesebuch für Städtebewohner / From a Reader for Those who Live in Cities*, the subject of David Midgley's essay – a collection not of songs this time but of role-poems and of bitter observations of the trials and strategies of modern living, conceived with the idea that they might be distributed on gramophone record as well as in his own pamphlet series, the *Versuche/Experiments*. And his involvement in film and radio was just beginning. He was perhaps attempting to re-function the institution of lyric poetry, to resituate it within the literary and wider social field, in much the same way as he was, at the same time, trying to revolutionise the function and purpose of the theatre with his *Lehrstücke* [learning plays].

(ii) 1933–47

Such experiments with the new technologies and with more public contexts for his verse were to some extent cut short by the arrival of a National Socialist government in 1933, and by Brecht's own departure into exile the day after the Reichstag fire (28 February – he had just turned thirty-five). At the same time, however, the renewed urgency of securing a wide distribution for a political message in these far from easy circumstances drew him further into experiments with the forms and media of his poems. In exile, he wrote poems (the 'German Satires' of the *Svendborg Poems*) for radio broadcast into Germany (and reflected on the exigencies of doing this in an essay 'On Rhymeless Verse with Irregular Rhythms')[18] and he contributed poems to pamphlets illegally smuggled into the country. In America, during the war, he and Ruth Berlau produced an anti-war booklet, the *Kriegsfibel/War Primer*, with 'photo-epigrams', terse four-line poems alongside pictures cut out of news magazines (we have included two examples in our illustrations). In the dying months of the war the Allied Psychological Warfare Division even dropped a Brecht poem on to the bombed cities of his homeland.[19] Although Brecht may not have known about that particular example, there is no question but that by this time he was content, indeed convinced, that poetry should be able to take a place in the modern world of communication, and to play a part wherever there was even a chance that people might talk, and read, and listen.

After 1933, few could hope the proletarian revolution was in immediate prospect. The poetry of the exile and of anti-Fascism had to reckon with a longer and more complex struggle. The defiant stance of 'Vorwärts, und nie vergessen',[20] (known in English as the revolutionary workers' song 'Forward, we've not forgotten'), was no longer adequate to the situation. The forum in which a Brecht poem might find its hearers was fragmented and endangered. The poetry of the later 1930s provides us both with our title poem and with our epilogue poem, and is discussed in several of the essays, notably those by Boa, Constantine and Ockenden (although these range more widely also). If the key collection of the exile years, the *Svendborg Poems* (mostly 1934–8), nevertheless seems somewhat under-represented, that is because another recent volume of critical essays, *Brecht's Poetry of Political Exile*, is devoted entirely to that collection. It should be treated as a companion to the present book.[21]

In 1938, comparing the *Svendborg Poems* with the *Domestic Breviary*, Brecht commented, 'From a bourgeois point of view there has been an astonishing impoverishment'. The richness of feeling and language in the *Breviary* had given way to a one-sided, cool, political agenda. 'Capitalism has compelled us to fight. It has laid waste to our surroundings. I no longer walk "in lonely contemplation in the woods", but amongst police spies.'[22] What more succinct expression of the necessity of a political aesthetic could there be? Brecht wants us to acknowledge the loss, it is something he comes back to time and again in the poems themselves. In one of the greatest of this period, not included in the *Svendborg Poems* (although it refers to the sea channel just beyond the bottom of his garden in Svendborg), he calls it a 'Schlechte Zeit für Lyrik' / 'Bad time for poetry' (*see also* p. 193):

> Ich weiß doch: nur der Glückliche
> Ist beliebt. Seine Stimme
> Hört man gern. Sein Gesicht ist schön.
>
> Der verkrüppelte Baum im Hof
> Zeigt auf den schlechten Boden, aber
> Die Vorübergehenden schimpfen ihn einen Krüppel
> Doch mit Recht.
>
> Die grünen Boote und die lustigen Segel des Sundes
> Sehe ich nicht. Von allem
> Sehe ich nur der Fischer rissiges Garnnetz.
> Warum rede ich nur davon
> Daß die vierzigjährige Häuslerin gekrümmt geht?
> Die Brüste der Mädchen

Sind warm wie ehedem.

In meinem Lied ein Reim
Käme mir fast vor wie Übermut.

In mir streiten sich
Die Begeisterung über den blühenden Apfelbaum
Und das Entsetzen über die Reden des Anstreichers.
Aber nur das zweite
Drängt mich zum Schreibtisch.

[Yes, I know: only the happy man
Is liked. His voice
Is good to hear. His face is handsome.

The crippled tree in the yard
Shows that the soil is poor, yet
The passers-by abuse it for being crippled
And rightly so.

The green boats and the dancing sails on the Sound
Go unseen. Of it all
I see only the torn nets of the fishermen.
Why do I only record
That a village woman aged forty walks with a stoop?
The girls' breasts
Are as warm as ever.

In my poetry a rhyme
Would seem to me almost insolent.

Inside me contend
Delight at the apple tree in blossom
And horror at the house-painter's speeches.
But only the second
Drives me to my desk.][23]

In the characteristic unrhymed lines and uneven, broken rhythms of the poems of this period, Brecht permits himself the fragments of an elegiac regret for the traditional stuffs of lyric poetry: natural idylls, pretty girls, blossoming trees. And for the forms which no longer seem adequate to this hard-edged, conflict-ridden reality: notice the dancing dactyls and hexameter echoes of line 8, or the hint of assonance in 'Mädchen/ehedem' – before he explicitly repudiates rhyme. This is a complex poetological poem, which enacts the very problems of which it speaks.

But the loss, as Brecht recognised, is also a gain. The old images and functions of poetry were also one-sided, and scarcely able to do justice to the complexity of modern life and thought. They could not speak to people's real experience and concerns. The political voice of these exile poems represents not just an impoverishment, but also an extension of the aesthetic. The visions of the *Svendborg Poems* are not narrow; rather, they give us a glimpse – as all good poetry should – of another, a better world. They sharpen our sense of what is wrong and what is right. They give us, as they gave Brecht's contemporaries, that quickening of consciousness which helps us to see what our own role and bearing (Brecht would call it 'Haltung') in the political world should be. It may be that those poems which speak most explicitly of Hitler's Germany and of Stalin's Russia have dated, and are hard to read today. In most cases, however, the moral and political outrage of the poems still resonates directly. 'An die Gleichgeschalteten'/'To those who have been brought into line', which was broadcast from Moscow in 1935, makes salutary reading in any modern society. What compromises have you made for your comfort or security? What accommodations have you reached with an establishment you like to think you have rejected? Can you know where this is leading?

> In order not to lose their bread
> In times of increasing oppression
> Not a few may decide
> No longer to tell the truth
> About the crimes the regime commits to maintain the exploitation, but
> Equally not to distribute the lies of the regime, so
> Not to reveal anything, but
> Also not to prettify anything.
> [...]
>   But this is the time
> While they still go in and out of the administration and the editorial offices
> Of the laboratories and of the factory yards, as people
> Whose mouths speak no untruths
> That they start to be harmful.[24]

Others still shock, make us pause for thought, even by their very simplicity:

> On the wall was chalked:
> They want war.
> The man who wrote it
> Has already fallen.[25]

That is the whole of one of the poems in the section of the *Svendborg Poems* entitled, like the later 'photo-epigrams', 'War Primer'.

As Brecht later wrote of his poems, 'Indeed, they are written from an attitude which someone only adopts if he can reckon with alert readers'.[26] The 'usefulness' of these poems lies not in the particularities of some political argument, but in that they encourage a critical, political bearing in the reader. Brecht argues elsewhere (in an essay entitled 'Lyrik und Logik')[27] that it is not the task of poems to prove something, like Pythagoras' theorem, but rather to provoke the characteristic pleasures and demands of the lyric: surprising the unwary, revealing tensions, provoking thoughts, communicating 'a thought or feeling which might be of some advantage, even for a stranger'.

In the face of such dark times and of the loss of community which exile and persecution entailed, one might have forgiven Brecht for retreating into the monologic voice of a more conventional lyric. But for him that was never an option. He had always understood poetry as a dialogue in a social context. Where that context is anti-Fascist exile, the society may be so ruptured that communication seems scarcely possible – 'Such poetry', he wrote later in his journal, 'is a message in a bottle'[28] – but that made it only all the more important to assert and to construct a sense of society and community in which his poems could be heard and could make sense. These poems are as full of 'we' and 'you' as they are of 'I'; and one entire section of the *Svendborg Poems* (IV) consists of addresses, appeals, pleas, praises and even epitaphs, some referring apparently to Brecht's own experience and others as explicit role-poems. Together, these forms of apostrophe and address begin to insinuate an international community of anti-Fascists at home and abroad, some already fallen in the struggle, others well and truly living: no triumphant collective, but a modest, fragmented, crucially dialogic community none the less. Even after he had

moved to distant California, where he found it perhaps most difficult to discover a voice and a function for his poetry (the wonderful
Hollywood Elegies almost exhaust themselves in a grim satire of
capitalist alienation[29]), we still find such communicative gestures –
especially towards and after the end of the war, when thoughts of
return and reconstruction were uppermost in his mind. This is the
period also when he worked on 'The Manifesto' (*see* Phelan).

The poems of exile spend a great deal of time reflecting on what
they can and cannot do, on who their readers may be and how they
may reach them. But they are not bogged down in poetological
grumbles. On the contrary, poem after poem homes in on an aspect
or a weakness of National Socialism, or a strength of its enemies.
Both individually, and in the multi-perspectival juxtapositions of
the collection, the *Svendborg Poems* tell us about Fascism, sound
warnings and cultivate attitudes which may mean almost as much
to us now as they did to Brecht's readers in the 1930s. These are the
famous opening lines of the last poem of the collection, 'An die
Nachgeborenen' / 'To those born later':

> Truly, I live in dark times!
> The guileless word is folly. A smooth forehead
> Suggests insensitivity. The man who laughs
> Has simply not yet had
> The terrible news.
>
> What kind of times are they when
> A talk about trees is almost a crime
> Because it implies silence about so many horrors?
> That man there calmly crossing the street
> Is already perhaps beyond the reach of his friends
> Who are in need?[30]

As Jan Knopf remarks in a recent study, there is no other writer
who has responded to political barbarism so precisely and determinedly with poems and songs as Brecht – and long before anyone
thought to ask the question whether there could be, or should be
poetry after, or about, Auschwitz.[31]

(iii) 1947–56

Writing about Brecht's poetry, and chiefly about poems of the later exile, the post-war Swiss writer Max Frisch made a distinction similar to Brecht's own remarks from the 1920s which I cited near the beginning of this essay. He contrasted, briefly, the phoney 'Rausch' [intoxication] of 'Poesie' with a real poetry, able to take its place in this world:

It is still a poem, even if I say it in a kitchen: with no candles, no string quartet or oleander. It has something to say to me. And above all: I don't have to forget anything in order to take it seriously. It doesn't presume a mood; it has nothing to fear from some other mood.

He characterises Brecht's own reading aloud of 'To those born later': 'clear and precise', 'matter of fact, presenting words like pebbles', 'communicative'.[32] One might perhaps say something similar about Brecht's own poetic language.

The first thing that strikes one about the poems of the later 1940s is the continuity of Brecht's concerns and of his poetic forms; above all, the unrhymed lines and irregular rhythms that are so familiar from the exile poetry. There is one great allegorical ballad, 'Freiheit und Democracy'/'Freedom and democracy' (1947), a scornful attack on the re-establishment of capitalist democracy in the western zone (modelled on Shelley's *The Mask of Anarchy*) which seems even to refer us back to the 'early' Brecht. Its forty aggressive four-line verses in rhyming couplets recall the anti-establishment protests of the *Kaiserreich* poems, and in particular the 'Legend of the dead soldier'. From 'Freedom and democracy':

One onetime parliamentarian
In Hitler's time he was an Aryan
Offers his services to the law:
Such zeal deserves to prosper more![33]

In this period, outspoken, compassionate poems about war give way, slowly, to outspoken, compassionate poems about reconstruction. At the same time, alongside many more personal poems – about returning, about Augsburg and the destroyed cities of Germany, about the burden of survival – Brecht tried once more to address a 'general public', the *Volk* with whom he had been out of contact for so long. He wrote cantatas and songs for public occasions; and he wrote children's verse again: no longer for his own children (the youngest, Barbara, was already nineteen in 1950 when he wrote the 'Children's Anthem' – *see* Wizisla), but rather for the new, post-war generation, in whose education he took great interest. At times, it seems, he is trying on the mantle of poet laureate of German socialism.

The newly founded German Democratic Republic (1949) of course offered great hope of a new beginning, but Brecht was not so naïve, nor was his sceptical imagination so tired that he could believe in the unproblematic achievement of some workers' Utopia. The signs were against that. 'The travails of the mountains', he wrote, 'lie behind us / Before us lie the travails of the plains.'[34] The relationship of the personal and the political is still absolutely central to this later poetry (nothing could illustrate that better than a private sketch of a national anthem, for children – see pp. 210–11). In some poems, this comes across apparently untrammeled; in many, however, and above all in Brecht's last great collection, the *Buckower Elegien / Buckow Elegies* it is veiled and uncomfortable. As the ostensibly socialist GDR revealed itself increasingly as a Stalinist bureaucracy, Brecht was manœuvred into an awkward ventriloquism: publicly, he still gave his backing to the regime; privately, he retreated to his country house in Buckow, thirty miles outside Berlin, where he could doubt. As Ray Ockenden demonstrates, it is certainly not, now less than ever, a question of thoughtlessly ramming messages down gulping throats.

Eisen

Im Traum heute nacht
Sah ich einen großen Sturm.
Ins Baugerüst griff er
Den Bauschragen riß er
Den Eisernen, abwärts.
Doch was da aus Holz war
Bog sich und blieb.

Iron

In a dream last night
I saw a great storm.
It seized the scaffolding
It tore the cross-clasps
The iron ones, down.
But what was made of wood
Swayed and remained.

Translated by Antony Tatlow [35]

The *Buckow Elegies* are a short collection of short poems, distilla-
tions of Brecht's techniques and political attitudes, urged from him
by the uneasy situation and his own status in the young GDR (at the
time of the workers' uprising in Berlin, 17 June 1953). The sentences here are simple, almost conversational, and yet their
cadences are arresting, unGerman even. Especially the parallel
clauses of lines 3 and 4 (of similar stress patterns, nearly rhyming)
and the interpolated adjectival noun of line 5, which give the poem
the poise and distance of a classical epigram. Throughout all his
poetry, Brecht exploits a highly inflected grammar, drawing on
dialect formulations, on Latin syntax, on English word-order sometimes, on the formulations of the Luther Bible, and on innumerable
other sources. Such carefully constructed sentences are disposed
just as carefully across the lines of a poem. Look at the violence
which falls on 'abwärts' [down] in this example, because of the
delay, and because it falls at the end of a line, the third consecutive
trochaic line-end. Notice the contrast between the almost
pompous, capitalised 'den Eisernen' [the iron one][36] and the more
matter-of-fact 'was da aus Holz war' [what was made of wood].
How important that a stressed 'blieb' [remained] should be the final
syllable in a shortened last line (an unambiguous trochee and iamb,
as against the two, three or even four stresses and ambiguous patterns of unstressed syllables in the preceding lines). What is this
building, threatened by what storm? If this is a dream, what, in reality, will remain? It is not the only bad dream in this collection.

Another striking characteristic of the poems of Brecht's last
decade is that they are fewer, fewer than half the number he had

written in either of the previous two decades. Perhaps this was, more painfully, a truly bad time for poetry. It is important to bear in mind that, although he received the news of Khrushchev's denunciation of Stalin at the 20th Party Congress in 1956, Brecht did not live to see the Hungarian uprising and its suppression (later in 1956), let alone the building of the Berlin Wall (1961). Nevertheless, there had already been sufficient signs that this new beginning was the wrong one. Brecht clearly found it easier, as a poet and perhaps in every other sense too, to live and to speak as a 'scourge of the bourgeoisie', or as a political exile – in other words, to indulge a creativity in and of opposition – than he did as a spokesman on the inside of the GDR. There is no gainsaying it, the poetry of his last years is less 'clear and precise', less 'matter of fact', less 'communicative', more circumspect than ever before.

Changing the wheel

I sit by the roadside
The driver changes the wheel.
I do not like the place I have come from.
I do not like the place I am going to.
Why with impatience do I
Watch him changing the wheel?

Translated by Michael Hamburger[37]

Continuities and contradictions

Even in this late period, however, our attention is drawn to the variety and eclecticism of Brecht's lyric, and of the sources on which he drew. In his youth, he was already wide-ranging in his reading habits, keen to borrow and exploit all that he found. He learned much from the linguistic experiments of German Expressionism, albeit he reacted against that aesthetic. He drew heavily on the Bible and on hymns, liturgies and catechisms. He was fond of particular Latin authors, especially of Horace and Lucretius (*see* Phelan), throughout his life. He read enthusiastically in the German baroque and amongst the English Elizabethans. He modelled some early sonnets on Pietro Aretino; and in many later poems Dante figures importantly. He tended to avoid German writers of the eighteenth and nineteenth centuries (except to parody them), but he found unlikely models elsewhere: from Rimbaud (*see* Brown) to Baudelaire, from Shelley to Kipling. From the English canon he also admired Swift and, later, Auden. In the late 1920s he was introduced to Japanese and Chinese literature (via the English translations of Arthur Waley) and he remained fascinated, even producing two short series of *Chinesische Gedichte* (1938–49). The occasionally inscrutable brevity of the poems of the *Buckow Elegies* has led some to identify an oriental influence here too.[38] And he read contemporary poetry as well, producing several versions (*Nachdichtungen*) of twentieth-century Russian and other poets, including even the young Ingeborg Bachmann, whose poems he tried to re-cast in his own idiom. This catalogue is not intended to be at all exhaustive or scientific. It may serve simply to recall Brecht's involvement with the tradition, and perhaps help to account for the variety of his own poetic voices and for the fruitfulness of his example in more recent German and European poetry (*see* Leeder). He insisted that one could revivify and sweep the dust off the classics, and at times too he styled himself a classic: in that lively tradition, with some of the authority, but none of the dust.[39] Repeatedly, this by turns arrogant and modest persona enters a dialogue with the poets of the past, sometimes even submerges itself in the tradition, becomes almost anonymous in its easy articulation of familiar forms and genres, in its determinedly impersonal messages. Then it resurfaces, suddenly and strikingly personal once more, and we recall the particular historical circumstances of the man Bertolt Brecht.

This fast-switching dialectic of the personal and the impersonal, of the particular and the general, is not only a matter of time and of the tradition. Each of Brecht's three great collections is defined also by a strong sense of place (surprising in a poet who seems to have little time for the local); and that place in turn is defined by his favourite elements, by water and by trees (surprising in a poet whose focus appears to be not nature, but the social): the river Lech and the chestnut trees of Augsburg in the *Domestic Breviary*; in the

Svendborg Poems, the fruit-trees in the garden and the arm of the sea which separates Fyn from its neighbouring islands and, beyond, from Germany; the poplars and firs and the lakes around his country retreat in Brandenburg in the *Buckow Elegies*. Many years separate the collections, and the meanings of these woods and waters shift and metamorphose, almost out of all recognition (as I hope even the few examples I have quoted demonstrate). Yet time and again they recall us, as it were, to the source and centre of this lyric voice. This is a poem of 1919, from the *Domestic Breviary*, with no thought yet for the political:

> In the pale summer when the winds above
> Only in the great trees' leaves a murmur make
> You ought to lie in rivers or in ponds
> As do the waterweeds which harbour pike
> The body grows light in the water. When your arm
> Falls easily from water into sky
> The little wind rocks it absentmindedly
> Taking it likely for a brownish bough.[40]

Like Baal, the subject, intriguingly generalised as 'man' [one, you], longs for symbiotic union and dissolution in the natural world.[41] From the exile period comes the short poem, 'Frühling 1938' / 'Spring 1938', quoted in full after the Foreword (p. 4). 'War' and 'little tree', 'my people' and 'my son', 'pointing the finger' and 'silence': all the interweaving of personal and larger political concerns is enacted here. And finally this, the opening of the first poem of the *Buckow Elegies*, a more problematic interplay of the natural and the cultivated (with months, not seasons, which may well have veiled political associations, *see* Ockenden):

> At the lake, deep amid fir and silver poplar
> Sheltered by wall and hedge, a garden
> So wisely plotted with monthly flowers
> That it blooms from March until October.
>
> Here, in the morning, not too frequently, I sit
> And wish ...[42]

Belatedly (although it's early morning), hesitantly (so many commas), wishfully, the poetic subject settles down once more in his familiar landscape and re-situates himself in his politics. It is customary to describe the *Buckow Elegies* as laconic, lapidary, coded even,[43] and yet, seen in this progression, these perhaps more tentative offerings insist, as much as any other Brecht poems, on an engaged and forward-looking dialogue with the reader.

Yet, however we may wish to stress those features which Brecht himself singled out – the poems' rootedness in concrete reality and real occasions, their determined gestures of productive communication – Brecht's is a poetic *œuvre* which, perhaps like any other great achievement in the lyric, derives much of its power from ambiguities and contradictions. The poems do not only seem to contradict and ignite each other, for, as Brecht wrote, 'every poem is the enemy of every other poem',[44] they are also individually full of tensions. 'The contradictions are our hopes!' was the motto Brecht chose for his great 'sociological experiment' in the Weimar Republic, *The Threepenny Lawsuit*.[45] It would make a good motto for his poems, too. For the burden of these tensions and contradictions is not despair, but, with the attitude of the true dialectician, cautious hope.

'Spring 1938' contains the dreadful recognition that the coming war 'may erase' the continent, but it ends with the tender, tenuously utopian gesture, preserving the young fruit-tree for a future harvest. 'The flower garden', quoted above, proceeds to a cautious (ambivalent) wish. Brecht's poems (unlike his plays) quite often risk a glance ahead. Take the last lines of 'To those born later':

> ... Oh, we
> Who wanted to prepare the ground for friendliness
> Could not ourselves be friendly.
>
> But you, when the time comes at last
> And man is a helper to man
> Think of us
> With forbearance.[46]

In the later poetry especially, the motifs of 'Freundlichkeit' [friendliness], the celebrations of humanity and the recollections of the pleasures of life (one poem is called 'Vergnügungen' / 'Pleasures') sit alongside the doubts, the fears and the miseries.

None the less, perhaps the most enduringly impressive statements, the poems which still have the power to move us to tears, are those expressions of outrage at injustice and of intense human pity. For a writer who has a reputation for rational, cool-headed analysis, and who is now widely vilified for his loyalty to the political goals of Communism (a once honourable cause), it is striking how consistently and hotly compassionate (and passionate) his poems are, from the ballad 'On the infanticide Marie Farrar' to another heart-rending ballad, the 'Kinderkreuzzug 1939'/'Children's crusade 1939'. One of the last poems that Brecht wrote expresses, I think, both his hope and his frustration with this aesthetic of pity and outrage.

> And I always thought: the very simplest words
> Must be enough. When I say what things are like
> Everyone's heart must be torn to shreds.
> That you'll go down if you don't stand up for yourself
> Surely you see that.

Translated by Michael Hamburger[47]

How could it not be enough, simply to tell it like it is? And yet of course the poem itself does not do that. On the contrary, quite apart from the fact that poems have seldom dealt with just 'the simplest words', we are told here that the poet *used to* think this. The simple 'must' – 'must' – 'that' – 'surely' assertions of the surface of the poem are accompanied by a shift in tenses from past to future, and a shift in address from generalisation ('everyone') to an alarming second person: 'Surely you see that'. We are made to ask what it is we should be defending ourselves against; we had not perhaps recognised that we were amongst those under threat. Only now, alerted by the turns of this poem and transformed into one of Brecht's 'attentive readers', are we ready to hear or to see what's what.

Disputation and laughter, and poetry

This book started life as a seminar, convened in 1998 in Oxford to celebrate the centenary of Brecht's birth. Most of the essays presented here originated as contributions to that seminar, and were developed, expanded and adapted in response to our discussions then. As a motto, the seminar took a phrase from the poem I have already mentioned, 'Visit to the banished poets': 'Streit und Gelächter' [disputation and laughter]. In the poem, on his way through the underworld to meet the poets, the anonymous 'I' passes by the hut in which their neighbours, the banished teachers, live, and he hears how they laugh and dispute (as the poets do as well later in the poem). It transpires that these are positive signs to Brecht of an active, critical and yet 'friendly' engagement. The poets have become teachers too – as Brecht aspired to. And their teaching carries us, not into a world of easy answers, but, predictably, into debate, into dialectics. The authors of the contributions to this book are themselves all teachers (some are poets too); it is not surprising that we should want to take up, to engage with, to argue with Brecht's pedagogy. So this is a book, not just of scholarly articles about poems in their historical context, but also of jovial disputation about a legacy and its reception, about the potential for a productive rereading of Brecht's poems in another century.

Brecht's rich and sober adventures in the lyric helped to form the literary language of the twentieth century. They both contributed to and extended the genre, as much as any works by Auden or Milosz, by Neruda or Seferis. In this sense alone they deserve an international audience. But one might still ask, is there no better reason to read Brecht today? Can his poems still appear both pleasurable and useful? In 'To those born later', Brecht presents the efforts of his generation as transitional, ephemeral even, and asks us, when we look on their works, to recall the dark times in which they lived 'with forbearance'. To some extent, Brecht's *œuvre* is clearly a monument of literary history, and a document of a dark time past. But it is more than that. In large measure, because we still recognise the conflicts and the aspirations of which Brecht spoke. The circumstances may have changed, but, in almost every way Brecht knew, the struggle today is still for a society worthy of a human life. In 1936, Brecht asked the question himself, 'Why / Should my name be mentioned?':

1
Once I thought: in distant times
When the buildings have collapsed in which I live
And the ships have rotted in which I travelled
My name will still be mentioned
With others.

2
Because I praised the useful, which
In my day was considered base
Because I battled against all religions
Because I fought oppression or
For another reason.

3
Because I was for people and
Entrusted everything to them, thereby honouring them
Because I wrote verses and enriched the language
Because I taught practical behaviour or
For some other reason.

On reflection, the poem continues, he is now content that he should be forgotten: 'Why / Should the baker be asked for if there is enough bread?' ... 'Why / Should there be a past if / There is a future?'.[48] By this turn the poem demands of Brecht's later readers that they confront this new question: have we really reached that point, is there today enough bread for all, what kind of future is there?

In 1942 Brecht noted in his journal, 'the battle of Smolensk is also for poetry'.[49] At first, that is an almost shocking thought: Soviet citizens were fighting for their lives and for their homeland against the troops of Hitler. But for Brecht the struggle was for a decent human society, a society in which culture would have its place and in which poetry – some sort of poetry, at least – might be possible. All of that was, he believed, under threat from the forces of Fascism. A poem, even innocent of all blatant political design, is a blow for human freedom, for free expression, for values endangered by the political and economic power of the few. In that understanding, it has a pretty impressive use-value. Would that we could honestly claim all our battles were for poetry.

1

Vom armen B. B.

1

Ich, Bertolt Brecht, bin aus den schwarzen Wäldern.
Meine Mutter trug mich in die Städte hinein
Als ich in ihrem Leibe lag. Und die Kälte der Wälder
Wird in mir bis zu meinem Absterben sein.

2

In der Asphaltstadt bin ich daheim. Von allem Anfang
Versehen mit jedem Sterbsakrament:
Mit Zeitungen. Und Tabak. Und Branntwein.
Mißtrauisch und faul und zufrieden am End.

3

Ich bin zu den Leuten freundlich. Ich setze
Einen steifen Hut auf nach ihrem Brauch.
Ich sage: es sind ganz besonders riechende Tiere
Und ich sage: es macht nichts, ich bin es auch.

4

In meine leeren Schaukelstühle vormittags
Setze ich mir mitunter ein paar Frauen
Und ich betrachte sie sorglos und sage ihnen:
In mir habt ihr einen, auf den könnt ihr nicht bauen.

5

Gegen abends versammle ich um mich Männer
Wir reden uns da mit 'Gentleman' an
Sie haben ihre Füße auf meinen Tischen
Und sagen: es wird besser mit uns. Und ich frage nicht: wann.

6

Gegen Morgen in der grauen Frühe pissen die Tannen
Und ihr Ungeziefer, die Vögel, fängt an zu schrein.
Um die Stunde trink ich mein Glas in der Stadt aus und schmeiße
Den Tabakstummel weg und schlafe beunruhigt ein.

7

Wir sind gesessen ein leichtes Geschlechte
In Häusern, die für unzerstörbare galten
(So haben wir gebaut die langen Gehäuse des Eilands Manhattan
Und die dünnen Antennen, die das Atlantische Meer unterhalten).

8

Von diesen Städten wird bleiben: der durch sie hindurchging, der Wind!
Fröhlich machet das Haus den Esser: er leert es.
Wir wissen, daß wir Vorläufige sind
Und nach uns wird kommen: nichts Nennenswertes.

9

Bei den Erdbeben, die kommen werden, werde ich hoffentlich
Meine Virginia nicht ausgehen lassen durch Bitterkeit
Ich, Bertolt Brecht, in die Asphaltstädte verschlagen
Aus den schwarzen Wäldern in meiner Mutter in früher Zeit.

Of poor B.B.

1

I, Bertolt Brecht, came out of the black forests
My mother moved me into the cities as I lay
Inside her body. And the coldness of the forests
Will be inside me till my dying day.

2

In the asphalt city I'm at home. From the very start
Provided with every last sacrament:
With newspapers. And tobacco. And brandy
To the end mistrustful, lazy and content.

3

I'm polite and friendly to people. I put on
A hard hat because that's what they do.
I say: they are animals with a quite peculiar smell
And I say: does it matter? I am too.

4

Before noon on my empty rocking chairs
I'll sit a woman or two, and with an untroubled eye
Look at them steadily and say to them:
Here you have someone on whom you can't rely.

5

Towards evening it's men that I gather round me
And then we address one another as 'gentlemen'.
They're resting their feet on my table tops
And say: things will get better for us. And I don't ask when.

6

In the grey light before morning the pine trees piss
And their vermin, the birds, raise their twitter and cheep.
At that hour in the city I drain my glass, then throw
The cigar butt away and worriedly go to sleep.

7

We have sat, an easy generation
In houses held to be indestructible
(Thus we built those tall boxes on the island of Manhattan
And those thin aerials that amuse the Atlantic swell).

8

Of those cities will remain what passed through them, the wind!
The house makes glad the eater; he clears it out.
We know that we're only tenants, provisional ones
And after us there will come: nothing worth talking about.

9

In the earthquakes to come, I very much hope
I shall keep my cigar alight, embittered or no
I, Bertolt Brecht, carried off to the asphalt cities
From the black forests inside my mother long ago.

Translated by Michael Hamburger[1]

'Of poor B. B.' – and others

Ronald Speirs

'Vom armen B. B.'/'Of poor B. B.' is a piece of poetic stocktaking. Conscious of the flow of time and of the questions posed to each individual by the ineluctable fact of personal transience, the poet surveys his life in the present, talks of his origins and considers the likely future and his attitude to it. Taking this poem as a starting-point, I would like to consider the nature of what I shall initially call 'the poetic personality'.

'Of poor B. B.' is the very last poem in the appendix to Brecht's first collection of poetry, *Bertolt Brechts Hauspostille/Domestic Breviary*, published initially as a limited edition in 1926 (under the title *Taschenpostille/Pocket Breviary*) and in a larger, cheaper edition the following year. Although not necessarily conceived with this function in mind – an earlier, free-standing version from 1922 exists[2] – the poem's position in the *Breviary* contributes to its meaning. As Wulf Segebrecht has pointed out,[3] it was common for books of religious edification, the general genre to which the *Breviary* belongs (it does not in fact conform strictly to the type of the 'Postille', a commentary or reflection on a passage cited from another work, frequently the Bible – hence 'post illa verba texta'), to close with a 'vita' of the author, who, like his readers, is a 'poor sinner' and who offers his life as an example of human frailty and of the redeeming power of Christ. Thus the poem opens, as such a vita should, by giving the name and place of birth of the author: 'Ich, Bertolt Brecht, bin aus den schwarzen Wäldern' [I, Bertolt Brecht, am from the black forests].[4] Ostensibly, at any rate, authors of such books of meditation, instruction and confession did not name themselves for the purposes of self-advertisement. They understood themselves rather to be speaking in all humility, presenting

41

their experiences as mere pages in the great book of life, where the story of salvation was written in countless examples, most of which passed unmentioned in earthly records; hence the epithet 'poor' (or other terms like 'wretch') as a gesture of *humilitas*, stressing by contrast the overflowing riches of Grace abounding. One explanation for the poet's partial obliteration of his name in the title of this poem could be that he wished to stress his awareness of and adherence to that tradition of humble self-presentation, lest anyone should understand the explicit mention of his name differently.

If the opening phrase 'Ich, Bertolt Brecht' also prompts thoughts of a rather different type of document, namely a person's last will and testament, another occasion on which an individual reflects on his or her past and thinks of the future and what they might bequeath to it, the association is entirely appropriate, since one of Brecht's chief models in this poem, and generally throughout the *Breviary*, was the fifteenth-century poet François Villon. Villon repeatedly addressed or referred to himself as 'poor Villon' (most famously in his poetic 'Testament': 'Here now closes the Testament / And here it ends, of poor Villon'), and Brecht could well have had in mind his poem 'Legacy' ('I, François Villon, scholar, declare …') when he began his poem 'Of poor B. B.' as he did.[5] Villon's poetry, however, is not so much an alternative source of inspiration to the tradition of 'Erbauungsbücher' [devotional books] as a particular strand within that tradition. Villon's poems, it is true, present a scandalous life, measured by the normal standards of decency and piety; they are poems which confess to all the violence, lust and wild drinking of this 'poor scholar', but confessional poetry it remains, and it is filled with pleas for mercy on its author's sinfulness. Whether all this is merely blasphemous lip service to religion and a mockery of devotional poetry cannot be decided for certain, but I suspect it is not. The poet Villon's closeness to the murderers, thieves and adulterers whom Christ came to save, strikes me as more of a challenge to the Pharisees of his age than to the Christian faith, for it is a life which, in the very 'poverty' of the poet's body and soul, personifies fallen humanity. More importantly for present purposes, Brecht's *Breviary*, at any rate, is not simply a blasphemous parody of the books whose forms and gestures it copies.

Rather, the collection is attempting to assess the sum of a life in a situation where none of the answers traditionally offered by books of piety seem to help, but in which the questions from which they arose – or to which they perhaps gave rise – continue to dog the poet. Blasphemy, parody or exorcism are not forms of behaviour inspired by dead letters; they are forms of engagement with something that is still felt to exercise power. As Brecht famously observed, when asked which book had influenced him most, 'You'll laugh: the Bible'.[6]

Thomas Mann described the relation of the *Zauberberg/Magic Mountain* to the tradition of the 'Bildungsroman' as an ironical and almost parodistic attempt at renewal.[7] Although the young Brecht would have hated being mentioned in the same sentence as Thomas Mann, the phrase can fairly be applied to the relation of the *Breviary* in general (and 'Of poor B. B.' in particular) to the tradition of books of edification. In other words, this poetry is not without its complications. To use a term which has become very popular in discussions of Brecht's poetry, 'Of poor B. B.' is a poem in which the poet puts on a mask, indeed a series of masks, to which he draws attention by speaking in various registers, mostly in a flat parlando manner, but sometimes in forms and phrases borrowed from the religious tradition and its blasphemous or unorthodox side-shoots, at others with a classicising flourish.[8] But all this talk of masks does not, I think, get us very far. For what poet does not wear a 'mask'? To write or utter any poem is to speak as a persona, in a stylised voice. More interesting, it seems to me, are the further questions: What kinds of voices and gestures does the poet adopt? How do they relate to one another? Is there a tendency to use a particular range of them or to use certain ones repeatedly? What is being signalled by the various forms of self-stylisation and their interactions?

Take, for example, the gesture of humility implied by the use of the anonymous initials 'B. B.', a gesture which is undercut immediately by the epithet 'arm' [poor], since this signals the poet's chosen kinship with Villon, who, had it not been for his poetry, would have remained as utterly unknown to posterity as the vast majority of his contemporaries. The intention to emulate Villon's survival in the 'monument more enduring than brass' of his poetry is written all over the impudent face peeking out from behind the rhetorical mask of humility. The initials could even signal the very opposite of humility; they could be laying claim, with arrogant self-confidence, to a fame so well founded that future generations of readers will know, even before they reach the first line of the poem, that it concerns Bertolt Brecht. And if effect permits the inference of intention, there is evidence that this is precisely what Brecht was aiming at: nowadays the lower case initials, once printed on the cover of a Methuen edition of his poetry, for example, are immediately recognisable, indeed unmistakable, to readers who belong to that anonymous, neutered collective – 'nichts Nennenswertes' [nothing worth talking about] – which the poet expected to occupy the globe briefly after his demise. Despite the fact that he protested his lack of faith in or respect for the future, the poet of 'Of poor B. B.' clearly wanted to survive into that future by leaving some trace of a voice that was just as particular, just as unforgettable as Villon's in a consciousness that outlived his own. Even in this demonstratively self-centred poem there is a need for at least a secular form of self-transcendence.

Incidentally, the man behind the poetic voice – the Bertolt Brecht whose legal persona still provides well for his heirs – bequeathed another very telling commentary on the question of masks and the man. In the same period as he wrote the *Breviary*, Brecht had a premature 'death mask' cast, and then had himself photographed holding the death mask up in front of his still-living face. You can read the picture in various ways, which seem interrelated to me. The dead mask indicates the desire of the living person to leave a visual record of his unique features post mortem, but it also indicates that his is a life in which the present is influenced to an unusual degree by awareness of the physical annihilation to come. The photograph may be saying on the one hand that behind the mask there is a real person. On the other hand, one can see the mask as a face which the man has pulled away, leaving behind it another, fractionally different face or mask, with the possible suggestion that layer upon layer could be pulled away like this. Taking these multiple, contrary readings together, one is led to the conclusion that if every face is a mask, every mask is also a face. In other words, there is, if not identity, then at least some kind of continuity in the personality that presents itself like this. Disguises do not simply hide; the choice of disguise also reveals.

Yet, though the pretended humility of 'poor B. B.' is undercut by the poet's evident determination to escape the anonymity of the dead, there is some truth in his profession of poverty. He, like other human beings, is poor simply because this mortal life is exiguous, however long it may be protracted. Hence the admonitory poem 'Gegen Verführung'/'Against temptation',[9] in the 'Schlußkapitel' [final chapter] of the *Breviary*:

> Be ye not deceived!
> Life is meagre stuff.
> Gulp it in mighty draughts
> You won't have had enough
> When you're forced to leave it[10]

Indeed, the poet is so conscious of being poor in a whole series of respects that his poetry can claim to be a legitimate, if heterodox, descendant of the tradition it parodies. His poetry, too, is instructional, intended to help the reader live more rightly in the face of death. Just as religious authors once urged their readers to acknowledge the desperate poverty of a life of sin and the assurance of eternal life beyond this world, Brecht teaches his readers to look hard at the poverty and brevity of mortal life as the first step to laying hold of such richness – in the form of sheer intensity of experience – as it is possible to know within the mortal span. He even offers them a share in an eternity of sorts: each may gaze at the enduring sky above (a 'Himmel' ['sky' or 'heavens'] that belongs to this world rather than an after-world) and feel the hardness of a stone beneath his or her back.[11] Such experiences are Brecht's resolutely physical version of the Goethean 'eternal moment'. These are gifts to be gained precisely from the acceptance of existential poverty, for the very brevity of our glimpse of the sky is what sharpens the appreciation of its permanence, its ever-changing constancy.

Yet the forms and language in which the poet's praise of the here-and-now is cast makes it plain that he is offering substitutes.

However much he may sing blasphemous psalms of praise to nothingness, to darkness, to forgetting, to a world without God, without any sense of sin or fear of punishment for sin, there remains, as 'Of poor B. B.' makes clear, an unremitting restlessness in the poet and an emptiness he can neither fill nor forget. Having been reared in a religious culture, the poet simply cannot get it out of his system. This poor sinner remains poor, not because he is plagued by thoughts of sin but because, although the concepts of sin and salvation are now redundant, they have nevertheless left him with feelings of dissatisfaction at life's exiguousness and with the need to construct an alternative rationale and justification for existence. It seems that he still has to sing psalms of some kind. 'Against temptation' may be anti-Lutheran in doctrine, but its chosen form is a chorale, because this form, and this form alone, will express the pathos of mortality in a world with knowledge of the absence of God (rather than one unburdened by any knowledge of God).[12]

The initials in the title of the poem carry a further implication. When spoken (and Brecht's poetry, particularly in the early years, was designed to be spoken or sung), the letters form, in German, the word 'Bebe' [baby]. The childish character of the poet hinted at in the title is stressed by the structural device of making the image of the baby in the womb both the starting-point of the poem and its point of return and closure:

> Ich, Bertolt Brecht, bin aus den schwarzen Wäldern
> Meine Mutter trug mich in die Städte hinein
> Als ich in ihrem Leibe lag.
> [...]
> Ich, Bertolt Brecht, in die Asphaltstädte verschlagen
> Aus den schwarzen Wäldern in meiner Mutter in früher Zeit.

Whereas the womb is normally associated with warmth and protection, so that expulsion into the outside world is accompanied by a 'Kälteschock' [shock of the cold], this particular foetus has evidently had a different experience, for it already knew the cold of the forests while still in the womb, before being carried into the cities to be born: 'Und die Kälte der Wälder/ Wird in mir bis zu meinem Absterben sein' [And the coldness of the forests / Will be inside me till my dying day].[13] One implication of this is that the foetus was so unusually sensitive to the cold that even the womb could afford no shelter. Another, suggested by certain oddities of the phrasing, is that the 'cold of the forests' does not simply penetrate the protective layers of the womb but is already part of the poet's own nature from the earliest stages of its development. As a creature from and of the 'black forests' ('Ich … bin aus den schwarzen Wäldern'), he and they are flesh of one flesh, sharing coldness as a common characteristic. The near identity or at least continuity of human life with that of the forests is further suggested by the term 'absterben', a verb normally reserved for the dying-off of a plant or a tree (or for the gradual loss of sensation in part of the body), and by the strange adverbial sequence in the last line of the poem, 'Aus den schwarzen Wäldern in meiner Mutter' [From the black forests inside my mother] – as if there were no essential difference between the world inside the body and the world outside: the foetus was in the forest within the womb.

Even if cold belongs to his nature, the poet is not entirely a cold-blooded creature. Rather, he *feels* the cold, both the cold within him and that around him. The foetus's need for protection from the cold is still present in the adult who seeks comfort in the small warmth of brandy and tobacco. In a world without transcendence, these things, along with newspapers, must serve as his secular 'Sterbsakrament' [last sacrament], supplied with which the poet will be 'zufrieden am End' [to the end … content]. At least, so he claims in stanza two. Stanza six tells a different story, for at the end of a night spent drinking and smoking in the city, he sees a grey dawn break with 'pissing' pine trees and their clamorous 'vermin', the birds, finishes his drink, throws away the stub of his cigar and falls into a 'troubled' ('beunruhigt') sleep. Neither the substitute, material 'sacraments' nor the tone of jocular blasphemy suffice in the end to ward off the unease of living in a world where the cold and poverty felt by the poet are not only physical.

Having known the cold of the world from the womb onwards, the poet's strategy is to accept calmly[14] what the young Brecht never tired of calling 'die Dinge, wie sie sind' [things as they are]. If the world is cold, one ought to meet it with coldness. In fact, however, the poet cannot quite muster the utter coldness that would guarantee insensitivity to the cold of the world. His conduct towards others is characterised rather by coolness, a compromise between self-protective coldness and the foetal need for human warmth. On the surface, he is friendly to people, a conformist who puts on a stiff hat 'nach ihrem Brauch' [because that's what they do], but privately he sees them, and himself, as 'ganz besonders riechende Tiere' [animals with a quite peculiar smell]. In the company of other men, whom he 'assembles around himself' with all the egocentricity of a child, he is careful not to disturb the optimistic consensus ('es wird besser mit uns' [things will get better for us]) by asking the awkward question: when? Like some pasha, he arranges 'a woman or two' on his 'empty rocking chairs' and gazes at them 'sorglos' [with an untroubled eye]. Here, in particular, he presents himself as emulating 'things as they are', for his warning to the women, 'In mir habt ihr einen, auf den könnt ihr nicht bauen' [Here you have someone on whom you cannot build], implicitly draws a parallel between himself and the 'earthquakes' he is sure will destroy the cities built across the surface of the earth, leaving only the cold wind to blow through their ruins. In a world destined for destruction, he affirms, men should take pleasure in the process of universal consumption: 'Fröhlich machet das Haus den Esser: er leert es' [The house maketh glad the eater: he clears it out]. Yet his empty rocking chairs evidently give him no pleasure, otherwise he would have no need to fill their emptiness with women. And why does he mention the fact that he is 'sorglos' when contemplating the women? The negative betrays the presence in his consciousness of what it negates. Incidentally, the suppressed source of anxiety – the brevity of time in general and of sex in particular – emerges plainly in some early verses varying the topos:

> But place a woman in the rocking chair
> Then time passes very slowly
> Which is very short[15]

Hence the poet is determined to be in control, to be on 'Gentleman' terms with his male acquaintances and to arrange 'a woman or two' (so that he is not tied by commitment to just one) as if on a stage for private viewing. Despite the poet's denial, the 'Sorge' [concern] that comes to haunt the ageing Faust is not absent from the life of 'poor B. B.' either, but rather breaks through the surface of ironic control repeatedly, in the unasked question about when things will get better, in the invective against the 'pissing' trees and the 'verminous' birds, in the vengeful apocalyptic vision of annihilating earthquakes[16] – and in the 'bitterness' which he fears might cause him to allow his 'Virginia', a symbol of tough coolness on the one hand and of a need for comforting warmth on the other, to go out at the last.

All the utterances of the poetic personality 'Bertolt Brecht' who speaks in 'Of poor B. B.' are characterised by contradiction and ambivalence. The poet puns on his initials, but the joke about the baby (or foetal) poet turns into an admission of unusual, lifelong sensitivity to the 'coldness' of forests and cities, of nature and culture alike. The claimed insouciance about the odd smell of the human animal ('does it matter?') and the carefree contemplation of the women in the poet's rocking chairs are at odds with the troubled sleep, the bitterness, the barely suppressed anger which culminates in the desire to see the coming of cataclysmic earthquakes. The citation of traditional books of piety and the tone of Luther's Bible ('Fröhlich machet das Haus den Esser') may be mockingly blasphemous, but it also draws attention to the poet's real emotional affinity with the Preacher of Ecclesiastes whose wonderful rhetorical lament at the vanity of all human endeavour as generation displaces generation is flattened to the seemingly dispassionate, stoical shrug of 'Wir wissen, daß wir Vorläufige sind / Und nach uns wird kommen: nichts Nennenswertes' [We know that we're only tenants, provisional ones / And after us there will come: nothing worth talking about]. The tone is different, but the anguish is the same; the wind invoked time after time in Ecclesiastes is the same wind as 'poor B. B.' imagines blowing through the ruins of the 'langen Gehäuse des Eilands Manhattan' [tall boxes on the island of Manhattan]. The guilty burden of the 'poor sinner' may have been cast off but the pitiable poverty of man's condition remains.

How does the persona 'of poor B. B.' relate to the poetic selves presented by Brecht at different stages of his career? Anyone who knows the activist, agitational voice he used from the end of the 1920s onwards ('Take your stand in the workers' united front / For you are a worker too')[17] will be struck by the contrast with the passive, isolationist, misanthropic view of mankind taken in such poems of the early twenties as the following:

> Jeder Mensch auf seinem Eiland sitzt
> Klappert mit den Zähnen oder schwitzt
> Seine Tränen, seinen Schweiß
> Sauft der Teufel literweis –
> Doch von seinem Zähneklappern
> Kann man nichts herunterknappern
>
> [Everyone is on his island
> Chatters with his teeth or sweats
> His tears, his sweat
> The devil drinks by the pint
> But from his chattering teeth
> There's not a scrap of sense to get][18]

The contrast of these sentiments in turn with those he expressed less than ten years earlier, at the start of the First World War, is equally stark. Consider, for example, a poem called 'Der heilige Gewinn' / 'The sacred prize':

> Das ist so schön, schön über all' Ermessen
> Daß Mütter klagelos die Söhne sterben sehn
> Daß alle *ihre* Sorgen still vergessen
> Und um des Großen Sieg nun beten gehen
>
> Das ist so schön, daß diese schweren Zeiten
> Fast wie ein Segen unser Haupt gestreift
> Daß dieses bittre und doch heil'ge Streiten
> In uns so opferstarke Kraft gereift
>
> [It is far lovelier than words can say
> That mothers, uncomplaining, see their sons die
> That all can put their private cares aside
> And pray that our great cause will triumph.
>
> It is so lovely that these grave times
> Touch our head almost like a blessing
> That this bitter and yet sacred fight
> Has made us strong and ripe for sacrifice.][19]

Where Brecht's twenties' poetry is blasphemous, self-centred, cynical, prepared to believe in nothing beyond intense individual experience, his earliest verse is idealistic, pious, inspired by a belief in community and a great cause ('des Großen Sieg' [the victory of the great]). The development from the patriotic poetry of 1914 to the agitational poetry he wrote from 1929 onwards takes the form of a double inversion, whereby the early idealism turns into the anti-idealism that dominates Brecht's verse between 1916 and the late 1920s, which in turn gives way to Communist-inspired idealism at the end of the 1920s. The key to the process is to be found in the fact that the changing positions are not simply different from one another but represent transformations of a single attitude or complex of attitudes. The ferocious egotism of the early 1920s would not have been so extreme and sustained had it not been for the strength of the patriotic idealism and the consequent disillusionment that set in about two years after the outbreak of war. Equally, the transformation of the cynical *enfant terrible* of the early 1920s into a committed Communist writer in 1929 (which surprised many, not least those on the political left who had not expected to find an ally in Brecht of all people) came about because a personality with a history of attachment to the values of community, and to struggle and sacrifice as the means of achieving those values, had been hidden within the cynic for almost fifteen years, giving rise to those tensions and ambivalences which pervade a poem like 'Of poor B. B.'. The idealism had been there all along, audible in the loudness of the poet's very denials, ready to re-emerge when 'die große Sache' [the great thing] (also called 'die dritte Sache' [the third thing]) had been found to replace 'das Große' [the greatness] of early patriotism, and once Brecht had become convinced of both the solidity and the achievability of his new cause. The double movement is one between extremes, for, as Brecht had confessed as early as 1916, his was not a personality attracted to the *via media*:

Kalt oder Heiß –
Nur nit Lau!
Schwarz oder Weiß –
Nur nit Grau!

[Hot or cold –
Anything but lukewarm!
Black or white –
Anything but grey!] [20]

The development indicated here in the sketchiest of outlines is, strictly speaking, the development of a fiction, a poetic persona who exists only as the speaker of verse. But I doubt that any sense can be made of the transformations of the lyric persona 'Bertolt Brecht' in purely poetic terms. It is not obvious to me that any law of poetic development would explain these changes, far less the necessity of these changes. The relationship between the poems Brecht wrote in the first fifteen or so years of his writing career is a psychological and moral one. In other words, the development of the 'poetic personality' cannot, in this instance at least, be understood in isolation from the development of the man who wrote the poems. For which biographical fallacy I expect to be shot at dawn by a literary-theoretical firing squad – but, exercising my rights as a writer, only in persona, of course.

2

Erinnerung an die Marie A.

1

An jenem Tag im blauen Mond September
Still unter einem jungen Pflaumenbaum
Da hielt ich sie, die stille bleiche Liebe
In meinem Arm wie einen holden Traum.
Und über uns im schönen Sommerhimmel
War eine Wolke, die ich lange sah
Sie war sehr weiß und ungeheuer oben
Und als ich aufsah, war sie nimmer da.

2

Seit jenem Tag sind viele, viele Monde
Geschwommen still hinunter und vorbei
Die Pflaumenbäume sind wohl abgehauen
Und fragst du mich, was mit der Liebe sei?
So sag ich dir: Ich kann mich nicht erinnern.
Und doch, gewiß, ich weiß schon, was du meinst
Doch ihr Gesicht, das weiß ich wirklich nimmer
Ich weiß nur mehr: Ich küßte es dereinst.

3

Und auch den Kuß, ich hätt ihn längst vergessen
Wenn nicht die Wolke da gewesen wär
Die weiß ich noch und wird ich immer wissen
Sie war sehr weiß und kam von oben her.
Die Pflaumenbäume blühn vielleicht noch immer
Und jene Frau hat jetzt vielleicht das siebte Kind
Doch jene Wolke blühte nur Minuten
Und als ich aufsah, schwand sie schon im Wind.[1]

Remembering Marie A.

1

It was a day in that blue month September
Silent beneath a plum tree's slender shade
I held her there, my love so pale and silent
As if she were a dream that must not fade.
Above us in the shining summer heaven
There was a cloud my eyes dwelt long upon
It was quite white and very high above us
Then I looked up, and found that it had gone.

2

And since that day so many moons, in silence
Have swum across the sky and gone below.
The plum trees surely have been chopped for firewood
And if you ask, how does that love seem now?
I must admit: I really can't remember
And yet I know what you are trying to say.
But what her face was like I know no longer
I only know: I kissed it on that day.

3

As for the kiss, I'd long ago forgot it
But for the cloud that floated in the sky
I know that still, and shall for ever know it
It was quite white and moved in very high.
It may be that the plum trees still are blooming
That woman's seventh child may now be there
And yet the cloud had only bloomed for minutes
When I looked up, it vanished on the air.

Translated by John Willett [2]

Love – Not – Memory.

An interpretation of 'Remembering Marie A.'

Hans-Harald Müller, Tom Kindt, Robert Habeck

1

'Erinnerung an die Marie A.' / 'Remembering Marie A.', said to be 'possibly Brecht's most famous poem',[3] has been the subject of sharply conflicting interpretations. Albrecht Weber describes it as 'the most tender and restrained of love poems',[4] but Jan Knopf sees it as 'a farewell to love'.[5] In choosing to examine this particular text, our aim is not merely to add to the existing stock of interpretations; we are guided by an interest in the theoretical and methodological problems of interpreting poetry.[6] To begin with, it is worth taking a look at the history of Brecht scholarship. The plea for closer consideration of that history should not be misunderstood: instead of seeking to uphold the ideas of the past, we are mainly concerned to falsify or modify them, and to generate new interpretations. But in order to articulate claims to innovation in a meaningful way, it is necessary to set those claims against a structured background of previous interpretations.

Looking at the history of Brecht scholarship as it specifically applies to 'Remembering Marie A.', one is astonished to find that no significant progress has been made in the interpretation of the poem since the study published by Albrecht Schöne in 1957.[7] This is all the more surprising in view of the fact that Brecht studies generally have made very striking progress, which could well have led to new interpretations. To cite only a few examples: Jan Knopf has clarified the history of the poem's genesis; Klaus Schuhmann has helped to place the work in context by identifying the related motifs in *Baal* and pointing out the intrinsic connection between the whole group of love poems written while Brecht was still in Augsburg; Herbert Frenken, drawing on the results of feminist research, has published an important monograph on the image of women in Brecht's poetry.[8]

Our allegation that no significant progress has been made in the interpretation of the poem since Schöne's study is of course based on a normative judgement, for which we shall endeavour to give reasons. Firstly, Schöne's structural description of the poem has served as a model for subsequent critics.[9] Secondly, his interpretation of the poem has convinced a large number of other interpreters. However, his reading of the intricate relationship between the forgotten lover and the remembered cloud is highly ambivalent. On the one hand, he claims that the past experience of love is preserved in the pictorial patterns of the clouds, which translate 'the image of the moment into the structured permanence of the art work' – this assumption makes it possible to interpret the poem as, in Schöne's words, 'a love song'. On the other hand, in the 'inability of the lyrical self to remember' he detects 'the possible undertones of an unwillingness to remember'. And here, Schöne poses a question that he leaves unanswered: 'In view of all this, can one still speak of a love song?'[10] It is probably the unresolved tension between statement and question, avoiding any definite interpretative commitment, which has enabled many critics to accept Schöne's reading, although their views differ in various points of detail.

Schöne's most outspoken opponent is Jan Knopf, who has published no less than four essays on this poem in the last fifteen years.[11] Knopf sees 'Remembering Marie A.' as 'a farewell to love', but instead of presenting an interpretation of his own, he confines himself to marshalling arguments against the view of the work as a love song. Where he discusses the actual text, he refers chiefly to the middle verse, which is described as 'completely destroying the apparently "sentimental" mood of the opening stanzas'.[12] This claim does not necessarily negate Schöne's interpretation. But Knopf takes his principal supporting arguments from the history of the poem's genesis, citing the original title 'Sentimentales Lied No. 1004'/'Sentimental Song No. 1004', in conjunction with a manuscript annotation in Brecht's hand,[13] and finally claiming that the work was not original but based on a song by the French composer Charles Malo, with a German text which Brecht is said to have parodied.[14] Individually and collectively, Knopf's arguments against the interpretation of 'Remembering Marie A.' as a love poem are less than convincing. However, our main objection to Knopf's interpretation is directed at his neglect of the 'cloud' and the sections of the poem devoted to it, which clearly leaves a large gap in the description of the text's structure. There is no improvement on Schöne's interpretation, which Knopf fails to refute, while his own reading is less comprehensive than that of his predecessor.

A similarly sketchy treatment of the poem's structure is found in the brief interpretation by Gerhard Neumann, in an essay dealing with gender roles and authorship, which sets out to show how Brecht's early love poems 'massively subvert the conventional pattern of European love poetry'. Combining traditional ideas with the vocabulary of poststructuralism, Neumann finds that 'instead of dramatising the memory of the loved one, Brecht's lyrical discourse enacts the obliteration of that memory'. Thus, according to Neumann, 'the poem itself dramatises the process of remembering as forgetting, and at the same time, the process whereby the beloved body is restored to nature, to the auratic element of the wind, the fleeting element of the cloud [...]'.[15] The stable opposition, crucial to the poem's structure, between the woman and the cloud, is therefore dissolved into a process of transformation, culminating in the destruction of memory.

Our own examination of 'Remembering Marie A.' is organised as follows. First, we shall discuss the basic conception underlying the poem – its ground-plan, so to speak. This section is descriptive in intention, and preserves neutrality with regard to the conceptions of meaning that might serve as a basis for interpreting the results of the description. In the next section, we shall subject the poem to a poststructuralist reading. In the final part of our paper, which should not necessarily be read in cumulative terms, we adopt an intentionalist conception of meaning as a framework for delimiting the poem's meaning.

We do not propose to engage in detailed discussion of the further conclusions that could be drawn from our analysis of the poem. However, it should be obvious that we are in favour of improving the culture of debate on interpretations and their results. All too often, programmatic controversies between different models and schools of interpretation have been pursued with a fundamentalist zeal which tends to obscure the fact that the number of operations for ascribing meaning to a text – by any school of interpretation, of whatever persuasion – is inherently limited. Until this range of operations has been satisfactorily reconstructed, research should devote more attention to the compatibility, comparability and quality of interpretative methodologies, instead of emphasising the incommensurability of different conceptions of meaning. Finally, in the evaluation of models and schools of interpretation, more thought should be given to the possibilities for combining interpretations with systematic or historical research programmes whose scope extends beyond the individual text.

2

The following analysis does not seek to describe 'Remembering Marie A.' on every possible textual level; it confines itself to reconstructing the poem's semantic aspect. Whereas the questions of metre, rhythm, phonology and syntax have been thoroughly investigated several times over, no one has so far produced a satisfactory description of the work's semantic constitution and structures.

At first sight, the poem appears to redeem the exact promise of its title. A lyrical self remembers a 'love so pale and silent' whom, once upon a time 'in that blue month September' he held in his arms 'beneath a plum tree's slender shade'. But in the second half of the first verse, immediately after sketching the situation of that September day, the remembering self loses sight of the initial subject, and focuses all its attention on the cloud floating high 'above us in the shining summer heaven'.

The entire poem is dominated by the opposition between these two spheres – the still life on the ground and the apparition in the sky. In the first verse, it already becomes apparent that the opposition has a wider significance, going beyond the basic topological contrast between high and low. The differences in the depiction of the two zones clearly imply that the speaker attaches different degrees of importance to them: thus, the stylistically conventional sketch of the scene under the plum tree is contrasted with the hyperbolic invocation of the cloud in the summer sky.

The latently hierarchical character of the opposition between the cloud and the loved one is explicitly developed in stanzas two and three. The lyric voice tells us that he can still remember the cloud, although so much time has passed since the day in question, but the memory of the lover's face has faded completely. Although whatever took place under the plum tree has been forgotten, the event in the 'shining summer heaven' has passed into a realm of timeless knowledge. But the white cloud not only guarantees the stability of memory, emphasised by the use of the future tense: to the lyric self, the cloud represents a condition of memory's very possibility. The only events still accessible to memory are those which the self is able to connect with the cloud – in the words of the speaker, 'As for the kiss, I'd long ago forgot it / But for the cloud that floated in the sky'.

In the final stanza, the initial topological opposition is extended to include the dimension of time. The semantic opposition between permanence and transience acquires a key structural importance; the idea of time's passing, which is crucial to this opposition, is illustrated by the image of the plum trees, the only motif which appears in all three verses and therefore shows a degree of continuity, but is defined in differing ways that also make it a symbol of transience. Meanwhile, the lyric self makes the white cloud a symbol of permanence, giving it the status of an element that stands above all forms of change. This representation of the dichotomy between transience and permanence supplies the basis for the internal differentiation of the symbolic spheres of which we spoke earlier. Since the lyric self regards the ontological transience manifested in the cloud as the precondition of psychological permanence or stability, it appears capable of immediately translating the 'seen' cloud into a 'known' cloud. For the lyric voice, the cloud of that September day – which 'blooms' and 'vanishes', and so belongs in the transitory realm of the plum trees, and which is lost from sight by the experiencing subject – achieves a certainty of transcendental status. The 'love so pale and silent', which was previously no more than a 'dream', albeit one 'that must not fade', only acquires a definite shape by being divided into two aspects, the one defined by time and the other outside it. In the final stanza, the lyric voice refers to the voiceless, colourless lover of the first verse by reference to 'that woman', who is associated with the plum trees and therefore with the passage of time, and the memory of the kiss, which is preserved from oblivion by its link with the cloud.

Yet the relationships between the first and last stanzas indicate that the cloud, characterised as the precondition of remembrance, is not the one observed on that September day. In the final stanza, the speaker makes a second attempt to remember the cloud, which conflicts with its first appearance in two respects. On the first occasion, it is said to be visible for an extended period before suddenly vanishing; the second time, it only appears for a few minutes but remains visible while it dissolves in the wind. The most emphatic statement by the lyric speaker, 'I know that still and shall for ever know it', would fall down, in performative terms, if the statement did not refer to an intelligible cloud that is distinct from its empirical counterpart.

The discrepancies between the two attempts to remember the cloud raise doubts about the reliability of the lyric voice, and thereby lead the reader back to the middle verse which we have so far neglected. It is here that the speaker reveals the basis of his repeated attempts to remember. Apart from the shift from the narrative past tense to the present, the feature that appears particularly significant is the sudden introduction of a fictive interlocutor, which clarifies the pragmatic constellation underlying the poem: we find that the lyric self is engaged in a dialogue with another person. In the light of this, even the opening lines of the first verse can no longer be interpreted as purely contemplative – they are an account shaped by a specific conversational situation and directed towards a specific partner. Instead of temporarily interrupting the flow of recollection, the reflections in the middle verse serve to show that the memories are part of an utterance addressed to a reflector figure. This has a major importance for the generic categorisation of the poem. The juxtaposition of forgotten love and remembered cloud already makes it clear that 'Remembering Marie A.' is not an example of naïve love poetry, and the relationship between the middle verse and the flanking sections shows that the text is neither an elegy of remembrance nor a wistful lament occasioned by the fading of memory – instead, it is a poem of reflection, a lyrical exercise serving to clarify the speaker's thoughts.

The text's basic communicative constellation is revealed in a stanza that occupies a particularly important position, in formal as well as pragmatic terms. The occasion for openly addressing the reflector figure is the question 'how does that love seem now?' – which marks the central axis of the poem and is the only interrogative in the entire text. A great deal of attention is thereby focused on the question, but its subject nevertheless remains unclear. The lyric self does nothing to change this: the admission 'I really can't remember' neither answers the question of love in general, nor does it respond to the enquiry regarding the former lover's current situation. Only in the context of the next two stanzas does it become possible to grasp the import of the opaque reply. The concessive 'And yet I know what you are trying to say', followed by 'But what her face was like I know no longer', implies that the speaker's first answer is framed by a concept of love which assumes the loved one's face to be an integral part of 'love'. However, this idea of love – emerging at the point where, in the German, the rhythmical turbulence is particularly marked – does not provide a clear answer to the initial question, because the concept defies assignment to a single pole of the fundamental dichotomy between the transitory and the permanent. Whereas the first reply characterises 'love' as forgotten, the next stanza indicates that love, like the cloud, belongs to the sphere of definite knowledge.

3

> A person uttering the word 'cloud' will neither think of its definition, nor
> will he see a particular mental picture of clouds as a natural phenomenon.
> The various concepts and images of the cloud, the emotions associated
> with the sight of it, and ultimately everything that may be connected with
> it […] can spring to mind at once, and yet there is no danger of confusion,
> since one sound welds it all together and preserves its wholeness.[16]

In our analysis of the text, we said that the textual conception of
'Remembering Marie A.' is characterised by a series of semantic
oppositions: for example, high versus low, the cloud versus the face,
knowledge versus memory, and transience versus permanence. On
closer inspection, these oppositions not only turn out to be intrinsically unstable; they are also involved in a series of relationships at
the syntagmatic level that pose considerable problems for any interpretation. Previous interpretations have sought to reduce these
problems, with the help of various assumptions, in order to assign a
determinate meaning to the text. Taking a different approach, we
propose in the following section of this paper to investigate the
multiplicity of relationships between the various oppositions, using
reading techniques taken from the repertoire of deconstruction.[17]

The problems of interpretation begin with the 'cloud', the
subject of several statements which, taken together, are either logically or empirically contradictory. These contradictions have been
handled in widely differing ways by previous readers. Whereas Jan
Knopf ignores them completely, Marcel Reich-Ranicki addresses
them openly but strips them of their problematic character by
superimposing a dialectical logic on the poem as a whole: according
to his attractively deft and uncluttered interpretation, the three
verses follow the familiar pattern 'thesis–antithesis–synthesis',
which Reich-Ranicki reads as a progression from memory to forgetting to a form of memory that is stable and lasting.[18]

In the context of a deconstructive interpretation, we are not
primarily interested in the logical or empirical contradictions
attaching to the cloud as a signifier with a definite meaning. What
interests us is the question how the linguistic sign 'cloud' – in con-

junction with, or in opposition to, other signifiers – contributes to the construction of meaning in the poem. According to deconstructive theory, a sign does not denote a represented object; instead, representation occurs as the retrospective effect of a semantic fiction.[19] On the basis of this concept of representation, and of the idea of the oppositional constitution of meaning, it is possible to describe the genesis of meaning in 'Marie A.' as a process involving three stages. The sign 'cloud' plays a key role in the constitution of the 'remembered' image. It serves as a point of reference for the emergence of a symbolic sphere that directly opposes it: the position of the white cloud in the sky corresponds to that of the pale lover on the ground. Once the scene under the plum tree has been set, the cloud has fulfilled its function and can therefore be allowed to fade away. This is done by giving the cloud the features of transience which in the scene of memory are assigned to the ground-level sphere of the plum trees and the woman; the cloud assumes the temporal dimension of its spatial opposition, and can vanish in the wind. The vanishing can therefore be understood as a displacement of the cloud as sign by a complex of signs that are distinct from the cloud yet developed from it. This abstraction of the signifier 'cloud' from definite spatial and temporal contexts coincides with its integration into the opposition between knowledge and remembrance.

The interweaving of the local and temporal relationships between the two symbolic spheres can be seen as a textbook example of Derrida's 'play of difference',[20] understood as the condition of possibility of the functioning of any sign. But finally, the cloud as signifier is removed from the order of the sign which initially forms the very ground of its emergence.[21] Precisely by vanishing from the scene of memory, the cloud assumes its key significance for the act of remembering; it becomes the sign that provides the basis for constituting and organizing the idea of memory. Thus, the development of the relationships between the cloud and the other signs and complexes of signs in 'Remembering Marie A.' can be read as a process of creating memory through literature – a form of memory that clearly remains a semantic fiction, because the indelible traces of its fabrication are revealed by the relationships between its signifying elements.

In terms of a theory of signs, the cloud acquires the significance assigned to it in the final stanza by effecting a transition from topological and temporal order to the opposition between knowing and remembering. In this key opposition, constituted in the middle verse, 'knowing' seems to denote a random and unlimited availability of ideas, while 'remembering' refers to the direct visualisation of those ideas. But these concepts, too – knowing and remembering – have to be examined in the light of the deconstructive premises that we outlined a moment ago in connection with the question of the reference of linguistic expressions. According to these premises, which systematically privilege the present over the past, the act of remembering cannot be seen as the mechanical retrieval of the stored contents of memory, nor can knowledge be regarded as an instantly accessible archive of consciousness. Statements pertaining to memory and utterances claiming the status of knowledge are organised around an absence that remains categorically excluded from representation; accordingly, memory and knowledge cannot exist without a symbolic Other – they are both fictional schemes.

The import of this, in considering 'Remembering Marie A.', is that the reflections of the middle stanza do not only contain the communicative basis of the memories explored in stanzas 1 and 3; they are also temporally anterior to these memories. The knowledge claimed in the central and final stanzas can only assert its own presence by referring to signifying structures. The memories in stanzas 1 and 3 are designed precisely to serve this purpose; thus, instead of representing a pre-existing context, they are constituted in order to function as a structure of reference for the statements in the central stanza, which have a primary status with regard to the situation and act of speaking. The relationship between the present of speech and the past of memory is therefore seen to be a relationship of close-meshed interdependence: knowledge is the ground of memory and memory the basis for the coming to consciousness of knowledge. Thus, the relationship between the temporal levels mirrors the idea already illustrated by the relationship between the two symbolic spheres in the poem – the idea of the constitution of meaning in the play of significative oppositions. The present of speech and the knowledge of the cloud remain involved in this game and are therefore above all suspicion of succumbing to a metaphysics of presence.[22] But love occupies a different, special position. Love, though it is introduced in the context of the unfolding of the dichotomy between knowledge and memory, is not implicated in the processes of oppositional meaning-creation: like the cloud, it is located within the sphere of knowledge, but the speaker can say of it, as of the woman, 'I really can't remember'. The unseen interlocutor's question 'how does that love seem now?' is therefore the question on which the entire poem is predicated. From a temporal and semiotic point of view, the signifier 'love' is anterior to the poem. It has a meta-semantic – or metaphysical – status; initially devoid of meaning in its own right, it nevertheless becomes the trigger for the production of meaning. Eventually, the signifier itself acquires a meaning, but of a kind that remains fully dependent on its poetic realisation in the process of allusion and counter-allusion that begins and ends with the cloud, generating the signs around which the processes of remembering and forgetting are organised, in a present that is undercut – in a manner analogous to the phenomenon of *différance* – by the negation of linear sequence, and is shown to be a species of 'future Nachträglichkeit', or deferred action. Any attempt to define the concept of love on the basis of a single link in this chain of allusions is doomed to fail. The concept cannot be defined solely in terms of remembering or forgetting – because of its metaphysical status, it never acquires a single meaning that can be formulated in propositional terms: its meaning, insofar as it has one, subsists entirely within the poetic process of 'Remembering Marie A.'.

4

For any programme of interpretation that aims at a delimitation of meaning on the basis of intentionalism, the contextualisation of the subject-matter has a decisive importance. The possible biographical context of 'Remembering Marie A.' need not detain us very long. As the object of his devotions herself recalls,[23] Brecht was involved in a protracted and unsuccessful attempt to win the favours of a woman called Marie Rose Aman. The relationship began in 1916 and ended in the autumn of 1920; and during this whole time it never advanced beyond the exchange of kisses. This, and the fact that Marie Aman also allowed other suitors to kiss her, aroused ambivalent feelings in Brecht: his letters to Caspar Neher indicate jealousy, possibly pain, and above all, anger.[24] However, the significance of these biographical details is eclipsed by the literary context of the poem, which completely integrates the empirical person into Brecht's poetic world: the similarities between the real Marie A. and the figure in the poem are almost completely irrelevant to the interpretation of the text.

Thematically, 'Remembering Marie A.' appears most closely related to the 'Epilogpsalmen'/'Epilogue Psalms'[25] which also originated in 1920 but were devoted to another of Brecht's lovers, Hedda Kuhn. The poems are defiant gestures of valediction, proclaiming the end of the affair and punishing the loved one with oblivion. But 'Remembering Marie A.' differs importantly from these works, not only with regard to the verse form, but also because of the carefully delineated image of the cloud – and for this reason we cannot agree with Jan Knopf's interpretation of the text as a simple 'farewell to love'. In Brecht's early poetry, the image of the cloud is generally associated with the figure of the loved one, and it is on this poetic context that we now propose to focus. In the 1919 version of Brecht's drama *Baal*, the protagonist addresses Sophie Dechant thus, after making love:

I'm calm now, like a child. It is the calm of the sky, high above, and evening, the trees yearn for it. There's a sweet gentleness in me also, like the acid of apples that have lain long and taste gentle; something swells my belly sweetly, it is full and yet light. And yet I'm at peace, cradled by your slim white knees as if in a gentle air full of breezes. We wander, you and I, through a drunken night, towards the morning. And you are the white cloud in the sky, and because we are walking at the same pace we are at rest for one another. When we look at each other we appear still, and yet we are walking and full of movement.[26]

This passage is a classic example of the characteristic Baalian outlook as it applies to love: a regressive image of symbiosis, an image of perfect rapture, of fusion with the universe, of mystical calm in the midst of movement. Symbiotic fantasies are a frequent and well-known feature of Brecht's early poetic world; white clouds and pale lovers crop up repeatedly in *Baal*. But these stock metaphors of love can have several different meanings. The crucial point is that, in the quoted passage from *Baal*, the woman and the white cloud both belong to the same, undivided world, whereas in 'Remembering Marie A.' they are assigned to entirely separate realms: here, the loved one is forgotten, but the remembered image of the cloud will be preserved for ever. Klaus Schuhmann has pointed to the pivotal role of Brecht's 'Ballade vom Tod des Anna Gewölkegesichts'/ 'Ballad of the death of Anna Cloudface'[27] in the process whereby these two spheres become disassociated. Here the idea of consigning the loved one's face to oblivion is combined with the cloud motif in a specific and unique way. Instead of merely juxtaposing the two images, the lyric voice describes how the face dissolves in the cloud: this idea is explored in the first five verses and confirmed in the final lines.

Ballad of the death of Anna Cloudface

1
Seven years went by. With gin and with whisky
He swilled her face right out of his brain
And the hole in the air grew blacker, and full of
The flood of liquor this brain became bare.

2
With gin and tobacco, with organs and orgies:
What was her face like, when she vanished from here?
What was her face like? Did it merge in the cloud-drifts?
Hey, there, face! This white page met his stare.

3
Wherever he travelled, on how many shores
(He didn't just go there as you would or I)
A voice cried out to him white on the waters
A voice from lips that were fading away...

4
Once more he sees her face: in the cloud drift,
Very pale by now. Since he lingered too long...

Once more in the wind he heard her voice, faintly
Far off in the wind which was driving the cloud...

5
But in later years he had nothing
Left but the cloud and wind, and they
Began to be silent as she was
And like her to fade away.

[...]

8
But always up to those hills that are wilting
Away high above in wild April's winds white
Like cloud-drifts fly his desires ever paling:
A face goes by. And a mouth falls mute.

Translated by Michael Hamburger[28]

Although the poem is set in a world of hard-bitten seafarers and adventurers, the tone shows that the transformation of the face involves a strong element of emotional conflict. In 'Remembering Marie A.', the loved one and the cloud already belong to distinct spheres, which are kept carefully apart and connected only by the abstract concept of love.

Brecht was evidently aware of the poem's emotional charge and of the significance of the relationship between the cloud and the loved one. This is indicated by the 'paratexts' in the manuscript annotations.[29] The least problematical of these is a note reading '21.II.20, abends 7h im Zug nach Berlin' [21.2.20, 7 p.m., on the train to Berlin], which serves to date and – as it were – to authenticate the poem. But there are two further paratexts that have a quite different function. The manuscript title 'Sentimental Song No. 1004' not only suggests a particular genre, it also alludes to the figure of Don Juan, who claimed to have had 1,003 love affairs in Spain alone.[30] It implies the presence of a speaker who has surpassed the achievements of even this legendary serial lover – a speaker, moreover, who does not wish to be identified with the relatively sensitive lyric self of the poem. The relationship between this cynical speaker and his lyrical counterpart is one of irreducible tension. A similar problem arises from the second paratext, which reads: 'Im Zustand der gefüllten Samenblase sieht der Mann in jedem Weib Aphrodite. Geh. R. Kraus' [To a man with inflated gonads, any woman will resemble Aphrodite. Kraus, District Medical Officer].[31]This text is worded as if it were the conclusion of a medical report on the poem: a doctor, called in to give an expert opinion, has diagnosed the work as a mildly pathological product of a poet with a clearly identifiable physiological problem. And the speaker of this paratext dispels any suspicion that he might be identical with the lyric self of the poem. Whereas one of the paratexts serves to certify the poem's authenticity, the function of the other two is apparently to establish a sense of detachment from the lyric self; the author seems uncertain whether to identify with or to disavow the lyric self, and so he does both – he signs the poem and at the same time disowns it. Only by excising the paratexts and replacing the final title[32] does Brecht eventually accept the lyric self.

'Remembering Marie A.' is a poem about remembering and forgetting, a renunciation and an affirmation of love. The affair with the empirical lover is declared to be over; her face and personality are consigned to the sphere of time and oblivion. But one aspect of love is rescued and preserved, as a permanent cognitive possession that time can never take away. The aspect in question is the idea of love, with its attendant fantasies of symbiosis, which is purged of all contingent elements and transformed into a Platonic cloud that eventually fuses with the universe high above. The biographical significance of such an attitude to love is a matter best left to interpreters with a more thorough grounding in psychoanalytic theory. Our own interest is drawn to what we see as a general premise of Brecht's lyric method. His division of the world into opposing spheres and his search for cognitive certainties appear to be based on a deep metaphysical need that could scarcely fail to leave its mark on his later work.

Translated by John Ormrod

3

Vom ertrunkenen Mädchen

1

Als sie ertrunken war und hinunterschwamm
Von den Bächen in die größeren Flüsse
Schien der Opal des Himmels sehr wundersam
Als ob er die Leiche begütigen müsse.

2

Tang und Algen hielten sich an ihr ein
So daß sie langsam viel schwerer ward
Kühl die Fische schwammen an ihrem Bein
Pflanzen und Tiere beschwerten noch ihre letzte Fahrt.

3

Und der Himmel ward abends dunkel wie Rauch
Und hielt nachts mit den Sternen das Licht in Schwebe.
Aber früh war er hell, daß es auch
Noch für sie Morgen und Abend gebe.

4

Als ihr bleiche Leib im Wasser verfaulet war
Geschah es (sehr langsam), daß Gott sie allmählich vergaß
Erst ihr Gesicht, dann die Hände und ganz zuletzt erst ihr Haar.
Dann ward sie Aas in Flüssen mit vielem Aas.[1]

The drowned girl

1

Once she had drowned and started her slow descent
From streams to where the great rivers broaden
The opal sky shone most magnificent
As if it had been her body's guardian.

2

Wrack and duckweed cling to her as she swims
Slowly their burden adds to her weight.
Cool the fishes play about her limbs
Creatures and growths encumber her in her final state.

3

And in the evening the sky grew dark as smoke
And at night the stars kept the light from falling.
But soon it cleared as dawn again broke
To maintain her sequence of evening and morning.

4

As her pallid body decayed in the water there
It happened (very slowly) that it gently slid from God's thoughts:
First her face, then her hands, and right at the end her hair.
Leaving those corpse-choked rivers just one more corpse.

Translated by John Willett [2]

Three 'Ophelia' poems

Ophelia

I
On the calm black water where the stars sleep
White Ophelia floats like a great lily;
Floats very slowly, lying in her long veils …
– You hear in the distant woods sounds of the kill.

For more than a thousand years sad Ophelia
Has passed, a white phantom, down the long black river.
For more than a thousand years her sweet madness
Has murmured its romance to the evening breeze.

The wind kisses her breasts and unfolds in a wreath
Her great veils softly cradled by the waters;
The trembling willows weep on her shoulder,
Over her wide dreaming brow the reeds bend down.

The ruffled water lilies sigh around her;
At times she awakens, in a sleeping alder,
Some nest, from which escapes a slight rustle of wings;
– A mysterious song falls from the golden stars.

II

O pale Ophelia! beautiful as snow!
Yes, child, you died, carried off by a river!
– Because the winds falling from the great mountains of Norway
Had spoken to you in low voices of bitter freedom.

It was a breath, twisting your hair,
That bore strange rumors to your dreaming mind;
It was your heart listening to the song of nature
In the complaints of the tree and the sighs of the nights;

It was the voice of mad seas, a great noise,
That broke your child's heart, too human and too soft;
It was a handsome pale knight, a poor madman
Who one April morning sat mute at your knees!

Heaven! Love! Freedom! What a dream, oh poor mad girl!
You melted to him as snow to a fire;
Your great visions strangled your words
– And fearful Infinity terrifies your blue eyes!

III

– And the Poet says that under the rays of the stars
You come at night to look for the flowers you picked,
And that he saw on the water, lying in her long veils,
White Ophelia floating, like a great lily.

Arthur Rimbaud, 1870
Translated by Wallace Fowlie

Ophelia

In her hair a nest of young water-rats,
hands heavy with rings splayed on the deep
like fins, she drifts through shadows of the great
primeval forest in its sunken sleep.

Wandering through the dusk the sun's last ray
plunges into the coffin of her brain.
Why her death? Why does she drift alone
where fern and weed and growth tangle her way?

A wind stands in the clustered reeds. It starts
the bats from hiding like a sudden hand.
Wings glistening with water-drops and dark,
they hang like smoke where the dark current bends,

like clouds at night. An eel across her breast
slips long and white. A glow-worm's light adorns
her brow. And leaves drop as a willow mourns
for her, and an agony whose voice is lost.

Georg Heym, 1911
Translated by Antony Hasler

Blithe Childhood

The mouth of a girl who'd lain long in the reeds
looked nibbled and bitten at.
When they broke open her chest the gullet was full of holes.
And then, in a grove beneath the diaphragm,
they found a nest of young rats.
One little sister lay dead.
The others were living off liver and kidney,
drinking the cold blood and had
lived a blithe childhood down here.
Just as blithe and swift was their death:
They threw the whole brood in the water.
Oh, how the little blighters squeaked!

Gottfried Benn, 1912
Translated by Tom Kuhn

Reading 'The drowned girl':
a Brecht poem and its contexts

Hilda M. Brown

Like 'Erinnerung an die Marie A.' / 'Remembering Marie A.'[3] with which, through the theme of memory, it has close affinities, this poem is taken from the *Hauspostille / Domestic Breviary* collection. Unlike that poem, however, 'Vom ertrunkenen Mädchen' / 'The drowned girl' exists in yet another context, that is to say, as an interpolated poem in Brecht's first drama, *Baal*. The question I want to pose in this paper is the question of *contextuality*. How important is it to view the poem within these different contexts? One could extend this enquiry to another context as well, to which I shall also make a brief allusion: this is the poem's relationship to a poetic tradition, of 'Ophelia' poems or 'Wasserleichenpoesie', a tradition which extends from the pre-Raphaelites and Rimbaud through to Paul Celan and Rolf Dieter Brinkmann. In the form of 'Untergangslyrik' [apocalyptic poetry] this tradition reaches a peak in the Expressionist decade, with contributions by such poets as Georg Heym and Gottfried Benn.[4]

One way of looking at the question of contextualisation is to examine the poem first as a free-standing entity (it was actually published separately under the title 'Die Ballade vom ertrunkenen Mädchen' in *Die Weltbühne* on 30 November 1922) and to treat it as 'poésie pure', adopting a 'werkimmanent' approach. Let us try out this method first and see how far it takes us.

The poem is based on a progression, which reaches a climax in the last line. The corpse of a young girl drifts downstream, following the pull of the current, gradually decomposing until, at the final stage in this process, it loses all those physical features which identify it as a 'human' being and becomes absorbed into the organic matter and plant-life of which the river is composed ('Dann ward sie Aas in Flüssen mit vielem Aas' [literally, 'Then she became rotting flesh in rivers with much rotting flesh']). The cyclical nature of biological processes is implied here; it is an idea which is not dissimilar to the biblical notion of 'ashes to ashes, dust to dust'.

At the same time, the onward-driving force of the river's current is partly modified through various motifs of retardation. The corpse's journey has started in what we must assume to be the fast-flowing mountain streams ('swam down from the streams') but the main focus in the poem is on its slow progress in sluggish rivers richly endowed with plant and animal life ('wrack and duckweed'; 'cool the fishes', 'creatures and growths'). Almost an eco-friendly environment, you could say (though some think it is a city river because of the word 'smoke').[5]

The poem's structure is defined by the two contrasting planes, upper and lower. Complementing the lower horizontal level of the drifting corpse is the dimension of the sky ('the opal sky'; 'the sky grew dark as smoke / And at night the stars kept the light from falling'). Arguably, the reference to 'God' in the last stanza might be linked with this higher level of the sky too (though opinions differ on this).[6] The mysterious opalesque hue of the sky in stanza 1 (the opal is a favourite motif in Expressionist poetry)[7] seems almost to have come into being for the express purpose of benefiting ('begütigen') the corpse. The alternation of morning and evening, light and dark, is likewise presented as a kind of favour on the part of higher, unseen powers towards the disintegrating physical body. The reference to God's 'forgetfulness' ('Geschah es, sehr langsam, daß Gott sie allmählich vergaß' [literally, '...that God gradually forgot her'] might suggest a final 'switching off' of this 'interest' from without. This function of memory too is presented as part of a process ('gradually').

Thus far, my interpretation has simply provided a bald description of the main structural features, drawing attention to certain ambiguities. To provide a more complete reading, one needs first to define the poet's attitude to what he is presenting; secondly, to elucidate the most difficult and ambiguous features, which relate to the 'sky/God' imagery. Finally, it is important to assess the significance of the poem's climax and its connection with the theme of 'forgetting'. All these issues are interconnected.

As to the first point, one receives a number of possible clues from *within* the poem, for example from its style and tone. The mainly five-stress lines – a mixture of trochaic and dactylic measures – is stately; the rhyme scheme is regular (a b a b, etc.) and avoids monotony by a judicious use of enjambement, which also mirrors the sense of a slow, stately but inexorable progression. The complete (and remarkable) absence of commas where one would expect them and a limited use of end-stopping strongly reinforces this sense of forward propulsion. Nothing is allowed to interfere with this sense of the inexorable; only the deliberately fragmented rhythm of the penultimate line, which reflects the piecemeal dissolution of the component parts of the body: 'First her face, then her hands, and right at the end her hair', provides a momentary interruption. But immediately in the final line the predominating pattern is resumed. Nothing about this highly accomplished presentation suggests disgust or revulsion at what, more commonly, might be regarded as a horrific disintegration of a human body. Even the parenthesis ('very slowly') has a softening effect on the subject-matter, underlining almost casually the idea of a slow, gradual process of disintegration which is characteristic of the impersonal forces of nature.

In short, it might seem as if the full range of aesthetic effects has been harnessed to beautify or glamorise a situation which normally would evoke revulsion. One critic talks of the impression of 'glassy artificiality' created by the poem's style.[8] Indeed, many other examples of aesthetic virtuosity could be cited. What is difficult to decide, on the evidence, is whether the impersonality and beauty are self-consciously assumed by the poet, possibly for ironical purposes. The question of the poet's perspective here is crucial. On the face of it, he is detached from his subject-matter. The title almost sounds like a report ('Vom ertrunkenen Mädchen' might even be translated: 'concerning the drowned girl'). The proceedings are presented in a matter-of-fact way in the form of a narrative: 'als' (line1), 'als' (line13), 'dann' (line16) [when ... when ... then]. But at the same time he includes more subjective, interpretative details: 'sehr wundersam' [most magnificent], 'beschwerten' [encumber]; and similes: 'als ob' [as if], 'dunkel wie Rauch' [dark as smoke]; things you would not expect to see in a report. These small but significant details point beyond the purely physical level on which the poem operates, that is, as a narrative account of the process of decomposition of a human body, to an evaluative or judgemental perspective on the whole process. This gives the poem an ambiguous tension between style and subject-matter.

No stanza seems more ambiguous to me than the third. Once again, this is because it hints at issues beyond the physical level of decay by focusing on the upper spatial dimension: the sky as opposed to the water and the dynamic tensions between the light and the darkness ('der Himmel … hielt nachts mit den Sternen das Licht in Schwebe' [literally, 'the sky … at night held the light in balance with the stars']) as well as morning and evening ('To maintain her sequence of evening and morning'). But the sharpness of the opposition between darkness and light is slightly blurred by the poet's presentation of the darkness of the sky as a vague murkiness ('like smoke') with which the brightness of the stars has to compete. Interesting here is the notion of a balance ('hielt in Schwebe') which *might* be construed as indicating a kind of cosmic order; a similar balance is implied by the alternating patterns of 'evening' and 'morning'. A feature of this stanza is the way in which these balancing forces in the natural world are presented firstly in cosmic terms ('sky', 'stars') and then in terms of what this implies for the human corpse. In the earthly domain, the practical implications of light and darkness are encapsulated in the times of day – morning and evening. But here there would seem to be more than a tinge of irony. The word 'Aber' [But] which marks the transition from the cosmic to the human level at the same time highlights the fact that this humanising of cosmic processes – setting them, that is, within the context of human perceptions and human experience – is achieved for no practical purpose. The suggestion that cosmic processes could serve human ends is subverted for the reader by the knowledge that the corpse cannot benefit any more from this apparent bounty of nature. What is important here is the discrepancy between the standpoint which is being *attributed* to Nature and the stark reality of the situation. The irony is produced by man's attempts to view his own significance in more grandiose terms than is warranted in the face of the larger, impersonal designs of Nature.[9]

Does this stanza provide us with an interpretative clue to understanding the problematic 'God/sky' imagery in general? Certainly, reading back from this to the first stanza, one can see there too evidence of the intentional (or pathetic) fallacy which has emerged powerfully and persuasively from the third. The suggestion implied in stanza 1 that the very strange, exotic ('wundersam') opalesque hue of the sky is somehow or other connected with the appearance of the drifting corpse may be regarded as another anthropomorphic fallacy. The proposition that what may well be a phenomenon explicable in purely physical terms is a kind of special show put on by Nature for the benefit of a human corpse appears in the sober light of day to be somewhat preposterous.

The sky imagery and the alternating pattern of light and darkness can be interpreted, then, in terms of impersonal cosmic processes which operate quite independently of man (despite his apparent wish to deny this). How does 'Gott' fit in these notions? It cannot be assumed that, as in biblical iconography, He inhabits the 'Himmel', unless as an (imagined) all-seeing eye looking down from an extra-terrestrial perspective. The sky (or heavens) – and its earthly manifestation as day and night – is a real, scientifically verifiable phenomenon. God, however, is in a different category, but a link between His role and that of the sky is established in the way He is attributed with human qualities, such as 'forgetting' (which presupposes His previously having 'known'). This feature of His existence – a man-dependent one – links up with the intentional fallacy which was found to be at work in the first stanza. There it was hinted that the sky's opalesque hue had been adopted in order to 'benefit' the corpse. Now it is suggested that 'God' who had briefly taken a benevolent interest in the girl, ceases to do so when she loses all traces of an identity. This train of thought seems to point in the direction of a post-Nietzschean position where religious ideas are unmasked and shown to be mere psychologising: 'God has forgotten' is as much as to say 'God is dead'. However, Nietzsche's stridency about this discovery is entirely lacking in Brecht's poem. There seems to be a mood of compliance with the state of things. One might therefore be reluctant to jump to the conclusion that Brecht is adopting a position of complete nihilism, as some commentators suggest.[10]

The climax of the poem comes, as I suggested earlier, in the final line. When the process of dissolution is complete and the corpse has been absorbed into the organic matter present in the river, its most distinguishing features are obliterated: face, hands and hair (the motif of hair, so often emphasised in pictorial depictions of Ophelia, already suggests a link with the long strands of the weeds and algae, connecting human and non-human biological matter). 'Dann ward sie Aas in Flüssen mit vielem Aas'. While not necessarily regarding this as nihilism – for, as I said, it is a state of affairs which Brecht seems to tolerate and accept – the absence of transcendence (in the form of 'God') is clearly stated. I see two possible interconnected readings here: firstly, Brecht's 'Diesseitigkeit' [this-worldliness] and acknowledgement of the physical laws governing all matter and acceptance of man's consequent insignificance, and secondly, his fashioning of this theme – self-consciously – into something which could be described as aesthetically beautiful and significant. This could be perceived as an 'answer' to the first discovery in the form of an expression of the creative impulse *malgré tout*.

I shall now turn to a few of the *contextual possibilities* I mentioned, in order to test out my 'immanente Interpretation'. As with so many of Brecht's works, the genesis of the poem is unclear and it has been suggested that it may even have been written *first* contextually, rather than as a free-standing entity.[11] Some see its origins as antedating even its appearance in *Baal* and point to the existence of a version entitled 'Vom erschlagenen Mädchen' which has been linked to a now lost 'Ballade von der roten Rosa',[12] dating from Brecht's Augsburg days early in 1919. The context here is very specific and relates to Rosa Luxemburg, who, along with Karl Liebknecht, led the Communist-inspired Spartakus uprising in Berlin in 1919, and was subsequently murdered, her body being thrown into the Landwehr canal from which it was eventually recovered. Interesting though this connection may be, I do not feel it is of much relevance to an interpretation of the later version, 'Vom ertrunkenen Mädchen', since this version of the poem deliberately avoids all reference to the *cause* of death, and concentrates entirely on the final stages of the corpse's days on earth before its dissolution. The earliest intimations of our poem appear in association with the second (i.e. 1919) version of *Baal*. Some of the familiar motifs are already present in a speech of Baal's addressed to the messenger, Baumann: 'sometimes I dream of a lake, deep and dark, and I lie down between the fish and look at the sky, day and night, until I rot'. Also close to our version of the poem is a speech by Johannes in this same version:

a very small corpse, half rotted ... Now there are rats and weed in her green hair, rather becoming ... a little swollen and whitish, and filled with the stinking ooze from the river, completely black. She was always so clean. That's why she went into the river and began to stink. [13]

This links the motif of the drowned girl directly to Johannes's fiancée, Johanna. But what is really interesting is that Brecht abandons this explicit link and the whole question of motivation in *all* subsequent versions of the play, *Baal*. And this despite the fact that Johanna is indeed still a victim of Baal's lusts and seeks her death in drowning as a result. Brecht simply places the poem in Baal's mouth as one of his poetic works and without any reference to the precise circumstances which have led to death. Baal reads it in a detached manner, as if it had nothing to do with him personally. The reader, of course, is well aware of his wiles, but is also being made to consider the proposition that he is re-fashioning (or, if you like, falsifying) experience in the process of creating poetry. As the young Brecht sees it, the creative process is decidedly amoral. Like many of Brecht's early works, *Baal* has a literary emphasis – the figure of the iconoclastic Bohemian poet Baal is based primarily on his cherished poet-heroes, the *poètes maudits*, Verlaine and Rimbaud.

Possibly because of the literary and amoral accentuation in this poem (and this is a common feature in many of Brecht's other works of the same period, poems and dramas), he sought to give it *another life* after his artistic and political 'Wende' around 1925–6. He now pressed it into service for the *Domestic Breviary* collection. This was published firstly as the *Taschenpostille / Pocket Breviary* in 1926, after protracted delays as Brecht craftily played off his two publishers, Kiepenhauer and Ullstein, against one another; then in 1927 under its new title *Hauspostille*. Now our poem is set within an *anthology* of diverse poems – ballads, lyrical works, etc. – written over a lengthy period (1916–25) and held together by an elaborate framework: the breviary. Here Brecht is parodying religious instructional literature. The basic model is the Lutheran instructional book (1544) of Veit Dietrich, which is intended as a pocket guide to keep believers on the straight and narrow, offering explanation and commentary on a biblical text. However, that does not stop Brecht from basing the individual sections ('Lektionen' [lessons]) of his *Domestic Breviary* on the Catholic equivalents: 'Petitions, Spiritual Exercises, Chronicles', etc. Our poem, 'The drowned girl', comes under the '5th Lesson' which is entitled 'Die kleinen Tagzeiten des Abgestorbenen' [The little hours of the deceased]. These 'Tagzeiten' are the 'canonic hours' in monasteries set aside for devotions; normally seven in all each day. The other poems in this group deal with the topic of death, e.g. 'Von den verführten Mädchen'/'Of the seduced girls', 'Die Ballade vom Liebestod'/ 'Ballad of the love-death', 'Legende vom toten Soldaten'/'Legend of the dead soldier'. The first of these is virtually a companion piece to 'The drowned girl'.[14] Corpses of drowned girls, entangled in weeds and algae, drift downstream. But the perspective is entirely different: the instigator of the suicides – the seducer – is identified as the first person; he registers a few pangs of conscience ('Gewissensbisse') but then, ambiguously, shows more concern and self-pity for the legacy of disease which the girls have transmitted than regret at their untimely demise.

Obviously, in suggesting that such subject-matter could be the focus for spiritual devotions, Brecht is parodying the form of the breviary and ridiculing religion in a manner which is calculated to provoke and shock bourgeois sensibilities. The overall framework as outlined in the Preface ('Notes for the use of the individual lessons') spells out the irony even more plainly. With reference to 'The drowned girl', the third poem (or 'chapter') in its group, we read 'the third chapter is to be read with whispering lips'. Further 'instruction' in how to read the poems is contained in the general injunction that the reader should conclude each and every reading with one of the poem 'Gegen Verführung' / 'Against temptation'. On duly turning to this poem, the reader finds a series of instructions which countermand all established religious teaching and stridently denounce any notion of an afterlife ('You die with all the creatures/And there comes nothing after'). In place of this Brecht proposes instead the philosophy of *carpe diem*, living life to the full: 'Slurp it in heady drafts'.

The effect of all this is to subvert the poems themselves, or rather to ensure that they are *not* viewed in the way I have been looking at 'The drowned girl', i.e. as a free-standing entity, a 'pure' poem. The injunction to concentrate all energies on the here and now, and the categorical statement that there is no form of transcendence or afterlife, acts, in the case of our poem, as a corrective to any ambiguity which might exist about the presence or otherwise of 'Gott' in the world or the hereafter. In its new *Domestic Breviary* context, the poem, with its originally gentle, maybe slightly reluctant toying with the possibilities of nihilism and its overtones of decadence and aestheticism is relativised by the crasser, unambiguous statements contained in 'Against temptation' and the elephantine humour of the 'frame'. By 1926 Brecht had distanced himself from his earlier phase of chaotic, often ambiguous experimentation and self-exploration. One might say that in the *Domestic Breviary* something almost akin to the effects of 'epic' theatre is being aimed at. Rather than rewrite or suppress certain poems which, for example, with their literary overlay and Symbolist influences, might now be a source of some embarrassment or misinterpretation, as indeed was also the case with his early plays,[15] Brecht can leave them as they are and manipulate them instead from without. A typically ingenious solution.

Finally, I shall very briefly draw attention to the wider contextual relationship of 'The drowned girl' to a whole tradition of poetry on a similar theme, the 'Ophelia' poetry, which focuses on the death by drowning of a beautiful young girl. The original source is known to us all, Gertrude's speech in *Hamlet*, IV, vii: 'There is a willow grows aslant a brook,/That shows his hoar leaves in the glassy stream/There with fantastic garlands did she come,/Of crow-flowers, nettles, daisies, and long purples...' This motif attracted many artists in the nineteenth and early twentieth centuries, both visual and literary. Among the former, the most celebrated were Delacroix (1844), Millais (1852) (see illustration 6), Edvard Munch (1896) and Alfred Kubin (1903–6). Among poets, Tennyson (*The Lady of Shalott*), Rimbaud ('Ophélie' and 'Le bateau ivre'), Georg Heym ('Ophelia') (see pp. 74–7) and Gottfried Benn ('Schöne Jugend' [Blithe childhood]) to name only a few.[16] The popularity of the literary motif seems to peak with the Decadence of the late 1890s and the early Expressionist movement, whose members were much influenced by various translations of Rimbaud's works (Alfred Wolfenstein, K. L. Ammer): 'apocalyptic poetry' was a favoured mode among this pre-First World War generation and it is subjected to many variations, ranging from Heym's visions of a decaying civilisation to Benn's unsparing clinical anatomisation of the manifestations of physical decay in the form of a post-mortem. Both Heym and Benn dwell on the horrific and grotesque aspects of the Ophelia theme – particularly repulsive in both are the references to the activities of the rats, a motif with which Brecht, as we saw, initially toyed, but then withdrew. Such details are not emphasised in Rimbaud's depiction of the smooth and stately progression of the corpse: 'Sur l'onde calme et noire où dorment les étoiles ...'[17] Brecht's treatment is not dissimilar to Rimbaud's in terms of description. And this is not entirely unexpected, given the powerful attraction the French poet exercised on him in the early Augsburg period. This influence reaches its peak in the early version of the drama *In the Jungle of Cities* (1921–2) in which whole sections from both *Les Illuminations* and *Une Saison en enfer* are set into the dialogue (complete with quotation marks).[18] Brecht's treatment of the Ophelia topos is very distinctive and original: and while Rimbaud's Ophélie preserves her identity (so had the Lady of Shalott!), that of Brecht's drowned girl is obliterated, as her decomposing body takes on another role within the cycle of nature.

Setting Brecht's poem within this tradition is helpful, I think, in identifying its essential qualities, in particular his personal approach to the question of death and decay and response to the contemporary debate about nihilism in a post-Nietzschean world. Above all, however, it emphasises his links with a *literary* tradition and the inevitably self-conscious annexation of motifs from this tradition. Rimbaud's epilogue to his 'Ophélie' introduces the poet's own voice ('Et le poète dit ...') and draws the reader's attention to the poet's role as a 'maker' and creator of the poem, and thus to the poetic level of reality which exists alongside the more mundane one. A parallel can be drawn here with the *Baal* version of 'The drowned girl' where it is presented by the poet himself as a self-consciously *literary* product, totally divorced from religion. But even an interpretation of the free-standing poem can benefit from association with other literary models, such as the Rimbaud version. In the poet's self-conscious application of high levels of aesthetic polish and formal and stylistic control in treating the subject's loss of identity and disintegration – an ironic disjunction between style and subject-matter – at least some measure of ambiguity attaches to the poetic process itself.

What in fact we have been dealing with is, of course, not *one* poem, but *three*. The miracle is that each text, however, is identical. Only the contexts change and produce perspectives which differ strikingly. The *Baal* context underlines the tendency to reinforce and exploit the aesthetic appeal of this rich and powerfully multivalent subject-matter. Setting the poem within the Ophelia tradition reinforces this impression. The *Domestic Breviary* context attempts to completely subvert any literary impressions or religious ambiguity that might be lurking in any of the poems: an almost Heine-esque example of 'Stimmungsbrechung' is achieved whereby an atmosphere of aesthetic completeness is rudely shattered by health warnings about the damaging effects of religious and/or aesthetic ambiguity. The free-standing poem, the 'Ballad of the drowned girl', tallies most closely with the *Baal* position. The aesthetic/religious dimension is at the forefront, but is much more tentatively, and more ambiguously handled than in the drama.

4

From *Ten Poems from A Reader for Those who Live in Cities*
'Part from your friends at the station'

I
Part from your friends at the station
Enter the city in the morning with your coat buttoned up
Look for a room, and when your friend knocks:
Do not, o do not, open the door
But
Cover your tracks.

If you meet your parents in Hamburg or elsewhere
Pass them like strangers, turn the corner, don't recognise them
Pull the hat they gave you over your face, and
Do not, o do not, show your face
But
Cover your tracks.

Eat the meat that's there. Don't stint yourself.
Go into any house when it rains and sit on any chair that's in it
But don't sit long. And don't forget your hat.
I tell you:
Cover your tracks.

Whatever you say, don't say it twice
If you find your ideas in anyone else, disown them,
The man who hasn't signed anything, who has left no picture
Who was not there, who said nothing:
How can they catch him?
Cover your tracks.

See when you come to think of dying
That no gravestone stands and betrays you where you lie
With a clear inscription to denounce you
And the year of your death to give you away.
Once again:
Cover your tracks.

(That is what they taught me.)

Translated by Frank Jones [1]

The poet in Berlin:

Brecht's city poetry of the 1920s

David Midgley

The city was not an altogether new theme in German poetry in the 1920s. The processes of industrialisation and urbanisation had left their mark on literary writing in the German-speaking world, as elsewhere, in the course of the nineteenth and early twentieth centuries. The perception of the modern city as the site of a depersonalised and dehumanised cultural condition is familiar to us from the writings of Rilke, as it is from those of Eliot; and in the poetry of Georg Heym and others, written in the years immediately before the First World War, the impulse to disrupt and overcome the processes of depersonalisation and dehumanisation expresses itself in imagery which demonises the urban world. But at the same time as industrialisation and the commodification of human creative effort were being interpreted as dehumanising tendencies, it was also recognised that the very abstraction of human and economic relations in the city was creating the conditions which provided new kinds of personal freedom and individual opportunity. In a famous essay of 1903 on the effects of urbanisation on intellectual culture, the sociologist Georg Simmel noted on the one hand the tendency for city life to reduce human relations to a system of commercial transactions and calculations, and on the other hand the differentiation and refinement of mental responses that comes with increasing specialisation of social and economic functions in the city.[2]

There are, however, certain senses in which the poetic treatment of the city underwent intensification in the 1920s and, partly as a consequence of a new intimacy with the life and language of the city, something qualitatively new entered into German poetry. Brecht's city poetry of the 1920s illustrates both sides of the picture. The world of human relations he depicts has definitely become abstracted and depersonalised, human individuals have become interchangeable and in obvious senses commodified. But at the same time, that abstraction of relations poses a new challenge to poetic expression, a challenge to identify and articulate the precise nature of such abstracted relations and their implications for the lives of the individuals who inhabit this city environment.

Brecht grew up in the small provincial town of Augsburg, and before he ever went to Berlin he contemplated the atmosphere of the big city as something alien and threatening, but also as the mode of social organisation which would undeniably dominate the world of the future. In a diary entry of 1921, which pre-dates his experience of Berlin (although he did have first-hand experience of Munich by that time), he muses on the challenge the city presents to the literary writer, and he does so in terms which are still strongly influenced by the stories of colonial adventure and pioneering conquest which he had absorbed in his youth and which provided the subject matter for some of his early ballads:

When I considered what Kipling did for the nation that is engaged in 'civilising' the world, I made the historic discovery that nobody up till now has actually described the big city as a jungle. Where are the heroes, the colonisers, the victims of the metropolis? Its hostile atmosphere, its stony hardness, its Babel-like confusion, its poetry, in short, is something that has yet to be recorded.[3]

Brecht, at the age of twenty-three, was approaching the issue of city life in heroic vein, as a subject which appeared to defy the capacity of poetic convention to voice its characteristic hardness, hostility and confusion, in a manner comparable to the way Kipling had expressed the idiom and the tensions of imperial conquest. In the course of the 1920s, Brecht made a number of attempts to present the world of the modern city in dramatic form, ranging from *Im Dickicht der Städte / In the Jungle of Cities* to *Aufstieg und Fall der Stadt Mahagonny / The Rise and Fall of the City of Mahagonny*, but it has to be said that the representation of city life in those projects remains rather sketchy and in any case subordinated to the main issues

Brecht is dramatising: in the one case, the notion of human existence as a struggle between vital potencies; in the other case, the perception of human society as ultimately subordinated to the demands of commercial exploitation.

What I want to argue about Brecht's city poetry, particularly as it develops in the mid-1920s, is that on the one hand it represents a more *modest* attempt to capture specific aspects of human relations in the city, and that on the other hand it leads to the development of an important *technique* for exposing the role of specific forms of discourse in the urbanised human society with which he is concerned. The technique I have in mind is not something that Brecht develops single-handedly; it is related to a trend in poetic writing in Germany after the First World War which belongs to what may loosely be called the 'cabaret' tradition of modern German poetry, and which achieves some of its most striking effects by combining phrases drawn from the various familiar idioms of the public world. Both Kurt Tucholsky and Erich Kästner worked within that tradition in the 1920s, but its real pioneer is Walter Mehring, and it is from Mehring's work that I want briefly to illustrate my point, before examining the senses in which Brecht's city poems also represent a productive development of that tradition.

Mehring genuinely wrote for cabaret performance, as Brecht, generally speaking, did not – although the two of them probably met up for the first time when Brecht was briefly engaged to perform two of his ballads in Trude Hesterberg's 'Wilde Bühne' [Wild Stage] cabaret in Berlin in January 1922.[4] When the theatre impresario Max Reinhardt sought to revive the pre-war tradition of literary cabaret in 1919, he recruited Walter Mehring off the street, as it were, where Mehring had been demonstrating with the Dadaists against the very bourgeois culture that Reinhardt might have been said to stand for, and put him to work inside the theatre. More precisely, Reinhardt employed Mehring as the 'conférencier' in his 'Schall und Rauch' [Sound and Smoke] cabaret, which operated as the late-night parodistic appendage to the mainstream repertoire of the Deutsches Theater. The text that Mehring wrote to open the show invokes a special kind of political role for lyric poetry, which explicitly adumbrates the sort of poetic effects I have in mind. After some ironic opening remarks about the esoteric character of this particular cabaret, Mehring invokes the precedents of classical antiquity – presenting the show as a satyr play, to follow the great historical tragedy that has just come to an end, namely the First World War – and goes on to suggest that the appropriate way for the artist to respond to a world that is dominated by the hackneyed phrases of nationalist fervour and Utopian socialism is to cultivate a lyrical virtuosity that asserts its command of 'political dialectics' in its manipulation of the various idioms of public life: the jargon of pimps and prostitutes as well as the argot of diplomats and the gobbledegook of politicians.[5]

Mehring's cabaret verses – which were published under the title *Das Ketzerbrevier/Heretic's Breviary* in 1921, several years before Brecht's *Hauspostille/Domestic Breviary*, and which parallel the blasphemous effects of Brecht's collection – are often stunning in the way they confront the bustle, the razzmatazz, the economic frenzy and the political platitudes of the post-war world with the debunking street-wisdom of the Berlin vernacular. The effects are often impossible to capture in translation, which is probably why Mehring's verses are little known outside the German-speaking world. But I have chosen a relatively accessible example to illustrate my point. 'Des Tippelkunden Frühlingslied'/'Tippler's spring song' uses the persona of a Berlin drunkard to convey a sense of undeluded alienation between the human individual and the ordered world of the city, and hints at the close association of church and state in the regulation of human lives. It is characteristic of the cabaret-style tradition of the 1920s, incidentally, that the refrain – in this instance, the allusive use of the proverbial phrase about the mills of God grinding slowly, but exceedingly small – takes on a variety of complexions as it reappears in the context provided by each new stanza in turn.

> Kommt der erste Frühlingstag an,
> Wird so schwach een'm,
> Und denn macht man
> Raus auft's Kaff.
> Wenn sich aus de sand'gen Kuhlen
> Blätter puhlen,

Würmer spulen,
Stehste baff!
Und denn liegt man sich zu aal'n, wo
Mang die kahlen
Letzten Häuser
Gottes Mühlen
Langsam mahlen.

Bürgers samt Familienkette
Stiebeln fette
Und adrette
Fein mit Ei!
Ob een'm unter dunst'ge Kiepen
Lause piepen
Wanzen ziepen,
Einerlei!
Jeder looft zur rechten Schmiede
Hundemiede!
Gottes Mühlen
Mahlen langsam!
Und solide!

Stochert man im weichen Mülle,
Jibbts die Hülle
Und die Fülle,
Hat man Schiß;
Manchmal find't man einer Schneppe
Blut'ge Schleppe,
Blonde Zöppe
Und Jebiß!
Für die Toten is's nich wichtig!
Jeld bringt's tüchtig!
Gottes Mühlen
Mahlen langsam!
Aber richtig!

Schließlich land't man treu und wacker
Ausjebaggert
Uff'm Acker,
Sacht nich: meff!
Leichenschauhaus zahlt die Rente
Und verwendt dir
Zu Zemente,
Altes Reff!
Nächstes Jahr deckt's Jroß-Stadtpflaster
Deine Laster!
Denn wo Gottes

Mühlen mahlen,
Wächst keen Jras mehr!

[When the first spring day arrives, you go all weak, and then you take yourself off out. As the leaves sprout and the worms crawl out of the sandy hollows, you're dumbstruck! And then you stretch yourself out where, among the last bare houses, the mills of God slowly grind.

The burghers with their families in tow strut along in their finery. If lice or bugs chirp out from under their steaming hampers, who cares? Each one trapezes home to his allotted place, dog-tired. The mills of God grind slow – and proper!

If you poke around in the rubbish (and there's all sorts to choose from), mind how you go; sometimes you find some old slapper's blood-stained dress, her blonde plaits, and her teeth! It doesn't matter to the dead. It still brings in the cash. The mills of God grind good and proper.

Finally, like a real gent, you end up clapped-out in the graveyard, you've breathed your last! The morgue'll pay your pension now, and turn you into cement, you old soak! Next year the city streets'll cover up your sins! For where the mills of God grind – the grass never grows!]

The sardonic jollity that we find in Mehring's verses is perhaps closer in mood to the songs Brecht wrote for the *Die Dreigroschenoper / The Threepenny Opera* than to his city poetry, although in this poetry we find Brecht, too, confronting the bleakness of a depersonalised society and articulating the tactical responses of individuals to particular conditions of urban life. The common feature in the poetry of Brecht and Mehring that I want to emphasise is the deployment of forms of everyday diction in constellations, which trigger insights into particular dimensions of the social world. The text in which Brecht arguably comes closest to the style of poetic composition pioneered by Mehring is one which was intended for the *Threepenny Opera*, but was not performed in the original production because the actress who was to sing it found it altogether too provocative; it is the 'Ballade der sexuellen Hörigkeit' / 'Ballad of sexual obsession', which is composed almost entirely of stock phrases used to characterise social attitudes and relationships, including some of an overtly sexual nature. But it is with the broader aspects of Brecht's experimentation in poetry, which speaks the language of everyday life, that I am concerned here.

Between 1921 and 1927, Brecht accumulated a considerable number of poems that evoke characteristic experiences of urban populations, and from among these he decided to include just ten in the 1930 collection *Aus einem Lesebuch für Städtebewohner / From a Reader for Those who Live in Cities*. Unlike the *Domestic Breviary*, in which the notion of the fleetingness of human existence is set in a cosmic dimension and which often express vitalistic and hedonistic responses to a sense of metaphysical emptiness, these poems focus on concrete social situations as the product of human actions and human attitudes. Some of them adopt an overtly instructional tone, whether in an encouraging manner – 'Die Städte sind für dich gebaut' / 'The cities were built for you'[6] – or in a spirit of admonition:

> If you had read the papers as carefully as I do
> You would have buried your hopes
> That things may yet get better.[7]

Others evoke nightmarish experiences of the transience, impersonality and alienation of human relationships, in a city environment:

> The woman I slept seven years with
> Greets me politely on the landing and
> Passes by
> Smiling.
> [...]
> It seems
> I have moved out. Someone else
> Is living here now and
> Doing so in
> My linen.[8]

Sometimes, the poem simply consists in the (studiously presented) imitation of an everyday utterance:

> I told him to move out.
> [...]
> When he came back the same night
> His bags were downstairs. That
> Shook him.[9]

It might imitate the brutal manner of an overseer addressing his workforce: 'Fall in! Why are you so late? Now / Just a minute! No, not you!'[10] Or it might stylise the emotional impulses of a situation into an almost theatrical speech with strong rhetorical effects, as in the insistent repetition of syntactical structures which prepares the way for the image of revenge in the following example:

> I know you all want me to clear out
> I see I eat too much for you
> I realise you've no means of dealing with people like me
> Well, I'm clearing out
> [...]
> When I come back
> Under a rougher moon, my friends
> I shall come in a tank
> Talk through a gun and
> Wipe you out.[11]

What is technically interesting about this group of poems in general is the way that fragmentary indications of the character of human situations in the city are constructed out of the discourse of city-dwellers themselves. What is fascinating about the *Reader* in its narrow sense is firstly the way it is deliberately organised, and secondly the manner in which everyday discourse is used in interaction with other specific poetic effects.

Before examining individual poems, it is worth setting the record straight about the rhetorical principles at work in the collection. In a recent book, Helmut Lethen presents Brecht's *Reader*, amongst other publications of the 1920s, as the expression of a 'doctrine of behaviour', a 'Verhaltenslehre'.[12] In an effort to construct a general theory of cultural change in Germany after the First World War, however, Lethen treats the text as if it were a direct and transparent expression of the author's attitude; with that aim in mind, he denies the ironic character of Brecht's *Reader* poems.[13] It is in fact perfectly easy to show how the presentation of ideas in Brecht's poems relates to the techniques which, in the classical tradition of rhetoric, combine to achieve an ironic effect: *simulatio* and *dissimulatio*. The effect we are dealing with in Brecht's case is akin to that of 'Socratic irony', which is to say that the significance of an utterance is initially kept hidden in order that it may be more deeply appreciated when it is revealed.[14] The way this typically occurs in the *Reader* poems is that the individual text simulates a speech situation (which may superficially resemble an act of instruction or advice, or the declaration of an attitude), and this speech situation is given a sense of context only in the last line (which typically appears in brackets). The effect can be a quite startling dislocation of the expectations created within the body of each text. The first poem sounds like a set of instructions to the reader on how to adjust to living in the city, until we arrive at the last line and are told, 'Das wurde mir gelehrt' [That is what I have been taught].[15] The second describes a seemingly singular moment in which an individual becomes alienated and isolated from the group with which he has apparently been used to working, but ends with the words, 'Das hast du schon sagen hören' [You have heard this said before]. And the third consists of a brutal and unadorned announcement that we want to take over your house, denounce you when they come looking for you, and even make you disappear like smoke up the chimney. But then we read, 'So sprechen wir mit unsern Vätern' [This is how we talk to our fathers]. It is also consistent with the rhetorical concept of dissimulation, incidentally, that this contextualisation is itself only brought about in vague or reticent terms. It is as if the author knows more than he is giving away; he alludes to the social dimension of the attitude the poem is expressing, but leaves the anticipated readers of the collection to puzzle over how best to make sense of the information they are given, in the light of their own experience, which is to say, their experience as city-dwellers.[16]

In other words, the manner in which Brecht presents city experiences in these poems is closely related to what he meant by the term *Gestus* [gesture] as he later applied it to his plays. There, the idea is that each scene points to a particular aspect of the social relations depicted in the play without necessarily making it verbally explicit; here, in the *Reader*, the effect is to isolate and point to a particular kind of social attitude, and to the manner in which it is linguistically constructed. This, Brecht is saying, is the way someone speaks in a certain situation. It is only in the final poem that we encounter an overt expression of intention in the manner of a direct communication from author to reader, and even here we are not given a key to what the collection as a whole signifies; rather, it is to the *manner of speaking* we have heard in the collection, and to what that signifies, that our attention is drawn:

> When I speak to you
> Coldly and impersonally
> Using the driest words
> Without looking at you
> (I seemingly fail to recognise you
> In your particular nature and difficulty)
>
> I speak to you merely
> Like reality itself
> (Sober, not to be bribed by your particular nature
> Tired of your difficulty)
> Which in my view you seem not to recognise.[17]

The collection, we are being told, is intended to *sound like* the harsh and unfeeling reality, which constitutes the life of the city. But the significance of the *content* of individual poems, the sense in which they do indeed reflect something of that 'reality' of city life we need to recognise, remains for the reader to extract by an act of interpretation.

There are just nine poems in the 1930 collection apart from the one just quoted, and on close inspection it is possible to see relations of both similarity and contrast between them. There are implicit connections between the poignant discovery of one's own superfluity in the second poem and the aggressive assertion of the interests of the young generation over those of the old in the third; between the fourth poem, which mockingly evokes the disciplined avoidance of stress, and the fifth, which presents someone who is determinedly overcoming her own fickleness; and between 6, 7 and 8, which describe varieties of response to failure or catastrophe. The ninth is the well-known and much anthologised poem which presents four different ways in which a man is offered a bed for the night, whereby the mode of address in each instance carries the markers of a particular kind of social relationship, from something that resembles family hospitality, albeit of a brusque kind, to the businesslike attitude of the whore. The resonance between the situations evoked in the individual poems – and indeed between the various linguistic registers employed within them – is, however, left to speak for itself. If the collection provides instruction for city-dwellers, then it does so, as Philip Brady has argued, indirectly and obliquely.[18] The requirement to interpret these poems by acts of inference is built into the composition of the collection. But when we examine the specific effects of individual poems, then it also becomes apparent how the *Reader* poems stand in a relation of tension – both with Brecht's own earlier poetry and with the general trend of the 1920s which I have highlighted. I should like to demonstrate this point with reference to the first and the fifth poems in the collection.

Readers familiar with Walter Benjamin's commentaries on Brecht's poetry will know that Benjamin interprets the first of the *Reader* poems – quoted at the head of this essay (p. 90) and also known under the title 'Verwisch die spuren' / 'Cover your tracks' – as expressing a conscious political strategy. He construes the furtiveness of the behaviour described in the poem as that of an underground agitator, and relates it to the position of the Communist as an 'exile in his own country'.[19] Benjamin explicitly relates his interpretation to the actual experience of exile from National Socialism after 1933, but he may have been encouraged in this view by the original wording of the last line, 'Das wurde mir *gesagt*' [That is what they said to me], which does indeed carry the implication of deliberate instruction. That impression is, however, significantly altered by the change which Brecht made to that last line in 1938,[20] precisely at the time when Benjamin was visiting him in Denmark and writing his commentaries. The wording of the new version, 'Das wurde mir *gelehrt*' [That is what they taught me], leaves open the possibility of interpreting the body of the poem as a set of conclusions drawn from experience, rather than as an explicit set of instructions.

There are, to be sure, clear overtones of political activity elsewhere in the collection. Poems 7 and 8 in particular evoke the experiences of being on the run and receiving political instruction. But even if the final stanza of 'Part from your friends at the station' contains lines about being betrayed and given away, the context in which these lines appear creates difficulties for a political interpretation. This first poem in the collection ostensibly provides a guide to survival tactics – keep yourself to yourself, mingle with the crowd, don't commit yourself – but it does so in terms which point beyond such seemingly practical guidance. For a start, the emphatic repetition of imperative verbs in stanzas 1 and 2 lends a peculiarly insistent pathos to the injunctions to keep the door shut and not to show your face: 'Do not, o do not, open the door' and 'Do not, o do not, show your face'. This is not the language of sober instruction or rational deduction, but rather suggests a strongly emotional response, even a panic response. In stanza 3, we might note, the urban environment is presented, not as the hard reality whose language we should learn (as the final poem indicates), but as a landscape that is there to be grazed without concern for the consequences, a site for satisfying the appetites of the individual, however anonymous he has become: 'Eat the meat that's there. Don't stint yourself.' If we put this injunction to consume in the here and now alongside the intimation of positively embracing death at the end of the poem, then we are not all that far from the vitalistic evocations of human endeavour and of ultimate absorption into the natural world that we find in the 'Choral vom Manne Baal' / 'Hymn of Baal the great' or the 'Ballade von des Cortez Leuten' / 'Of Cortez's men' in the *Domestic Breviary*.[21] But there is a particular twist to the presentation of the notion of death in this instance, which takes us, if anything, further away from Benjamin's political interpretation.

If, as initially appears to be the case, this poem offers advice to a newcomer on how best to protect himself in the city, then what sense should we make of stanza 5, in which even the moment of death is presented as an occasion to erase the traces of individual existence, to avoid having a gravestone which advertises your name and betrays you by displaying the date of your death? If we apply the expectations of traditional rhetoric to this element in the poem, and try to account for it as a case of *amplificatio* – as the deliberate exaggeration of something self-evidently repugnant – then we find the poem's apparently serious advice on how to adjust to the demands of city life collapsing into absurdity.[22] A more plausible suggestion is that death is evoked in the manner of the baroque *memento mori*.[23] The fact that this motif is presented here as an intentional action for which we should prepare – 'Sorge, wenn du zu sterben *gedenkst'* [Be careful when you come to think of dying] – might perhaps be seen as an assimilation to the speech situation of instruction which the poem is apparently imitating. But however we view it, the introduction of this motif of the anticipation of death gives the poem an impetus running beyond the framework of preparation for living in the city. It is an allusion to death which might reasonably attract the comment which Brecht himself made with respect to the prominence of the death theme in the *Badener Lehrstück / The Baden-Baden Lesson on Consent*, when it was published in the same volume of the *Versuche / Experiments* as the *Reader* collection in 1930: 'Dem Sterben ist im Vergleich zu seinem doch wohl nur geringen Gebrauchswert zuviel Gewicht beigemessen' [Too much emphasis is put on dying, given its negligible usefulness].[24] The precise manner in which it is introduced in the poem also makes it difficult to view the motif in this instance as an example of the knowledge of death providing a sense of the framework for an *ars vivendi* in the here and now, which has been seen as characteristic of Brecht's poetry of the early 1920s.[25] When viewed in conjunction with the intimations of pathos in earlier stanzas of 'Part from your friends at the station', moreover, the death motif here seems to carry the implication of an emotional impetus, which is not consistent with the logic of an instruction to avoid identification, but which runs on, as it were, in *parallel* to it and aims at the total effacement of personal identity: don't open the door, don't show your face, save nothing for the morrow, don't take responsibility for anything, leave no sign of your existence behind you after your death. This sense of emotional impetus at least lends credence to one aspect of Lethen's interpretation of the poem, when he comments: 'Das Ich ergreift die Flucht nach vorn – wo der Tod wartet' ['The lyric 'I' flees ahead into the future – where death awaits'].[26]

What I want to suggest about this poem, then, is that it articulates two parallel lines of argument, which find their common theme – their slogan, so to speak – in the refrain 'Cover your tracks'. One of them aims at public communication, and consists in the rhetorically disciplined presentation of survival tactics, which the final line of the poem identifies as a summary of experiences learned from the environment. The other expresses emotional responses to that environment of a personal and intimate nature, and tends ultimately to a total obliteration of self. I am sceptical about the possibility of drawing any conclusion of a general nature from the presence of this latter motif, as Lethen does, whether in relation to the personal psychology of Brecht or to the cultural climate of Germany in the 1920s. But I do see it as evidence that both the personal character of lyric poetry in its traditional sense and themes which are characteristic of Brecht's personal career as a poet are carried forward, in the *Reader* poems, within the envelope of a poetry which is becoming more obviously orientated towards intervention in the social domain. The precise implications of that development in Brecht's poetry become clearer if we now consider the fifth poem in his sequence alongside the first.

The dominant theme of the fifth poem is self-overcoming. The sentiments voiced are those of a woman who is determined to take advantage of whatever favourable opportunities present themselves to her, and to assert herself against whatever holds her back. She has fought against drink, drugs and sexually transmitted disease, and by implication she has also fought against the self-contempt which expresses itself in the recurrent phrase, 'Ich bin ein Dreck' [I'm dirt]. Like the drunkard of Walter Mehring's song, this is someone with an intimate knowledge of life at the bottom of the heap. But unlike Mehring's drunkard, she is not simply resigned to being ground down and turned into 'cement' at the end of her life. The self-image which supplants her self-contempt in the final stanza is that of the 'hard mortar' with which cities are built. It is an image of a substance that is as common as dirt, but which is capable of hardening to provide the binding force that will hold a structure in place. The self-evident seriousness of this poem is further highlighted by its position in the sequence of Brecht's *Reader*: it is preceded by one which ironises a keep-young-and-beautiful routine, and it is followed by one which exposes the self-deluding character of the effort to put a bold front on commercial failure.

But what is remarkable about this poem in its context is not the theme of self-overcoming in itself, nor the way it makes explicit those elements in the woman's own make-up which *need* to be overcome, but the precise terms in which her programme of self-overcoming is evoked. Her self-contempt relates to her recognition that the best she can expect of her own nature is 'weakness, treachery and degradation'. She can resolve to throw off the drink and the drugs when she sees what they are doing to her, but the self-assertion on which she prides herself takes place in the terrain of her own sexuality. In stanza 4 she responds to the recognition of her diseased state by seeing it as a challenge to recover her sexual allure:

> Who
> Would ever have thought a woman like me
> Would ever make men crazy again –
> I began again at once.

She is manifestly trying to put herself in control, but it is a self conceived in terms of sexual assertiveness, and that remains the measure of her achievement, even as she notes that to assert herself in this way requires the exercise of emotional self-control and the suppression of warmth and receptivity towards the men in her life:

> I have never taken a man who did not do
> Something for me, and had every man
> I needed. By now I'm
> Almost without feeling, almost gone dry
> But
> I'm beginning to fill up again, I have ups and downs, but
> On the whole more ups. [27]

When, in the following stanza, she speaks of controlling the impulse to display her jealousy of sexual rivals, then it is precisely the external display of emotion that she wants to avoid, rather than the emotion itself. The impulses which govern her sense of purpose in life are, again, those which we find celebrated in Brecht's earlier poetry; they are those of the human organism seeking, above all, the gratification of its vital urges in life.

There is a clear dialectical tension between the first and the fifth poem in the *Reader*: where the one draws out a trajectory of self-effacement, the other describes a programme of self-assertion. But there is also a dialectical tension within the fifth poem itself. It evokes a social force which sees its time as having come and which adopts the self-discipline necessary to assert itself, but it also shows that social force to be ultimately driven by the demands of the flesh. Through these internal tensions, it again throws light on the relationship between two conceptions of poetry which vie with each other within the framework of the *Reader*. The first poem remains ambiguous, I suggested, because the personal emotional theme is not integrated with the ostensible public purpose, but runs in parallel to it, and because the two themes meet only in the refrain 'Cover your tracks'. In the fifth poem, the tension between the personal and the public is effectively resolved, not only because the woman's life story is made public in the act of telling, but because the trajectory of that personal life is one of competent integration into the social world. This is the sense in which I see the fifth poem as epitomising the impetus behind the composition of the *Reader* as a whole. It retains a sense of the tension between personal motivation and the demands of the social world, but it also shows the character of the social world being constituted out of the impulses of individuals. By combining the articulation of personal impulses with the rhetorical demands of the public domain, we might say, Brecht's city poetry shows the elements of individual experience through which the development of the social world will have to be effected, and indeed that such development cannot be effected other than through personal experience.

5

Praise of Communism

It stands to reason, anyone can grasp it. It's not hard.
If you're no exploiter then you must understand it.
It is good for you, find out what it really means.
The dullards will say that it's dull, and the dirty will say that it's dirty.
It has no use for dirt and no use for dullness.
Exploiters will speak of it as criminal
But we know better:
It's going to stop them being criminal.
It's not a madness, rather
The end of all madness.
It is not the problem
But the solution.
It is the simple thing
Which is so hard to do

Translated by John Willett [1]

In praise of doubt

Praised be doubt! I advise you to greet
Cheerfully and with respect the man
Who tests your word like a bad penny.
I'd like you to be wise and not to give
Your word with too much assurance.

Read history and see
The headlong flight of invincible armies.
Wherever you look
Impregnable strongholds collapse and
Even if the Armada was innumerable as it left port
The returning ships
Could be numbered.

Thus one day a man stood on the unattainable summit
And a ship reached the end of
The endless sea.

O beautiful the shaking of heads
Over the indisputable truth!
Brave the doctor's cure
Of the incurable patient!

But the most beautiful of all doubts
Is when the downtrodden and despondent raise their heads and
Stop believing in the strength
Of their oppressors

[...]

Translated by Martin Esslin [2]

The eulogistic mode in Brecht's poetry

Elizabeth Boa

Brecht's poem 'Über die Bauart langdauernder Werke' / 'About the way to construct enduring works'[3] constantly plays on an ambiguity: are the works in question poems or the Communist project to build the good society? Such ambiguity implies that poems and project are intimately linked. The poet then reflects on the future readers, or builders, of the good society:

> Wer verleiht den Werken Dauer?
> Die dann leben werden.
> Wen erwählen als Bauleute?
> Die noch Ungeborenen.
>
> Frage nicht: wie werden sie sein? Sondern
> Bestimme es
>
> [Who gives works duration?
> Those who'll be alive then.
> Whom to choose as builders?
> Those still unborn.
>
> Do not ask what they will be like. But
> Determine it.][4]

But the as-yet-unborn of Brecht's time have now overthrown the edifice of Communism, and it seems clear that the poet and others of his persuasion have failed to determine what the future generations would become, who were to read the poems and further the project. Right at the beginning, the poet suggests that works last until they are completed: as long as they still require effort ('Mühe'), they do not crumble; works of really great design are those which are incomplete. Here, Brecht subtly keeps his distance from a rhetoric of closure, whether the political promise of final arrival in Utopia or an aesthetic of the closed verbal icon. But now that, far from reaching completion, the Communist project has collapsed, what of the poems? This chapter is devoted to works which are among the most politically engaged of all Brecht's *œuvre*, those poems in eulogistic mode, which celebrate Communism and the Communist Party, famous and anonymous heroes and great moments in the history of class struggle, victims of Fascism, and attributes and qualities useful to the cause. In this bad time for political lyrics, have such poems died along with a failed project or do they still elicit that effort in the reader which poems must if they are to last? Are some of the poems of that great design, that incompleteness which challenges readers still to work on the meaning they gesture towards, a meaning which perhaps transcends the particular brand of Communism which has just collapsed? In the final section, on the other hand, 'About the way to construct enduring works' takes a more modest turn: the wish to make long-lasting works is not always to be welcomed; short-lived works may be useful at the time and may then be properly forgotten when the occasion has passed. Yet Brecht's time is perhaps still close enough for even minor works, devoted to a now lost cause, to retain some grip on readers, looking back over the troubled history of the last century and the epochal change at its end. In reading a selection of poems in the eulogistic mode, my primary concern will be analytical, to explore how the poems seek to determine the reader's response. (Think of that magisterial 'Determine it'). Of course readers can resist the poet's determination yet still feel, for their own reasons, that the effort of engagement was worth it, or they might decide that the poems belong in the dustbin of history along with other failed projects.

In selecting which poems to consider, I looked initially to titles which signal praise, such as 'Lob der Partei' / 'Praise of the Party', 'Lob des Kommunismus' / 'Praise of Communism', or 'Lob des Revolutionärs' / 'Praise of the revolutionary'.[5] An important group of such poems belongs in two plays, the didactic play *Die Maßnahme* / *The Decision* and *Die Mutter* / *The Mother*. Several of these poems Brecht then included as a section in the collection *Lieder Gedichte*

Chöre/ Songs Poems Choruses, which he prepared while living in exile in Denmark and which was published in Paris in 1934.[6] After some general points on the eulogistic mode, it is to this group I shall mainly look.[7] A further group consists of dedicatory titles such as 'An einen jungen Bauarbeiter der Stalinallee'/ 'To a young builder of the Stalinallee'.[8] Or there are the celebratory addresses to anti-Fascist heroes, such as 'Adresse an den Genossen Dimitroff, als er in Leipzig vor dem faschistischen Gerichtshof kämpfte'/ 'Address to Comrade Dimitroff when he was fighting in the Fascist courtroom in Leipzig'.[9] A related form is the memorial paean of praise, such as 'Kantate zu Lenins Todestag'/ 'Cantata on the anniversary of Lenin's death', a poem which includes 'Praise of the revolutionary' as Part 8.[10] There are also anniversary addresses, such as 'Der große Oktober'/ 'Great October'[11] which signals unmistakably the mode of eulogy in its opening hymnic invocation: 'O great October of the working class!'[12] Some narrative poems could be drawn in under the eulogistic mode, for example some of the chronicles in the *Svendborg Poems*, such as 'Die Teppichweber von Kujan-Bulak ehren Lenin'/ 'The carpet weavers of Kujan-Bulak honour Lenin', 'Die unbesiegliche Inschrift' / 'The invincible inscription' or 'Inbesitznahme der großen Metro durch die Moskauer Arbeiterschaft am 27. April 1935'/ 'The Moscow workers take possession of the great Metro on 27 April 1935'.[13] In the overall mode of eulogy, different moods can be distinguished, notably the celebratory but also the elegiac, as in epitaphs such as 'Auf den Tod eines Kämpfers für den Frieden'/ 'On the death of a fighter for peace',[14] dedicated to the memory of the pacifist editor and journalist, Carl von Ossietsky, who was awarded the Nobel Peace Prize in 1935: having been sent to a concentration camp in 1934, Ossietsky was forbidden from accepting the prize and died in 1938 only two years after his release from imprisonment. Or there are the two epitaphs 'An Walter Benjamin, der sich auf der Flucht vor Hitler entleibte'/ 'To Walter Benjamin, who took his own life whilst fleeing Hitler' and 'Zum Freitod des Flüchtlings W. B.'/ 'On the suicide of the refugee W. B.'[15] In their very brevity and unusual lack of any note of hope, these two pieces celebrate and mourn a friend and a master of the short form. Only the last sentence of the second of the two poems –

'All this was plain to you / When you destroyed the torturable body'[16] – silently implies a contrast between the vulnerable body and the impregnable spirit informing Benjamin's work. Minor occasional works such as these recall events still close enough to touch readers today. Likewise, Brecht's address in honour of Georgi Dimitroff, the Bulgarian secretary of the Communist International, who was accused of complicity in the Reichstag fire, remains a still useful poem, especially now that, following unification, Dimitroff has lost his memorial street name in East Berlin. (Dimitroffstraße is now Danziger Straße.)

With the exception of epitaphs in which mourning holds the balance with celebration, Brecht's eulogies are liable to provoke discomfort in modern (and even more so in postmodern) readers. The modernist aesthetic has, by and large, shunned the public voice of the poet-orator or bardic spokesman for the body politic; the mood of mourning or despair, or the cynicism of disappointed idealism, the ironic or blackly absurd rather than the celebratory, have prevailed in the modernist canon. As for postmodern readers, no other category in Brecht's prolific poetic output will so irritate such a reader, for despite the dark times of their writing, these are poems shaped by a grand narrative and committed to ultimate faith in progress. In 1934, when *Songs Poems Choruses* was published just as the Nazi regime was establishing its grip, the exiled poet's political imperative was not to proclaim the end of enlightenment, as the cultural pessimists who helped pave the way for National Socialism had done, but to keep faith in the possibility of redirecting the course of history in a progressive direction. Formally, many of Brecht's eulogistic poems draw on a classicising tradition, which was strong in the Age of Enlightenment. Commenting on the group from *The Decision* and *The Mother*, Peter Whitaker sees them as sharing, despite their less formal discipline, a similarity in attitude with the classical ode, suggesting that 'the calm, precise authority, the controlled enthusiasm of the ode attract him here'.[17] In defining the ode as a form, Roger Fowler notes that odes were often written to celebrate public occasions and lofty universal themes.[18] He cites Horace and Pindar as the main models, more especially Pindar, whose odes derived from choral lyrics in drama, which were to be chanted to music by a dancing chorus. Many of Brecht's eulogies celebrate public occasions and lofty universal themes and those in *The Decision* and *The Mother* are to be chanted or sung by a chorus. The missing element is the dance or that Dionysian inspiration, which Goethe appropriated in his Pindaric dithyrambs of the 1770s with their vision of larger-than-life heroes, such as Prometheus or the wander-genius striding alone through a mythic landscape. Rather than the towering individualism of the *Sturm und Drang* [Storm and Stress], however, Brecht's odes look back to an enlightened sociability, which allows the poet to speak for the public out of a shared ethos. To cite Fowler again, 'The Pindaric ode was "occasional", that is to say composed for a specific and important public event (e.g. to honour the victors in Greek athletic games)'.[19] Brecht so honours the labour force which built the Moscow underground. If the Pindaric ode was occasional, implying a communal ethos informing public events, the Horatian ode is more personal and reflective, more 'quietly serious', as Fowler puts it.[20] Some of Brecht's eulogies are in that more reflective Horatian manner.[21] This manner has more space for irony and may also be seen to look back beyond the Enlightenment to the Renaissance and to works such as *In Praise of Folly* by the humanist Erasmus or the essayistic reflections of Bacon or Montaigne – Brecht's 'In praise of doubt' or his 'Praise of dialectics' exemplify such a tendency. Or there is his 'Praise of the stab in the back'[22] which, through its title, gives a satirical twist to an invective calling on the workers to turn a war of nations into a class war, by stabbing their leaders in the back rather than fighting fellow workers from another country face-on.[23] Here celebration modulates into castigation of workers who have not seen the light. Yet even such invective rests, if not on an already shared communal ethos, then on faith in an ultimate universal humanity, which will transcend class differences and the folly of nationalism. Fowler remarks, in conclusion, that since the Romantic age, the ode has declined in fortune to become the outmoded prerogative of poets laureate. Christa Wolf has recently been castigated as a 'Staatsdichter' [state poet], whose work lent false lustre to an oppressive dictatorship. Is Brecht, at least when practising the eulogistic mode, just the jobbing poet laureate of a discredited ideology?

Turning from reflections on how Brecht's eulogies might be placed within poetic tradition, I want now to consider more specifically the interplay of poetic form and ideology. Some of the eulogies are among the most doctrinal of Brecht's works. In propounding the creed, they deploy various devices to deal with a tension within Marxism, between a sceptical method of critical analysis and the collective discipline of a party dedicated to a Utopian end. The audience the poems construct has somehow to merge the thinking individual and the class, for only through class-identification can the individual participate in historical agency, which of necessity must be collective. To be effective, however, collective action must be shaped and directed; it must be spearheaded by the Party. Thus the individual would-be activist or critical sceptic is subsumed under the overarching order of the Party, guardians and interpreters of 'die Klassiker' [the classics].[24] In 'Praise of the Party', Brecht uses this odd, impersonal and capacious term to designate Marx, Engels and Lenin. The use of such a term shifts the emphasis from the individual thinkers to their reception through generations of interpretation and struggle, so that the exhortatory voice in the poem speaks with the authority of a whole tradition. To convey the collectivist doctrine and the role of the Party, while also remaining in dialogue with the recalcitrantly singular reader of poetry, involves questions of representation in a double sense. (Poems as part of dramatic performance for a public in the theatre raise slightly different issues to be touched on below.) How can the poet represent, in a vivid and engaging way, the abstract doctrine of a not-yet-existent good society and a collective endeavour? One method is to deploy representative figures. But in what sense do the figures represent and how legitimate is their representative function, whether they are anonymous or named, and whether the named are famous leaders such as Lenin or unknown foot soldiers in the cause? Implicated in such questions are the twin semiotic and political senses of the term 'representation', roughly speaking, 'to signify' or 'to depict' on the one hand, and on the other 'to speak for' or 'to act for': in German, 'darstellen' on the one hand and 'vertreten' on the other. Whereas the masses cannot be depicted, an individual can be portrayed so as to stand for or signify ('darstellen') the masses. But such figures are also deployed to speak for the masses or are shown to act on their behalf ('vertreten'). Brecht's eulogistic poems constantly play upon this ambiguity. The poems allude to representative figures in the political sense, such as Lenin, for example: whether Lenin legitimately spoke for the workers of the world is clearly questionable and the hagiographic traces are for today's readers surely the most off-putting element in Brecht's eulogies. The term 'die Klassiker' too is liable to make even readers who value the Marxist tradition cringe a little and even more so a poem like 'Lob der UdSSR'/'Praise of the USSR', celebrating the great hope of resistance to National Socialism. *The Decision*, in which this poem appears, was written between 1929 and 1930, before the show trials of the 1930s and the Hitler–Stalin pact. Yet even this poem is perhaps a still useful reminder of historical ironies, for the Soviet Union eventually did prove Hitler's undoing, but in a Great Patriotic War, not a class war.

Besides historical figures and events, the poems also depict anonymous workers or foot soldiers in the cause, exemplars who stand for a whole class but who are also deployed to speak for the class. Here the devices are designed to persuade the reader that the representative function is legitimate in both senses, that the figure is typical and therefore can legitimately speak for the class. In 'Lob des Lernens'/'Praise of learning',[25] for example, a voice exhorts a man in a hostel for the homeless, a man in prison, a woman in the kitchen and a man in his sixties to learn their ABC and read books; the three representative men and one woman, characterised by minimal details of location, age and gender, have to learn so that they can take over the leadership. The notions of class and of typical exemplar are interdependent and demand the paring away of difference: the excision of supposedly accidental or inessential differences is necessary to uncover that class identity which legitimates the notion of typicality in the individual member of the class. But in poetic rhetoric, the logic moves in the reverse direction: palpable and concrete details serve to overcome the abstraction of class; they emblematically signify the class and adumbrate its looming presence. In 'Praise of learning', the addressee shifts from the four differentiated types of the homeless, the prisoner, the woman in the kitchen and the sixty-year-old, characterised by place, age and gender, through a more abstract man who is freezing and hungry, finally to a comrade. By the end, the differences have fallen away, or rather been transmuted into signifiers of a shared identity, so allowing the collective designation of 'Genosse' [Comrade] to emerge. In 'Praise of the stab in the back', national differences must be pared away to uncover the class identity of the opposing armies on the field and the civilian workers back at home, who service the war economies in different countries, economies which are really part of an overarching international capitalist system, which profits from increased arms production and hence from war. In this poem, Brecht sets forth the doctrine of class war, conducted on the economic front and the war front, in abstract doctrinal terms, but he adds a few telling details, metonyms which carry the primary emotional impact: thus places (trenches or factories) and implements (plough, switchboard, drawing board, cooker and sewing machine) build up the concept of class. The poem constructs a collective addressee for the call to class war out of a few emblematic details, which transmute from signifying different people into signifying their collective identity, as national or gender difference (between the opposing armies or between users of ploughs and users of sewing machines) falls away to allow class identity to stand forth. In 'Praise of the revolutionary', homely everyday details such as the pay packet ('Lohngroschen'), or the water to make the tea, form part of a list of revolutionary demands, which culminates in state power, so linking together the individual worker, the Party worker and the state to be taken over. In their pathos, the details legitimate the arrogation of state power. Sparse details in the poems, such as soup or water for tea, are supplemented in the plays, from which some of the poems come, by a whole range of props and costumes, though Brecht's staging, always parsimonious compared with the naturalist theatre he followed on from, deploys 'defamiliarising effects', which magnify the significance of details, changing their meaning from merely signifying a milieu to signifying a world view. But even in the poem on its own, the juxtaposition of tea water and state power suggests how the small-scale individual task relates to the vast project, or rather they show not so much *how* it relates but simply assert *that* it relates, so implying that the individual revolutionary and the Party are one. Such techniques of representation – the metonymic detail signifying the person through his function, the part standing for the whole, the one standing for the class, or the leader standing for the led – are not, of course, peculiar to Marxism, but are stock devices of poetry through the ages and of the construction of a constituency through political discourse.[26] The technique is no different from that in the lines by Shirley (1596–1666) which schoolchildren used to learn as examples of metonymy: 'Sceptre and crown / Must tumble down, / And in the dust be equal made / With the poor crooked scythe and spade'. But where Shirley celebrates Death as the great leveller, Brecht looks to revolution. And that is the trouble: for readers now, at a time when the Communist project has so recently foundered, are liable to be afflicted by double doubts as to the legitimacy of the representation in both senses of the word.

Of course, the poet himself has arrogated a representative function to speak *for* the masses, even while he also stands apart as one of the intellectual élite, who warn and admonish and interpret the classical texts *to* the masses.[27] But Brecht adopts many measures to collectivise the position of educator, to pluralise his voice. The poems are highly dialogic; they evoke speaker(s) and addressee(s) in many ways. In 'Praise of Communism', for example, a first-person plural 'we' addresses a familiar single 'you', so that the implied reader oscillates between, or occupies, both positions as part of the 'we' being spoken for *and* as the 'you' being addressed. The subject position the poem constructs is thus singular *and* plural, individual *and* collective. Frequent use of exclamations and questions contributes to the effect of oral dialogue, creating the illusion of presence, which counteracts the abstraction of a theory embracing whole classes and the movement of history at large. Another device is to progress within the poem from addressing a singular to a collective 'you' (from 'du' to the familiar plural 'ihr'). In 'An die Frauen'/'To women' and 'Das Lied von der Suppe'/'Song of the soup',[28] this device brings the reader to the threshold of that class-consciousness which transmutes the individual into a representative of the collective. Like the shift from tea water to state power in 'Praise of the revolutionary', the last two verses of 'To women' break open the naturalistically-evoked domestic milieu by posing a puzzle to the now plural women being addressed in the poem and to the now pluralised female reader: what is the way out of a bad situation? Well, the way out must at least start with getting out of the kitchen and so the kitchen-sink milieu is opened up.

'To women' and 'Song of the soup', though not in the eulogistic mode, are worth looking at here to illustrate yet a further device within the context of *Songs Poems Choruses* as a collection, namely the effect of reading poems in sequence.[29] The sequence of poems from *The Decision* and *The Mother* conducts the reader from a seemingly hopeless position, through emerging class-consciousness, and culminates in a series of eulogies setting out the creed. The sequence serves also to unobtrusively get rid of differences, other than class difference, and to assimilate all sorts of categories into class identification. 'To women' stands at the beginning of this process and demonstrates, in the sardonic tone of an impatient teacher, the pointlessness of women's traditional domestic labour as a mere palliative measure, which is in effect counter-revolutionary, in trying to make the unbearable bearable instead of changing it. This message is conveyed through the pathos-laden domestic details of a worn old jacket, which no amount of brushing can rescue, or the watery soup, which no amount of care in cooking can make taste better. Thus women are called upon, by implication, to repress maternal femininity as constructed in class society and to assimilate to the revolutionary proletariat. Yet the pathos of the metonyms keeps maternal femininity half in play in evoking the dignity of poverty and the nurturing, caring instinct, which the poet wants to expand from the familial into a wider social arena. If the full force of the poems derives in some degree from their position in a collection, as elements in *The Decision* and *The Mother*, other factors come into play. In *The Mother*, much more than in 'To women', as a poem in a collection, maternal femininity is appropriated as raw material to be transmuted into the fuel of revolution, a strategy repeated or aimed at in several of Brecht's major plays.[30] Women are called upon to repress love for a person or to sublimate care for their own children, to feed into service to the cause. The problem of achieving sufficient depersonalisation and collectivisation comes in acute form in *The Decision*, where the young worker is called upon (and fails) to repress, for strategic reasons, his pity and his immediate sense of comradeship, and is finally brought to accede to his own death and disposal in a lime pit in order to save the cause. The expunging of difference in the interests of collective identity here reaches an extreme in the willed disposal without trace of the body, that envelope we all move in and which sometimes pleasurably, sometimes painfully, always obstinately differentiates us from one another. The eulogistic mode then blooms in full flower to celebrate the emergence of collective identity, as differences such as gender or even the bodily separation of individual human beings is dissolved. In the context of *The Decision*, 'Praise of the Party' celebrates not human beings with the usual two eyes, but a giant with a thousand eyes:

> One single man may have two eyes
> But the Party has a thousand.[31]

Thus, the recalcitrantly separate body is literally disposed of in a lime pit and metaphorically assimilated into the giant body of the Party with its thousand eyes.[32]

In the plays, the plot intensifies the drive towards merging the individual into the collective through the submersion of difference. The plays also intensify the pluralisation of the poetic voice, which becomes more literal than in the poem on its own, in that several of them are spoken by the chorus. Thus, in *The Mother*, the didactic poem, 'Praise of learning', is recited by a collective of revolutionary workers in answer to a reactionary schoolmaster, who has just poured scorn on the Marxist analysis of exploitation. The inclusion of the poem in the collection *Songs Poems Choruses*, by contrast, runs the risk that, without the dramatic framework, the pedagogic tone will grate or elicit the question: who is to educate the educators? In the play, the answer is clear: teachers, as lackeys of the powers that be, must give way to the collective, who learn not only through books but through revolutionary action, so overcoming the division between theory and practice. Yet as a poem on its own, 'Praise of learning' leaves more apparent the distance between didactic speaker and the spoken for, than when ventriloquised through a dramatic chorus which conceals the poet behind a collective mask. As Klaus-Detlev Müller notes, the poems transmit the philosophical level of the plays: spoken by the chorus, they transcend the specific learning model demonstrated in the action and generalise from it.[33] But for such a technique to work, the spectator must be convinced by the philosophy. Otherwise, the effect risks being a reduction of the figures to puppet mouthpieces for an unseen authority. It will depend greatly on the style of acting whether the eulogistic choruses create a sense of an intellectual enterprise shared between actors and audience, or of a subjection of actors and roles alike to an ideological superego, which speaks through them as the voice of authority, to which the audience too is called upon to accede. 'Das Lob der dritten Sache' / 'Praise of the third thing',[34] from *The Mother*, comes dangerously close to a post-Oedipal idyllic triangle, as mother and son talk about the third thing, the great thing that is common to them both, which occupies the point in the triangle reserved for the father. At times, a hinted ideal identity of individual and mass, of leader and led, of poet–spokesman and people, of human agent and creed, creates the impression that individual figures may not just represent ('vertreten'), but somehow embody ('verkörpern') the larger entity, partake of its essence, or, even more disturbingly, be swallowed up into it. Greek actors wore masks to conceal their ordinary faces behind the heightened dramatic role, but behind the illusion of heroic individuation, as Nietzsche argued, the mask in Greek theatre concealed Dionysus, the once whole, now torn, god of all things, so that the choric rhythms evoked a unity beyond the tragic illusion of separate identity. In *The Mother*, the poet speaks doubly masked, behind his actors, themselves masked choric mouthpieces for a future unity, which will overcome current division and restore a lost wholeness. The god here is not Dionysus, of course, but the moving spirit in world history. If alienating acting keeps the audience always critically aware of the actor behind the role, the songs and choric eulogies invoke an imaginary power, the driving force of history, the Real of which the concrete figures are masks or shadows and which the actors too serve.

Furthermore, sometimes this imaginary power breaks through when the representative figures are no longer human beings at all, but personified abstractions as in religious allegory. For along with echoes of the classical ode celebrating civic occasions, or of Renaissance humanism and Enlightened reason to be pitted against the barbaric unreason of the times, Brecht's eulogies frequently echo religious discourse, especially in their use of personification of moral qualities or of institutions such as the Party. In 'Praise of Communism', for example, only the title uses the noun 'Communism'. Throughout the rest of the poem, the constantly repeated personal pronouns 'er' [he] and 'ihn' [him] hover between the merely grammatically correct observance of gender and full personification:[35] 'Er ist vernünftig, jeder versteht ihn. Er ist leicht' [It stands to reason, anyone can grasp it. It's not hard] or further down, 'Er ist gegen den Schmutz und gegen die Dummheit' [It has no use for dirt and no use for dullness].[36] Brecht's syntax is here so easy and light that it conveys the illusion of Communism as truth itself embodied in syntax. Yet rising like a rock from the limpid stream is the last sentence: 'Er ist das Einfache / Das schwer zu machen ist' [It is that simple thing / Which is so hard to do]. In retrospect, so readers now might wryly feel, such an epigram says it all, an 'all' too massive, however, and evoking too many different responses, dependent on political views and sense of history, to be summarised here. 'Praise of the revolutionary' might seem to reverse the movement towards subsuming the single human being into an imagined greater agency driving the movement of history, for it disposes of the superfluous many, with positively Nietzschean vigour. A faceless collective of 'Viele sind zuviel' [some get in the way; literally many are too many][37] makes way for the single 'he', the hero who carries on the revolutionary work of the dead comrade in the previous poem in the sequence.[38] This singular revolutionary has, however, become a concept rather than a person, for he consorts not with human beings, but with personified abstractions. The eponymous hero asks 'property' where it comes from and 'opinions' to whom they are of use and sits down at table in company with 'dissatisfaction'. These are personifications of the sort you might meet in Bunyan's *The Pilgrim's Progress*; they invoke an already known creed, from which they draw their meaning and belong in a theodicy justifying the movement of history in the name of a final end. The giant Party with a thousand eyes in 'Praise of the Party' is another such Bunyanesque figure, albeit a Giant Hope rather than a Giant Despair. Most readers today, however, even those who regret the passing of 'that simple thing which is so hard to do', will rejoice at the disappearance of this all-seeing presence, which might seem to have ominously foreshadowed the network of unofficial spies pervading GDR society.

Early on, I suggested that Brecht's work reflects a tension within Marxism between the collectivist doctrine of a party dedicated to a Utopian end and a sceptical method of critical analysis. There is a case to be made for saying that Brecht's eulogies from *The Decision* and *The Mother* serve an authoritarian vision which, far from being sceptical, parallels many elements of religion: 'die Klassiker' as scripture; the Party as the Church Militant; a papal Lenin; the people who partake of the spirit, but who may be alienated from the godhead and are exhorted to see the light by poets and prophets, exegetes of the doctrine; the Revolutionary who, like Bunyan's Christian, has become the embodiment of a creed. Stylistic echoes in the sentence structure of biblical German, lost in the English translation, make the parallels overt:

> Wo er [der Revolutionär] sich zu Tisch setzt
> Setzt sich die Unzufriedenheit zu Tisch
> Das Essen wird schlecht
> Und als eng wird erkannt die Kammer.

> [Where he [the revolutionary] sits at table
> Dissatisfaction is sure to sit there too.
> The food will be bad
> And the room be found too cramping.] [39]

Yet the irony in these lines is that the language of faith is here used to question established power, as indeed do the Beatitudes in the Sermon on the Mount. The poem thus solicits a double frame of mind, of faith and of scepticism: 'He'll say to property: / Where do you come from?' This is a question still worth asking. The following lines turn back, however, to bite the questioner's adoption of the language of faith: 'He'll ask opinions: / Whom do you serve?'[40] Rather often in this set of poems, the self-reflexive moment is actually lacking, the awareness that scepticism should properly begin with the articles of faith.[41] The revolutionary is blind to his own condition of subjection to dogma. Where does that leave readers now? Of course, readers of religious or political texts need not accede to the doctrine, still less need they bow to a Church or a Party, but can perform what David Constantine calls a 'conversion into usefulness', which will turn doctrinal or historical specifics into Utopian possibilities in present struggle.[42] Yet in the case of the poems at issue, it may be advisable rather to hang on to the sceptical questioning and resist the Utopian moment, or to see the Utopian moment precisely as the scepticism which resists full subjection to a belief system.

I want now to pick up on the sceptical counterweight, in some of the poems, as an antidote to the pressure towards faith, which has so far been my main topic. Thus 'Praise of the Party' is followed in *Songs Poems Choruses* by a sequel entitled 'Wer aber ist die Partei?' / 'But who is the Party?'.[43] This offers a definition of who makes up the Party which, following the thousand-eyed giant, restores human dimensions and shows that the Party is not a monolith, but an arena of debate and argument, from which action will flow. Brecht here reverses the order in the play, where the giant Party follows as the culminating outcome of the work of the many.[44] 'But who is the Party?' begins with the assurance that the Party does not sit in a room with telephones making secret decisions; you, I, we are all the Party. So far, so good. The next lines, however, are less reassuring: 'Comrade, the clothes it's dressed in are your clothes, the head that it thinks with is yours'.[45] This is fine if the movement of thinking is two-way, between the members and the organisational centre, but the lines could offer a more sinister reading, suggesting a penetrating mental subjection to ideology. The next line reassures again, with its emphasis on solidarity under attack: 'Where I'm lodging, there is its house, and where you suffer an assault, it fights back'.[46] In 1930, the date of the play, and even more so in 1934 when the collection appeared, the need for solidarity to oppose Fascism was evident; individual heroism was bound to fail. The many tactical mistakes and the tragic failure of the left, itself divided, to forge a united front along with liberals should not detract from recognition that the Communist opposition to National Socialism was more substantial than that of any other grouping. The rest of the poem continues then with an urgent sequence of warnings to the individual not to cut himself off from us, the Party members: to follow the right path, without taking the membership along, is to follow the wrong path; through argument, the individual can put his case and win over the membership; to act in isolation is counter-productive. In the play, the delivery of the poem by the chorus to the young comrade in itself enacts an exemplary performance of debate and persuasion, in the interests of effective action. But the plot takes an authoritarian line in showing how the dissident individual must bow to the collective will, or be disposed of. In the 1934 collection, by contrast, the change in the order of the two linked poems re-humanises the giant Party and the sequel has an open ending on an urgent plea: 'Don't cut yourself off from us!'.[47] Like that 'simple thing which is so hard to do', this is another heart-stopping moment for readers, who with hindsight might feel that the exhortation 'Don't cut yourself off from us!' had better have been addressed to the Party, rather than to the young dissident. Circumstances were very different later in the century, of course, but the anti-Fascist struggle became the heroic myth of the GDR's origin and served to legitimate the GDR authorities in their dealings with those who would not toe the line, and in the end the SED did cut itself off from 'us'.

Of Brecht's eulogies, one a later generation might most wish to convert into current usefulness is 'Praise of dialectics', in which the sceptical and the Utopian appear as two sides of one coin. For it is a total scepticism towards the necessity of things as they are which grounds Utopian faith in the possibility of change for the good:

> Those still alive can't say 'never'.
> No certainty can be certain
> It cannot stay as it is.[48]

The poem is a call to the ruled to rise up against rulers: it is our responsibility if we are oppressed, just as it is ours if we overthrow oppression. But the stark oppositions between ruler and ruled, oppressors and oppressed, victors and vanquished, which the poem works with, are not easy to convert meaningfully in our time of asserted cultural difference, of post-colonial ethnic conflict, of a globalising economy which increasingly eludes control by political rulers. In the poems discussed here, the universal rationalism, the proletarian historical agent, the class war between two defined camps, seems out of time, as does the tone of stoic asceticism in such frugal details as worn jackets and watery soup, for we live now in an age of popular consumerism. The supermarket, the internet and unprecedented prosperity of large swathes of the world population coexist with the ravages of starvation and disease afflicting unprecedented numbers of people. The contrast between wealth and poverty is starker than ever, but the ruler and ruled, the oppressor and oppressed are hard to define and do not line up as simple opposed forces. Such poems as 'Praise of dialectics' or 'Praise of Communism' offer the peculiar pleasures of moral assurance combined with syntactic order. They have something of melodrama: the work of the anonymous hero in 'Praise of illegal work',[49] though performed in a shadowy underworld, will one day be recognised, for he lives in truth. These are poems without subtexts – it is like looking at a clear stream without hidden depths. Melodrama offers the powerful pleasures of moral assurance and righteous indignation.[50] But the poet's spare language, the frugality of images, the logically ordered, authoritative sentences, the meditative movement of verse which demands attention to the detail made salient by positioning in uneven lines, all these add coolness to the passion of melodrama, so that mind and emotions stand in controlled tension. A reader of today might well feel jealous, not of the political conditions of the poet's time, but of the stark simplicity of the choice between good and evil, which such poems so logically, so lucidly lead us towards. Even if we who are later born cannot, or will not, follow the path as signalled, Brecht's eulogistic poems should certainly not be consigned to the dustbin of history, for they strikingly illuminate a frame of mind at a time in history which we need to understand if we are to understand the trajectory of the failed project and the role of intellectuals, whose thirst for righteousness led them to hold faith for so long.

A last example of Brecht's eulogistic poems, this time one which needs little conversion for current usefulness, is 'In praise of doubt'. A somewhat later poem than the group I have been discussing, it was written in 1939, around the time Brecht was working on *Leben des Galilei / Life of Galileo* and just after his address 'An die Nachgeborenen' / 'To those born later' of 1934–8,[51] with which it shares a magisterial grandeur of tone. Works planned on a really big scale are unfinished, so the poet claims in 'About the way to construct enduring works'. 'In praise of doubt' addresses unfinished business. It closes not with the promise of arrival in an ideal society, but on the prospect of continuing interrogation of power by doubt. In the closing lines, the poet addresses a leader:

> You who are a leader of men, do not forget
> That you are that because you doubted other leaders.
> So allow the led
> Their right to doubt[52]

Although the word 'Führer' in the first line might suggest Hitler, the immediate addressee for the closing admonition, couched in lightly ironic tones of modest reasonableness, is surely Stalin. The modest suggestion was, of course, no more effective than Swift's modest proposal. But the address to a leader, any leader, also draws the poem into the wider ambit of the 'Fürstenspiegel', or guide for the conduct of princes, a literary mode which followed in the wake of Machiavelli's *The Prince* (1513) and flourished in eighteenth-century Germany. That the poet adopts the mask of counsellor to princes and disguises the mighty addressee, rather as Lessing did in a pre-revolutionary absolutist age in transporting his prince to Italy, deepens the irony, for Brecht's and Lessing's contemporary audiences knew full well who was meant. Until the end, however, most of the poem is addressed to listeners in the familiar second-person plural, by an affable teacher or enlightened preacher, seeking to persuade by reason. The plural addressees figure in the first two verses of preliminary admonition, then fade into the background as the poet develops his argument and lays out a sequence of fields in which to practise doubt: first history; then medical science, which progresses because doctors doubt the diagnosis of 'incurable'; then politics, where the poet praises doubting the oppressors' strength as the fairest doubt of all; then philosophy, in a slightly long-winded passage, echoing the long time philosophers take to overthrow a hallowed truth; then the military, clerics and theological apologists for the world as it is; then labour and economics. After the fields for practising doubt comes a character-typology, satirising those who never doubt but also the wrong kind of doubters. The key technique required for expertise in doubting is dialectical argument or contradiction; thus, for example, the first field of history is full of invincible armies in flight and collapsing impregnable fortresses. The dialectical method reaches its culmination in the two verses just before the closing address to a leader. Having until now advocated doubt, here the poet warns against doubt which becomes despair:

> Therefore, if you praise doubt
> Do not praise
> The doubt which is a form of despair.[53]

To act without sufficient grounds may lead to mistakes, but to ask for too many grounds risks inaction. This call finally to cast doubt aside and take action might have made a satisfying ending, but the poem continues on its zigzag path to that last admonition to a generic leader, behind whom an all too specific face lies scarcely hidden, to allow the led to doubt.

'In praise of doubt' offers many pleasures: witty paradoxes; comic thumbnail sketches; games with German semantics such as that 'Zweifeln, das ein Verzweifeln ist' [doubt which is a form of despair]; games with German syntax and the division of sentences between lines, such as the one word 'instructed' ('Belehrt') in a splendid isolation which demands resistance; the self-reflexive twist as the doubter doubts doubt; the slightly archaic flavour of the poet–pedagogue's eighteenth-century or baroque German, which has a tinge of self-mockery. Brecht in magisterial mood is not to all tastes, of course. But here, in this poem of 1939, the paradoxical combination of the message of doubt, yet the sovereign assurance of tone, comes across as comforting and as a rallying call against the despair, which is evoked towards the end only to be banished, a rallying call which the exiled poet is surely addressing also to himself and answering in the stance of assurance. The echoes of past styles of German, in arguing for reason and the sceptical method, gesture towards a universe of discourse and a German tradition opposed to National Socialist ideology and its irrationalist myths of Germanness. And if Brecht can be criticised for the exclusion elsewhere of doubts from his poetry, this poem closes with an admonition to you know who, placed in a salient position as the last words which the reader will take away. The poem offers no direct message to readers now, of course, no political blueprint. But, in our time of capitalist triumphalism, of glaring global inequalities, of threats even to global survival, of leaders still denying the led the right to doubt, praise be to the frame of mind which 'In praise of doubt' seeks to induce and itself expresses.

6

Manifesto of the Communist Party

A spectre is haunting Europe – the spectre of Communism. All the powers of old Europe have entered into a holy alliance to exorcise this spectre: Pope and Czar, Metternich and Guizot, French Radicals and German police spies.

Where is the party in opposition which has not been decried as Communistic by its opponents in power? Where the Opposition that has not hurled back the branding reproach of Communism, against the more advanced opposition parties, as well as against its reactionary adversaries?

Two things result from this fact:

I. Communism is already acknowledged by all European Powers to be itself a Power.

II. It is high time that Communists should openly, in the face of the whole world, publish their views, their aims, their tendencies, and meet this nursery tale of the Spectre of Communism with a manifesto of the Party itself.

To this end, Communists of various nationalities have assembled in London, and sketched the following Manifesto, to be published in English, French, German, Italian, Flemish and Danish languages.

Karl Marx and **Friedrich Engels**, *The Communist Manifesto*
Translated by Samuel Moore (1888)

On the Nature of the Universe

Look at a man in the midst of trouble and danger, and you will learn in his hour of adversity what he really is. It is then that true utterances are wrung from the depths of his heart. The mask is torn off; the reality remains.

Consider too the greed and blind lust of status that drive pathetic men to overstep the bounds of right and may even turn them into accomplices or instruments of crime, struggling night and day with unstinted effort to scale the pinnacles of wealth. These running sores of life are fed in no small measure by the fear of death. For abject ignominy and irksome poverty seem far indeed from the joy and assurance of life, loitering already in effect at the gateway of death. From such a fate men revolt in groundless terror and long to escape far, far away. So in their greed of gain they amass a fortune out of civil bloodshed; piling wealth on wealth, they heap carnage on carnage. With heartless glee they welcome a brother's tragic death. They hate and fear the hospitable board of their own kin. Often, in the same spirit and influenced by the same fear, they are consumed with envy at the sight of another's success: he walks in a blaze of glory, looked up to by all, while they curse the dingy squalor in which their own lives are bogged. Some sacrifice life itself for the sake of statues and a title. Often from fear of death, mortals are gripped by such a hate of living and looking on the light that with anguished hearts they do themselves to death. They forget that this fear is the very fountainhead of their troubles: that it is that harasses conscience, snaps the bonds of friendship and in a word utterly destroys all moral responsibility. For many a time before now men have betrayed their country and their beloved parents in an effort to escape the halls of Acheron.

Lucretius, *De rerum natura*
Translated by R. E. Latham

Returning generals

Brecht's 'The Manifesto' and its contexts

Anthony Phelan

During the Second World War, and particularly in the first months of 1945, Brecht developed a plan for a long poem which would rewrite a significant part of *The Communist Manifesto* in classical German hexameters, his 'Didactic poem on the nature of human beings', or more simply 'Didactic poem'.[1] Brecht described his plan to Karl Korsch in the spring of 1945:

I am trying my hand at a didactic poem in the respectable metre of Lucretius's *De rerum natura* on something like the unnature of bourgeois relations. *The Manifesto*, which I present in the two central cantos, forms the kernel.[2]

The dates of Brecht's interest in Lucretius, his *De rerum natura*, and in a modern adaptation are suggestive. Early fragments indicate that Brecht first became interested in the Roman poet in 1933, then began to plan a Lucretian epic in 1939, and returned to his project in a renewed form in January 1945, with an attempt to versify *The Communist Manifesto*.[3] His plan develops between January and March until the scope of the poem included four cantos: the first is on the difficulties involved in coping with the nature of society and would also include a brief critique of contemporary socialist litera-ture, drawing on the third section of *The Manifesto*; Brecht's second and third cantos would present the first and second chapters of *The Communist Manifesto*, on the bourgeoisie and on the proletariat and its relationship to the Communist movement respectively; while the last canto would reveal the monstrously intensified barbarisa-tion of society, in terms which seem to refer specifically to Nazi atrocities.

Brecht's major effort up to September 1945 was expended on four versions of 'The Manifesto', a paraphrase of Marx's and Engels's chapter on 'Bourgeois and Proletarians', planned as his *second* canto. In this paper, the successive versions of 'The Manifesto' appear as M[2] which absorbed the substance of Brecht's first attempt of January 1945, M[3] and M[4].[4]

Brecht called on a number of collaborators to help with the technical difficulties of the hexameter, including his son Stefan, Lion Feuchtwanger and Karl Korsch; and even, at a later stage, Rudolf Alexander Schröder. At various times Brecht also asked working-class friends for their advice, and the poem was supposedly read at workers' gatherings. Brecht's *Journal* notes laconically: 'read The Didactic Poem [...]. Effect surprising.'[5] In reality, the effect may have been rather different. Ruth Berlau noted that he 'read the text in such a strange way, so remarkably stiffly, that no one could understand him. The American comrades had no idea what to do with it, but our comrades had no notion of what Brecht had in mind either.'[6]

The collective labour devoted to the work and the intensity of Brecht's engagement mark the important place the versified *Manifesto* held in his understanding of his poetic task. His notes and sketches reveal that he thought it would be possible to revive the impact of the original. In the *Journal* for 11 February 1945 he wrote:

The *Manifesto* is itself, as a pamphlet, a work of art; yet it seems possible to me to renew its propagandist effectiveness today, one hundred years later, equipped with new and armoured authority, by removing its character as a pamphlet.[7]

Approaching the centenary of *The Communist Manifesto*, a new and original historical perspective has been opened up. Brecht's thought is worth following closely. He recognises *The Communist Manifesto* as an artwork because of its qualities *as* a political pamphlet. Brecht implies that through its form and rhetoric, the work of Marx and Engels is, in a particular sense, dated. A hundred years on, the historical pamphlet published in 1848 can be abandoned in order to renew its impact. It can gain in authority by being recognised as a classic, and not merely as an historical curiosity. Towards the end of the war, significant historical moments are brought to a conscious coincidence at a critical time, and Brecht seizes on Lucretius to enable the emancipation of the critical force waiting to be unleashed in *The Communist Manifesto*.

There are three factors to be considered early in 1945: Brecht himself, *The Communist Manifesto* and the *De rerum natura*. Marx and Engels's prologue is notoriously dominated by the spectre haunting Europe, but Brecht takes this reference to the anxieties of the Holy Alliance and makes of it an insistently *contemporary* opening for his own poem. His work on the text emphasises the historical continuity of the Communist presence *through the war*.

> Wars are destroying the world and midst rubble a ghost is walking.
> Not born in the war, in peace too sighted, o long since.[8]

Hence the realistic detail in the M² version – 'Even in offices seen, heard even in lecture rooms, betimes/Climbing upon giant tanks and flying in death-bearing bombers' – is rewritten in M³: 'At times then it puts on a steel hat/Climbs into enormous tanks and flies with death-bearing bombers'.[9] The military helmet is not merely an attempt to modernise. Brecht is establishing the context of the war as a critical condition for any contemporary encounter with the argument of *The Communist Manifesto* that 'The history of all existing society is the history of class struggles'.[10] The move from this recollection of the Second World War to the stark claim of *The Communist Manifesto* presents Brecht with a problem: M² summarises the teaching of the 'classics', Marx and Engels, as a revision of the history books. Older historiography recounts 'the deeds of enormous persons', their destiny, the movement of their armies, the splendour and destruction of their empires. The critical perspective brought to bear on such Rankean pageants is reminiscent of 'Fragen eines lesenden Arbeiters'/'Questions of a worker who reads'.[11] Instead of adopting the 'peasant view' of individual privation and labour, however, Brecht needs to introduce the Marxist view of class struggle.[12] In M² his difficulty is still evident:

> ... But to the classics
> History is mostly the history of the struggles of classes.[13]

The word 'mostly' here speaks volumes: the tanks and bombers evoked in Brecht's prologue recall a war which did not on the face of it demonstrate the truth of the Communist theorem, so that the fact that Marx and Engels 'mostly' read history as a history of class struggles is introduced almost apologetically. Subsequent drafts shift the uncertainty from Brecht's contemporaries to the scepticism of Marx and Engels:

> ...However, the great
> doubt-driven teachers search through the old books for other things
> And they teach us: History is the history of CLASS-
> STRUGGLES.[14]

Here, M³ nods in the direction of Engels's footnote glossing 'the history of all hitherto existing society' as 'all *written* history'. This gives Brecht's poem some room for manœuvre in its transformation of the classics' historiography as classical epic.

The wars of Brecht's prologue are the war which he could see approaching its end in Europe after the last German offensive of December 1944. His hexameter version of the *Manifesto* is framed by the historical moment in which Brecht takes up again the Lucretian thinking he had begun in 1933. Hence he even negotiates argumentational difficulties raised by his insistence on the immediate wartime context.

One of Brecht's clearest gestures in the prologue is a desire to recover the waning interest of the working class in the Communist analysis. They are its addressees in 'Much you have heard of it' in M², expanded in M³ into an explicit programme of restitution:

> Falsehood about it from foes, from friends too
> Falsehood is what you have heard. This is what the classics *do* say [...][15]

The same anxiety, that the working class may turn its back on Marx and Engels, and his response in the 'Manifesto' project are apparent in the *Journal* for 3 March 1945, where Brecht imagines himself caught 'between the didactic poem and the dreadful newspaper reports from Germany. Ruins and no signs of life from the workers.'[16]

Because the German working class had not yet responded to the failure of National Socialism, Brecht needed to reveal the power of the Communist analysis by giving it the critical and objective status of his epic make-over. His adoption of a Lucretian model for this engagement with *The Manifesto* is particularly apposite to the moment of national defeat and prospective allied victory. Lucretius provides a way of staging Brecht's own relationship to this moment.[17] After the fragmentary 1933 texts based on Lucretius, the Roman poet next makes an appearance in *Die Trophäen des Lukullus / Lucullus' Trophies*.[18] Here, Lucretius is Lucullus' interlocutor in a conversation about historical fame. Lucullus is widely recognised in Rome as the conqueror of Asia, but his reputation has become a danger in the face of Pompey's imminent return, after successfully completing the Asian campaigns begun by the ageing general. Such victories may be ambiguous: as Lucullus says, 'Altogether this is a month of fear, isn't it? Fear has become rampant. As always after a victory.'[19]

In *Lucullus' Trophies*, one victor is shown as a challenge to another. In Lucullus' case, his fame makes him a threat to Pompey, but equally he fears the loss of fame – just as he begins to fear not death itself, but the fear of death. In response, Lucretius quotes lines supposedly suppressed in *De rerum natura* and which Brecht in fact pastiched on the model of Knebel's translation, which forms the basis of the passage quoted earlier by Lucullus. These nineteen lines were subsequently revised, and it seems at least likely that Brecht intended to include them in his projected Lucretian poem.

Lucretius' additional lines explain that loss of life is merely the extreme instance of the pattern of *theft* which governs social relations in commodity exchange, patrilineal inheritance, and ultimately even in art and science:

> Just as the priest knows tricks to get alms from penurious tenants
> while the doctor finds industrial disease is a goldmine.
> Who in a world like this can confront the concept of dying?
> 'Got it' and 'drop it' alone determine how life will develop.
> Whether you snatch or you hold, your hands curving like talons.[20]

The pessimism of this 'Lucretius' echoes *De rerum natura* III: 68–71 on the pursuit of wealth but anticipates the transformation of all the professions into paid wage labourers, both in *The Communist Manifesto* and in Brecht's poem.[21] Brecht was evidently thinking along the same Marxist lines when he composed the lines for Lucretius in the story.

Lucretius can be detected in another text at about the same time. 'Viele sprachen vom Krieg' / 'Many spoke of the war'[22] reflects on the willingness of human beings first to treat war as an elemental force of nature, then to reject it passionately in its aftermath only to embrace its imperatives once again: 'So short was the time between imprecation and praise'. The pacifism of this sequence recalls *De rerum natura* III where the thought of a lost limb is used to establish the separation of mind from the vital force of spirit.[23] In his Lucretian fragment, Brecht converts Epicurean scepticism into his own gesture of analytical distance, when faced with the prospect of renewed hostilities. The classical point of reference highlights the continued need for a different understanding of wars, which is neither metaphysical nor simply moral, but essentially class-political.

The materialism of *De rerum natura* can be seen as part of a constellation which associates warfare and victory in war (and therefore, as Lucretius wryly points out, someone's *defeat*) with the exploitative force of theft implicit in capitalist commodity exchange.[24] By contrast, the Lucullus of the *Trophies* seeks enduring fame in Roman history by his *gift* of the cherry tree, the real trophy of his Asian campaign, to western agriculture and western tables. By the time Brecht returns to the Lucullus material in his subsequent radio-play of 1939–40, however, even the gift is insufficient to save him. The frieze of his conquests provides enough evidence of innumerable defeats for ordinary people and the poor.

Lucullus confronts the anxieties and ambiguities of 'victory' in the company of Lucretius and in the light of the poet's materialist account of the experience of loss as expropriation. In 'The Manifesto', the Lucretian component raises the question of the political significance of the Western Allied victory for a German working class which has lost touch with *The Communist Manifesto* and its view of history. A couple of years later, in his ballad 'Freiheit und Democracy' / 'Freedom and democracy',[25] Brecht sketches another triumphal procession which, like Lucullus' in the radio-play of his trial, provides ample evidence to betray the true rapacity of the Western Allies. In bitter sarcasm, industrialists, teachers, doc-

tors, scientists, and other intellectuals are denounced as ideologi-
cally complicit with National Socialism and its genocidal policies. In
its turn, this poem is reminiscent once again of *The Communist
Manifesto*'s analysis of the liberal professions: 'The bourgeoisie [...]
has converted the physician, the lawyer, the priest, the poet, the
man of science, into its paid wage labourers'.[26] Brecht's 'Manifesto',
engaging at an earlier moment, seeks to reorientate his readership
in relation to the end of the war by reconnecting the outcome to
the classical history of class struggles.

Lucretius emerges from this collocation with Lucullus as a *model*
for the poet who teaches and philosophises. Less complexly than
other role models such as Empedocles or Lao-Tsû, Lucretius exemplifies a poetic practice which Brecht can emulate.[27] Mittenzwei's
claim that Brecht is interested only in exploiting the material he
could borrow from antiquity fails to recognise this self-identifica-
tion.[28] The first aspect of the Lucretian role model is the sheer
difficulty of the poetic undertaking. Lion Feuchtwanger, who
attempted the awkward task of correcting Brecht's versification,
explained that forcing the technical terminology of *The Communist
Manifesto* into the hexameter rhythm had been the principal difficulty. He cites terms such as 'bourgeois', 'bourgeoisie' and
'proletariat' as resistant to the dactylic line.[29] Feuchtwanger's complaint is very specific. The retention of Marxist political vocabulary
makes versification unusually difficult. Brecht recognised the problem himself, but remained remarkably resilient. Brecht was not
simply incompetent, however: he was a reasonably good Latinist,
and there are many turns in his lyric writing which draw on the
resources of the dactylic hexameter. In retaining the specialised
vocabulary of *The Communist Manifesto*, Brecht is rather making a
specifically Lucretian move. *De rerum natura* sets itself the task of
communicating the materialist thought of the Greek philosopher
Epicurus, within a Greek form which is properly the metre of epic.
In tackling this transposition, Lucretius faces exactly the problem
which Feuchtwanger believed had proved insurmountable for
Brecht's project. He has to import into his poem a range of Greek
terms, which either cannot easily be accommodated by the fabric of
the poetry, or which will not readily submit to translation or para-

phrase. Lucretius makes the point himself: 'It is not easy to elucidate in Latin verse the obscure discoveries of the Greeks'.[30] This
general lexical and metrical difficulty is dramatised by the Roman
poet's relationship to Epicurus who 'was first to raise mortal eyes in
defiance, first to stand erect and brave the challenge'.[31]

The resistant note of Lucretius' *obsistere contra* in this act of defiance makes the authentic Brechtian gesture. In this presentation,
Lucretius frames Epicurus' thought in his own exposition; and the
same pattern of elaborated citation from the work of another
thinker is repeated by Brecht's relation to *The Communist Manifesto*.
His text does not simply present the text of *The Manifesto* in verse
form, as if he himself had no relation to the process. The images of
modern warfare, tanks and bombers in the opening of Brecht's
poem stress the altered context of *The Manifesto*'s articulation. But
precisely the form of that presentation is the focus for the huge
effort involved. Brecht's *Journal* describes his work as sheer industry
('Fleißarbeit', 11 February 1945). In a significant way, then, Brecht
too reworks a classic text.

Finally, the hexameter itself continues to carry the epic aspirations which it had for Lucretius. The Roman poet adopts for *De
rerum natura* a metre dignified by the models of the *Iliad* and
Odyssey. His own poem has the length and grandeur of epic, but
addresses a philosophical and scientific theme. In this sense, and
particularly in the light of his own scientific pretensions, Brecht has
a forerunner in Lucretius as well as a model. He adopts a metre
which predecessors, in a tradition from Klopstock to Mörike, had
used for historical purposes, but reclaims it for his own political
project. This epic dimension of *De rerum natura* resonates with
Brecht's own methods in epic dramaturgy. The estrangement of
experience, by various means of distancing and quotation, is
repeatedly activated to achieve an understanding which is not
possible from a position of immediacy and intimacy. Brecht characterised the effect of epic theatre as a transposition of first-person
experience into the third person of narrative, so that each element
can be separated out for scrutiny. In the versification of *The
Manifesto*, the process of distancing is unusually clear. This takes
place at two levels: 'The Manifesto' is not itself a manifesto, but a

poem which deals with *The Communist Manifesto* – it is, significantly, a poem about *The Communist Manifesto*, the poem of *The Communist Manifesto*. This shift has remarkable consequences: the rhetorical qualities of the text of Marx and Engels, interpellating its partisans and calling a corresponding political party into existence, are stripped away to encourage a reading – a reading of history and, in the end, a very close and vocal reading of *The Communist Manifesto* itself.

In the opening lines, the ghost whose name is Communism is duplicated by a friendly spirit, who befriends the children of the industrial suburbs, peeps into impoverished kitchens and visits exhausted workers outside mines and shipyards, and in prisons. Brecht's epic account of *The Manifesto* restores the threat that human friendliness presents, as the continuity of a proper human concern, to victorious generals. In particular, the spectre of *The Manifesto* appears in Brecht's poem via a metaphor drawn from a specifically German tradition. Büchner's *Hessian Messenger* with its motto 'Peace to the huts! War on the palaces!' is ineradicable.[32] The earlier draft retains the palaces – 'honoured guest in the quarters of poverty and fear of palaces' – but in M³, where *modern* bourgeois villas replace these feudal palaces, the huts of the poor are restored: 'honoured guest in the huts it sits, care of the villas'. Brecht's poem hence, and once again, locates the significance of *The Communist Manifesto* in a cultural as well as political tradition, recognising the force of a materialist posture from Lucretius, via Marx and Büchner in the same generation, to Brecht himself and the Second World War.

Against the falsifications of friend and foe alike, Brecht's poem declares what the classics, Marx and Engels, have to say: 'If you read history, you read of the mighty deeds of great persons'. Brecht begins his summary of the Communist doctrine by explaining that class interests are historically subordinated to the successful prosecution of wars against external enemies. The ruling class, Brecht stresses, can make use of many different means to guarantee its own supremacy – despotism, warfare or sly treaties ('schlaue Verträge', M³, line 36) – but this is not a significant issue for Marx and Engels at this point in the early argument of *The Communist*

Manifesto. The civil truce or 'Burgfrieden' (M3, line 46) which privileges external conflict over internal class struggles provides a further pointer to the allied victory:

> If a truce unites the hostile classes against the external
> Enemy in real need or an artificially laid trap
> Alas, what both had fought for, victory's gained by one only.[33]

This lesson is for the immediate context and recalls Lucullus once more – who is the beneficiary of allied victory? The USSR or the capitalist West? For some fifty-five lines the opening of 'The Manifesto' insists, in different ways and at different levels, on the continuity of class struggle through the final stages of the war. Brecht's next task is to transpose the main ideas of Marx's and Engels's first chapter 'Bourgeois and Proletarians'.

Brecht's version moves between proximity to the text of *The Manifesto* and varying degrees of distance, as part of its method of citation; but the dominant effect of the verse is its narrative energy. Marx and Engels describe the development of colonies and overseas markets:

The discovery of America, the rounding of the Cape, opened up fresh ground for the rising bourgeoisie. The East Indian and Chinese markets, the colonisation of America, trade with the colonies, the increase in the means of exchange and in commodities generally, gave to commerce, to navigation, to industry, an impulse never before known, and thereby to the revolutionary element in the tottering feudal society, a rapid development.[34]

Brecht renders this (and part of what precedes it) in M3 as follows:

> So thus there arose what now passes, the epoch of the bourgeois
> Once a mere serf he became a chartered burgher
> Enclosed land became city where close-walled
> The mighty guilds flourish. The walls do not hold the cloth
> And trade awakens the slumbering land. On the coast
> Maritime cities build great ships which reach towards new shores
> Keen they sail around Africa, America in their bold sights
> And the market in China, the east Indies and opening up
> The new world, the accumulation therefore of money and products
> Set industry in such great motion and mightily steps forth
> From feudal society the new lord and master, the bourgeois.[35]

In M3 and M4, Brecht stresses the contemporary context by adding the phrase 'which is now passing' to *The Communist Manifesto*'s 'our epoch, the epoch of the bourgeoisie'. But the sense of historical distance from the original is less significant than the historical sweep of the narrative as an epic of economic innovation.

A number of important features of Brecht's practice in rewriting can be observed. Most vivid is his transformation of the bare outline of economic history in *The Communist Manifesto* into a sequence of events and human actions.[36] Marx and Engels give no sense of the dynamics of trade which, in Brecht's account, 'awakens the slumbering land'; nor do they imagine the business of shipbuilding. Via the adverbs 'tapfer', 'fleißig' ('bold' and 'industrious', or 'keen' in my version), Brecht actively re-imagines the abstract 'discovery of America' and 'the rounding of the Cape' in Marx. This is a stunning effect of simultaneous realisation and distance: the rounding of the Cape is seen as the result of shipbuilding and navigation, but the dry and clichéd tone of the adverbs suggests a hackneyed heroic account of such 'bourgeois' achievements, in simplified schoolbook history. The reader is invited by these cited elements to take a quizzical look at the familiar (and, it is implied, ideological) version of events. The substitution of the poetical word 'Gestade' ['shores' or perhaps 'climes'] for the dry modern tone of 'ein neues Terrain' [new ground] in *The Manifesto* unmasks the Romantic image of what is in reality the precondition of rapacious exploitation. The passage is doubly epic: it narrates the sweep of national histories as the heroic emergence of the bourgeoisie, but simultaneously the poem is epic in Brecht's sense: by identifying a series of emblematic moments the poem subjects the irresistible progress of history to analysis – and demonstrates that this had been the narrative method of *The Manifesto* too.

In M4, inverted commas expound a similar ideological analysis: *The Manifesto* describes the dominance of the cash nexus in capitalist production and notes that 'it has drowned the most heavenly ecstasies of religious fervour, of chivalrous enthusiasm, of philistine sentimentalism, in the icy water of egotistical calculation'.[37] Brecht retains in paraphrase Marx's icy water, but *exemplifies* the expressions of human values which *The Manifesto* sketches in the abstract:

... 'noblesse oblige', 'chivalry' and
'Faithful retainers', 'love of the land', 'honourable trade'
'Serving the cause' and 'my inner calling', all was swamped
By the icy jet of calculation.[38]

Like most of M[4], this is very close to M[3]. The revealing change is the addition of quotation marks. Brecht makes a double point. His transcription of 'callous cash payment' follows *The Manifesto*, and the reworking emerges as a close engagement with the source in rhetoric and vocabulary. At a different level, Brecht strives to re-imagine the force of *The Communist Manifesto* beyond its own rhetorical effects: this is at least implied in the Brechtian 'epic' moments, when Marx and Engels are themselves subject to the distanciation of the *Verfremdungseffekt* [defamiliarising effect] – 'As the classics show'; 'The teachers show in great detail'.[39] (Simultaneously, in the passage quoted from the fourth draft, Brecht demonstrates the sentimentalism of the clichés that he highlights. Human values such as 'chivalry' or 'honourable trade' are unmasked as ideological falsifications – just like the bold and industrious bourgeois of histories of economic exploitation.

In the earlier passage from the third draft, Brecht's poem retains the terminology of *The Communist Manifesto* in relation to the markets of China and the East Indies in order to stress the contrast of economic realities (the accumulation of money and commodities) with myths of 'bold seafarers'. This framework permits the emergence, 'industrious' and 'bold', of the bourgeois, 'der Bürger' in final dramatic position. Here Brecht again engages with a particular German tradition which values the solidity of middle-class life, as in the celebration of bourgeois virtues in the comic Book III of Goethe's *Hermann und Dorothea*, a poem which Brecht cites among the works from which he has learnt.[40]

Brecht is also getting to grips with the text in immediately verbal ways. The close reading of *The Manifesto*'s first chapter which underlies his transcription makes his poem highly sensitive to the details of the Marxist lexis he adopts. This process of citation and paraphrase is too complex to catalogue in full. What is most important, however, is the *conjunction* in the text of proximity to as well as distance from *The Communist Manifesto*. For instance, where the bourgeoisie 'has left remaining no other nexus between man and man than naked self-interest, than callous "cash payment"',[41] Brecht gives 'Suffering no other bond between people than their naked int'rest / And the callous cash-payment' – a direct citation of the original removing only its rhetorical repetitions.[42]

In section 7 of Brecht's notes on his own literary apprenticeship, 'Where I have learnt', in which he discusses the value of reading Virgil's *Georgics* as well as Lucretius, he recommends the hexameter in German, especially Voß's and Knebel's verse translations because, through its use, the German language appears 'gehandhabt', manipulated or handled like some physical resource.[43] This skilful handling, he tells us in a footnote, is also evident in the versification by Goethe of his earlier prose version of *Iphigenie* and in Schiller's *Don Carlos*. The effect of hexameter, then, is to reveal the truth and force of the original by a kind of calculated stiltedness, which is one of Brecht's most characteristic verbal gestures. Line by line, in the edginess and awkwardness of his writing in 'The Manifesto', we can sense the intensity of his simultaneous act of reading and rewriting: through the struggle of citation and paraphrase Brecht can imagine the novelty of *The Manifesto* for himself, while making it newly accessible to others.

The first chapter of *The Manifesto*, 'Bourgeois and Proletarians', deals first with the rise of the capitalist class and then, after a transitional passage about overproduction and the crises of the capitalist economy, with the emergence of the proletariat which, formed as a class, is to seize the weapons of the bourgeoisie for its own purposes. The transitional passage ('A similar movement is going on before our eyes')[44] is couched in particularly dense and abstract language in *The Communist Manifesto*. This provokes Brecht to find vivid illustrations and examples of the process and consequences of overproduction. In a characteristic Brechtian insight, 'The Manifesto' presents overproduction in relation to hunger:

> Hunger from long ago plagued the world when the granary was empty
> But now, no one understands it, we go hungry because it is too full.
> Nought in the pantry can mothers find to fill little mouths with
> While behind walls there rots, stored towering high, the good corn.[45]

It was this mystery of overproduction and waste that famously drove Brecht to read Marx, and especially *Das Kapital* (Capital), in the first place. The sweep of the historical dialectic here is concretely imagined in terms of the working-class experience of hunger, inadequate clothing, homelessness and unemployment. In this way, the transposition of analytical discourse into narrative yields a vignette of real life which might indeed suit the demands of public performance, as Duncker had anticipated when he called it 'eine Form für den großen Vortrag in der Öffentlichkeit' [a form for grand public performance].[46]

At two points, Brecht's poem significantly expands on the text of *The Communist Manifesto*.

> Of course, what are pyramids to us now and Rome's viaducts
> Cologne cathedral, migration of peoples, the march of the Huns or crusades
> Us who've seen buildings and ventures gigantic like all those
> This all overturning class makes, which always and ev'rywhere
> Breathlessly overturns what it created, and lives from this downfall?
> Ceaselessly it changes machinery and products
> Unthought of forces it draws from the air and from water
> It creates new materials never before seen on earth.
> (Thrice for one generation the cloth of a garment changes
> Different you feel in your hand the handle of knife and of fork
> Many times. Upon new formations our eyes are constantly falling.)
> So too it changes people, drives peasants into the factories
> Drives tradesmen in droves to new and wild climes
> Villages rise up and cities, wherever it digs for ore
> At once dead and emptied of people, when it withdraws. Speedier riches
> Were never seen in these places, nor poverty faster.[47]

These lines in M4 represent the passage in *The Manifesto* which celebrates the unexampled innovation of the bourgeoisie, culminating in the recognition that 'all that is solid melts into air'.[48] What is striking here is the way in which *The Manifesto* is re-thought in *contemporary* terms. There is a parallel in Brecht's version of the bourgeois subjection of nature to human purposes by the application of technology, the cultivation of previously undeveloped land,

and the canalisation of rivers. In M³, however, Brecht goes beyond Marx's and Engels's nineteenth-century account to include the exploitation of mineral oil, the petrol engine, turbines, hydroelectric power, newspapers, radio, and manned flight.[49]

In the passage contrasting bourgeois capitalist innovation with the achievements of antiquity, Brecht is clearly returning to themes he had considered before and more cynically in *Man Equals Man* and *Mahagonny*. Taken together, however, these developments of *The Communist Manifesto* clearly reveal a further dimension that is important to Brecht. When the elaboration of Marx and Engels in M³ moves on to aviation – 'Men in guidable airplanes'[50] – Brecht returns to a moment of technological progress which had acquired huge significance for him, as an emblem of innovation understood as the very possibility of change.[51] Although he faithfully transcribes *The Communist Manifesto*'s belief that no earlier century had 'even a presentiment that such productive forces slumbered in the lap of social labour', his poem 'The Tailor of Ulm' in reality shows that the dream of human flight had always presented the challenge of atheist modernity to religious ideology.[52]

Even here, however, we should note how the constraints of the hexameter encourage the rather quaint neologism 'lenklich' [guidable], which is retained in the next draft. The hint of eighteenth-century diction, nodding to Voß and Goethe, coins the invention of manned flight afresh as an astonishing moment in the human story which Brecht's didactic poem has to tell; but it is part of the *story* for all that. In the earlier passage these technological advances are paralleled by Brecht's attention to more domestic innovations – in textiles, artificial materials, design and even building materials and techniques.[53]

Brecht's updating frees the classic text from its own historical moment in order to promote not merely its contemporary relevance, but rather the necessity of a continuing and active engagement with its arguments. An engagement with the argument of *The Communist Manifesto* was crucial in the historic moment of Allied victory, if the defeat was not to be visited upon the German working class as such, rather than on the Nazi regime and, in Brecht's view, its capitalist collaborators. In recasting the his-

1. Marie Rose Aman, the model for 'Remembering Marie A.'

2. Brecht with his guitar, 1916

3. and 4.
Original manuscript of
'Remembering Marie A.'

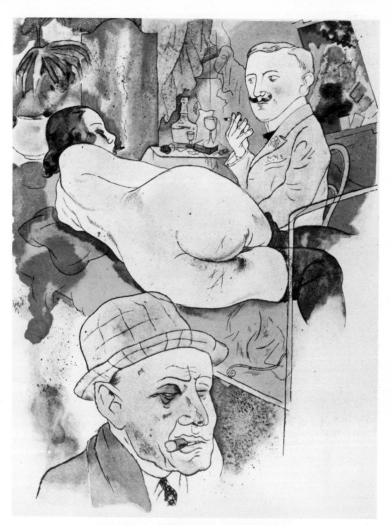

5. △
Ecce Homo by
George Grosz, 1921,
watercolour from
the *Ecce Homo*
series 1922/3

6. ▷
Ophélie by
John Everett
Millais, 1851–2

7. Brecht and Margarete Steffin playing chess in Svendborg, c 1935

8. Brecht's house in Skovosbostrand bought in 1933

Here are the cities in which once our 'Heils!'
Acclaimed our war machine as it paraded.
But these are nothing to the thousand miles
Of foreign cities that it devastated.

9. Photograph and poem from Brecht's *War Primer*

10. Brecht, the young playwright in Spichernstrasse, Berlin 1927

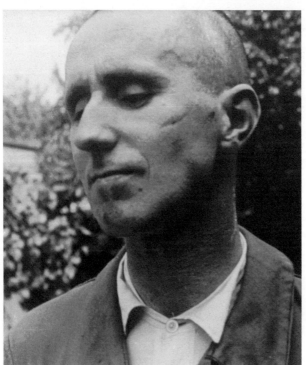

11.
Brecht in Berlin, 1928

12. 'The cases are packed': Brecht in Hardenbergstrasse, preparing to leave Berlin, 1933

13. △
Brecht in Santa Monica in the 1940s,
photographed by Ruth Berlau

14. ▷
Brecht in Zurich for the production of
his plays, 1949

Hymne

Anmut

~~Arbeit~~ sparet nicht noch mühe

Leidenschaft nicht, noch verstand

deutschland

Auf dass ~~unser~~ deutschland / blühe

Wie ein andres gutes land.

~~—~~

Dass die vö/lker nicht erbleichen

Wie vor einer räuberin

So wie andern völkern.
Sondern uns die hände reichen

Hin uns denn die hände hin.
Wie den andern völkern hin.

wieil
Und ~~wenn~~ wir dies land verbessern

Lieben und beschirmen wirs

Und das liebste mags uns scheinen

So wie andern Völkern ihrs.

15. Original manuscript of Brecht's 'Children's Anthem'

torical conspectus of *The Manifesto*, Brecht can establish the epic status of the working-class task at this moment; but he also configures himself as a latter-day Lucretius, providing new access to the insights of 'the classics'. In doing so, he conspicuously avoids the fate of those intellectuals, the poets among them, who become the wage labourers of the bourgeoisie. His class-treachery, characteristic in *The Communist Manifesto* of 'times when the class struggle nears the decisive hour',[54] is recast in terms familiar from elsewhere in his work:

> Further, as individual nobles went over to the youthful
> Bourgeoisie, fighting nobility, so there flees now
> Many a bourgeois from the bourgeoisie, a ship, not yet sinking but
> Compassless upon threatening seas and to bursting full of
> A wild self-destructive crew, and they bring their skills and their knowledge.[55]

This ship of state is retained, in one way or another, in Brecht's subsequent drafts. We need not look too far to see which port it hails from: the wild and self-destructive crew is transparent as a reworking of Brecht's own preoccupation with pirates in the half-serious, anarchic Romanticism of poems in the *Domestic Breviary* and particularly the 'Ballad of the pirates'.[56] (He had already reworked his own passage with the pirates in the extraordinary poem 'How the ship "Oskawa" was broken up by her own crew',[57] in which drunkenness at sea becomes an act of class warfare. The reappearance of the pirate theme here repositions Brecht himself, once more, in the historical configuration of *The Communist Manifesto*, Lucretius, and the end of the Second World War. Such recurrent fantasies of piracy, destruction, and drunkenness have their origin in the high tradition of European modernism, in Rimbaud's 'Le bateau ivre'. In attributing the imaginary repertoire of piratical violence to the bourgeoisie, Brecht has himself abandoned the Utopian critique of society which is still implied in the *Domestic Breviary* and its personae, and which in some ways drew on the Expressionist reading of Rimbaud for its own version of nihilism and *Weltschmerz*. By alluding to this anarchic resistance to the rising bourgeoisie, and therefore to the part it had played in his own formation, Brecht at least in part mounts the critique of the resources of 'contemporary socialist literature', which he had promised in his letter to Korsch.[58]

Perhaps more importantly, he makes clear his own commitment to Communism, bringing to the contemporary understanding of *The Communist Manifesto* his own skill and his knowledge of and admiration for a classical tradition which, he seems to have thought, might revive the politics of *The Communist Manifesto* in the classically dangerous moment when victorious generals arrive.

7

Sonnets by Bertolt Brecht and Margarete Steffin

Brecht: Als wir zerfielen einst in DU und ICH
Und unsere Betten standen HIER und DORT
Ernannten wir ein unauffällig Wort
Das sollte heißen: ich berühre dich.

Es scheint: solch Redens Freude sei gering
Denn das Berühren selbst ist unersetzlich
Doch wenigstens wurde 'sie' so unverletzlich
Und aufgespart wie ein gepfändet Ding.

Blieb zugeeignet und wurde doch entzogen
War nicht zu brauchen und war doch vorhanden
War wohl nicht da, doch wenigstens nicht fort

Und wenn um uns die fremden Leute standen
Gebrauchten wir geläufig dieses Wort
Und wußten gleich: wir waren uns gewogen.[1]

Steffin: Dir zugeeignet und dir ganz gewogen
Bin ich, seit ich den Mut zum Du gefunden.
Was immer mir auch fehlt, ich muß gesunden
Solang mir deine Liebe nicht entzogen.

Das kleine Wort, das damals wir ernannten
Das unauffällig machte das Berühren
(Unwiderstehlich machte das Verführen)
Durch Monde ist es Hort deiner Verbannten.

Das Wort ist mir Umarmung, ist mir Kuß.
Die ich so lange auf dich warten muß
Ich küsse es in jedem deiner Briefe.

Und weine ich, wenn ich es lese, ist
Es nur, weil du dann wieder bei mir bist
Und ich bin ohne Wunsch. Als ob ich bei dir schliefe.[2]

Then when we fell apart in ME and YOU
And when our beds stood HERE and over THERE
We chose an inconspicuous word to share,
A word as if to say: I'm touching you.

Short shrift, you'll think, if you can only *say*
For touch itself can't ever be replaced
And yet at least 'it' was safe and chaste,
Preserved like something pawned and locked away.

My own in name, and yet for now foreclosed
Not much use, but not at least in danger
Not quite to hand, but still not out of reach

And when we met in company with strangers
We'd let the word fall casually in speech
And know at once: that we were well disposed.

Translated by Tom Kuhn

Entirely yours, and more than well disposed
Since I discovered how to dare say 'Du'.
I'm cured of all my wants, made whole by you
As long as from your love I'm not foreclosed.

The little word we chose as guarantee
That if we touched it would be unattested
(And your advances couldn't be resisted)
Has been a haven for your refugee.

The word performs what real kisses do.
However long I have to wait for you
I kiss it every time in every letter.

And if I, reading, cry aloud, well then
It's simply that I feel you here again
And am content. As if we were in bed together.

Translated by Tom Kuhn

Two sonnets, after Brecht

On seducing angels

Angels aren't for ravishing – unless it's quick.
Just drag him straight into the entrance hall
Shove your tongue right down his throat and stick
Your finger up him, turn him to the wall
And when he's good and moist, lift up his gown
And fuck him. Should he groan as if in pain
Hold him hard, bring him on: once and again –
That way he'll lack the strength to strike you down.

Remind him that he has to move his bum
And tell him he can go ahead and touch
Your balls, that he must just let go and come
While earth and sky are slipping from his clutch –

But while you're fucking don't look in his face
And see his wings unruffled, feathers stay in place.

Michael Morley[3]

When I'd brought the pair of them the news
that up among the living nowadays
no one actually gets killed since ownership

had been abolished, the man
who certainly wasn't her husband
lifted his hand attached by chains to her hand,

looked at her, then asked, 'If no-one can
own anything, then nothing can be stolen, right?'
I nodded, but saw that at his touch she turned

bright red. He noticed too. 'I haven't seen that happen,
not since the first guilty moment when our lips ...
So now you mean there's not the slightest risk?'

And off they went, the chains that bound them tight
then seemed to weigh no more than paperclips.

Jamie McKendrick[4]

Brecht's sonnets

David Constantine

There are nearly seventy finished sonnets in Brecht's collected poems; another six or seven unfinished; and half a dozen more poems that have fourteen lines but may not strictly be called sonnets.[5] The earliest of his sonnets date from 1913, the latest from 1948.[6]

Brecht had periods of sonnet writing, the first in 1913 when, as a beginner in lyric poetry, he did what most would have done then and tried the sonnet. In his journal on 20 May 1913 he wrote: 'The following is an attempt at a sonnet'. The sonnet thus produced was 'Die Gewaltigen'/'The mighty'.[7] He wrote another five that year, and a poem of fourteen lines but no sonnet rhyme-scheme, called 'Der Narr'/'The fool'. Formally these early sonnets are interesting in their mixing of metres and their frequent variations in lengths of line. 'Emaus'/'Emmaus' indeed is, as to form, the least conventional, most experimental sonnet in Brecht's entire *œuvre*. Designated a sonnet in his diary,[8] it is set out as six very long lines and two hemistiches. The long lines rhyme halfway and as they finish, so that an almost conventional scheme (abba cddc efg egf) is there to be discovered. Chiefly these early sonnets advocate a zestful and even violent engagement with life, already rather in the manner of the hard men and the pirates of the *Hauspostille/ Domestic Breviary*. Thus 'the mighty', in the poem of that name, 'go through dense grey fog/In their fiery eyes the crimson glow/Of spilt blood – but with clear consciences/They stride towards judgement';[9] and have young Eugen Berthold's approval.

Two other fourteen-line poems, 'Die Schneetruppe'/'Snow unit' (early 1915) and 'Und als sie wegsah'/'And when she looked away' (1919), complete the tally of Brecht's early dealings with the sonnet form. The first, dedicated to Brecht's Uncle August and published in the local newspaper, the *Augsburger Neueste Nachrichten*, fuses Nietzschean vitalism with the non-combatant's enthusiastic patriotism: 'You die then as though drunk on the noblest kind of giving/ In the deepest, most triumphant sense of divine life'.[10] The second, arranged in its rhymes 5+4+5, is fit to be sung by Baal:

> Der Himmel war wie Milch. Ich dachte kühl.
> Und lachte mit den Gliedern, die ermattet waren.
> Und dann war nichts zu tun. Ich bin von früh
> Bis spät den Mississippi abgefahren.
>
> [The sky was like milk. I was thinking coolly.
> And laughed with my limbs that were fatigued.
> And then there was nothing to do. From early
> Till late I sailed down the Mississippi.][11]

So much for Brecht's earliest sonnets. Brecht himself did nothing further with them. But he made the rest of his sonnets, written between the mid-1920s and 1948, into a considered, distinctive and coherent part of his whole lyric work. He gathered many of them into titled collections, in fair copy. And nearly all of the sonnets left over after that gathering do seem to 'belong to' one or another of those collections. These are the collections:

(i) *Die Augsburger Sonette*, 1925–7. Contains twelve sonnets, but of a further twelve written in the same period, ten are similar in tone and subjects and could be added to those collected.[12]

(ii) *Sonette* and *Englische Sonette*. There are thirteen sonnets in the first collection, three in the second, written in 1932–5 and all addressed to Margarete Steffin. Five or six more, written 1937–40, might be added to them.[13]

(iii) *Studien* (*Studies*). These are eight sonnets on literary and artistic subjects, six of them written in 1938. Another five or six sonnets, written around that time, might be added to them.[14]

Of those four (effectively three) collections only one, the last, *Studies*, was published in Brecht's lifetime: in 1951, in *Versuche* (*Experiments*), volume 11.

Of Brecht's total sonnet *œuvre* after 1919 (about seventy, if we include the unfinished and the fourteen-line poems not strictly sonnets), most (fifty-four or thereabouts) were either gathered by him into definite collections or 'belong' in one or other of those collections. And nearly all of the few strays, written outside the main periods of sonnet-writing, in tone and/or subject are drawn to the collections. For example 'Empfehlung eines langen, weiten Rocks'/'In favour of a long, broad skirt' (around 1944), 'Über die Verführung von Engeln' / 'On seducing angels' and 'Saune und Beischlaf'/'Sauna and copulation' (both 1948) would be quite at home among the *Augsburg Sonnets*.[15] That is of *some* interest. We can say that the sonnet seemed to Brecht suitable for certain, quite restricted kinds of poetic undertaking.

I make that point – an obvious one – to emphasise how conscious Brecht was of the character and usefulness of different poetic forms, and how adept he was at exploiting them. He wrote ballads, chorales, music-hall songs, marching songs; psalms, epigrams, odes, elegies, idylls; he wrote in iambics, trochaics, hexameters, free verse; he rhymed when it suited him, didn't when it didn't; he wrote lyrically, reflectively, at length and with brevity; he wrote poems of lament, of grief, of rage, of celebration. That tribute is by no means exhaustive. The variety of his poetic craftsmanship is astonishing. I can't think of a poet who paid more and such close and unprejudiced attention to the poetic forms and possibilities placed at his disposal by tradition, by his own and by other languages' traditions.

Brecht was, to put it mildly, a contradictory man, and as such he needed things to contradict. Dozens of poetic forms and traditions served him in that way. But contradiction does not necessarily annihilate the thing it contradicts. The contradiction I have in mind (Brecht's sort, I think) draws its lifeblood out of the continuing life of what it contradicts. If this is a dialectic, it is not one that resolves itself into a synthesis. The desired or at least the achieved effect (the truth of the writing?) lies actually in the antagonism, in the continuing struggle of diction and contradiction. That applies to these sonnets, applies to us in our reading of them (our relationship with them), and may, I think, also be the truth of the particular relationship out of which many of them came, that with the brave and poetically gifted Margarete Steffin.

It will be helpful, thinking about contradiction, to consider the 'Sonett vom Erbe' / 'Sonnet on the legacy':

Als sie mich sahn aus alten Büchern schreiben
Saßen sie traurig mürrisch bei mir, die Gewehre
Auf ihren Knieen, und folgten meinem Treiben
Gehst du bei unsern Feinden in die Lehre?

Ich sagte: ja. Sie wissen, wie man schreibt.
Und zwar die Lüge, sagten sie, die Lüge.
Ich freute mich der Rüge
Sie standen auf: ich sagte hastig: bleibt!

Das sind die Leute, die uns
Die uns das Brot in dünne Scheiben schneiden
Und ihres Volkes Schlägern raten: schlagt es!
Was können sie dich lehren? Sagte ich: zu schreiben.
Und was zu schreiben? Sagte ich: ihr sagt es
Sie schneiden euch das Brot in dünne Scheiben.

[In the room with me, their guns across their knees,
When they saw me writing out things from old books
They followed my doing with sad and sullen looks:
Are you taking lessons from our enemies?

Yes, I answered. They know how to write.
Write lies, they said, write lies, indeed they do.
I liked this setting me straight.
They rose to leave. In haste I said: Don't go.

These are the people who ——
Who cut the loaf thin when they cut for us
And counsel those who beat the people: Do!
What can you learn from them? I said: To write.
Write what? I answered: What you said:
They cut the bread thin when they cut for you.]

Translated by David Constantine [16]

Written around 1938 and not quite finished (it wants the rest of line 9 and perhaps some adjustment of the rhyme scheme in the sestet), the poem was probably intended for the *Studies*. Indeed, its title would serve for that whole collection and for other associated sonnets of the time whose subject, and practice, is present dealings with the culture of the past. The question of the legacy – whose is it? what to do with it? – was critical among German exiles in the 1930s, was so again in the GDR, and of course always is critical to any writer orientating himself or herself in tradition. 'Sonnet on the legacy' is one such self-orientation, but it also and properly, given the writer's real circumstances, addresses the further question: what can the writer do for and alongside the combatants in their common struggle? And it asserts that, for the struggle, you can learn the craft of writing even from the enemy.

The sonnet form itself stands in an interesting relationship to both those issues. Sonnets have been written in the languages of Europe for seven hundred years. Any writer using the form engages, consciously or not, with that long tradition and the best writers by the force of their own sonnets alter it. In his 'Sonnet on the legacy', Brecht acknowledges the tradition he belongs in, reflects on his own relationship with it, and enquires whether that particular tradition – the sonnet – can be made to serve his present needs. That specific dialectic is part of, or representative of, the larger one that the writer must engage in with all 'the legacy'.

Might the sonnet be useful in the struggle? 'Kohlen für Mike'/'Coal for Mike' (1926)[17] was offered in the wish that it might, in its own way, be as materially helpful as the lump of coal thrown over the fence by Mike's comrades to his widow. Brecht in exile wanted to write poems that would be of material help in the struggle against Hitler. In 'Sonnet on the legacy', he stands in the same relationship to the armed fighters as he did to the brakemen in 'Coal for Mike', wanting to help, with a poem. He wrote only one sonnet to serve in that way: 'Vorschlag, für den Krieg mit Hitler schießbare Radioempfangsgeräte zu bauen'/'Suggestion that for the war with Hitler radio receivers be manufactured that could be fired from guns'. Written, like 'Sonnet on the legacy', in or around 1938, addressed to the workers of the Soviet Union and probably intended, like the *German Satires*, for the Free German Radio, the poem proposes an action akin to the writing and polemical dissemination of poetry, namely bombarding the misguided German workers with little radios from which would issue arguments likely to convert them:

> Suggest they should ally themselves with you.
> Tell them the reasons. Shell them with the reasons.
> Many a one may be struck and come over to you.[18]

Again the association, in wishful thinking, of the poem with the more material aid or instrument: coal, rifles, artillery, radios. It is the wish that poetry should be, as Seferis says it is, 'strong enough to help'.[19] The question is always, of course: in what way is poetry best suited to help?

That is the only sonnet serving as the poet in 'On the legacy' hopes his verse will serve, as a weapon in the struggle.[20] Quite simply, Brecht did not think the form suitable for that particular pupose. The looser forms of the *German Satires* worked far better.

'Sonnet on the legacy' is an apologia for Brecht's irrepressible love of all manner and variety of writing. Certainly, he learned and borrowed everywhere, and very often from 'the enemy'. This sonnet suggests that his appropriation of models and traditions always had the committed purpose of serving the struggle. What he learned from the enemy, he could use against them. Needless to say, in spirit and in practice he was far less strict than that. And 'Sonnet on the legacy', depicting him at his most committed, is written in a form, the sonnet, which of all forms was the one he wrote in nearly always at his least committed. Most of them, even including the *Studies*, have to do with sex and many are pornographic. He had in mind to present the *Augsburg Sonnets* under the caption 'Meine Achillesverse'/'My Achilles verses';[21] which is to say, punning on 'Achillesferse'/'Achilles' heel', that he viewed their subject as his weakness and the sonnet as the form most suitable for indulging it. He wrote to Helene Weigel in August 1927 that he was writing pornographic sonnets 'as always when I'm doing nothing and on my own'.[22] Taken together, the sonnets are the least pointedly political genre in his poetic *œuvre*, though all but the first half-dozen post-date the *Domestic Breviary*. Many do have political point, of course; but they achieve it in a peculiarly equivocal way. Indeed, his most usual practice in the sonnets is to contradict the self – the committed comrade – who appears in 'On the legacy'. It is in the sonnets that he is at his most personal, sensual, selfish, quixotic and intractable. The form seemed to him suitable for trying out the least politically aligned aspects or versions of his complex and contradictory character.

Brecht's dealings with his models were always independent. He was never overwhelmed by them. Usually his dealings were critical, often they were actively hostile. His radically blasphemous appropriation and abuse of breviary, psalm and chorale in the *Domestic Breviary* is a good example. There is something of that tension in every poet's independent dealings with traditional pre-existent forms, indeed with poetic form altogether. A phrase of Hölderlin's – 'liebender Streit' [loving quarrel][23] – may be used to describe that coming together of free creative spirit with tradition and with the necessary shaping constraint of a particular form. In Brecht's case the quarrel is scarcely ever loving. Most often it is violent, and his self-assertion is an act of insult.

Brecht was not by any means a radical transformer of the sonnet *form*. Among his contemporaries, Rilke and Anton Schnack were much more adventurous, as was, among his predecessors, the seventeenth-century poet Gryphius. One hallmark of Brecht's sonnets (and of much of his other poetry too) is minimal punctuation; but his only repeated formal transgression – after the experiments and uncertainties of the very earliest attempts – is the line that exceeds the iambic pentameter by one or more feet. This occurs so frequently, and in sonnets which are otherwise regular in their rhymes and pentameters, that it reads rather like a signature. For example, line 5 of 'Was ich von früher her noch kannte, war' / 'Things I remembered from those past days were': 'Drum weiß ich nichts von ihr als, ganz von Nacht zerstört' / 'So all I know of her, by night undone'. Or line 4 of 'Die Opiumraucherin' / 'The opium smoker': 'Und: daß sie nur den dritten Teil vom Leben braucht' [And two-thirds of the time she won't be living].[24] He rhymes very obediently and fully; works in quatrains and tercets (with some licence in the arrangement of the tercets); or (less often) in quatrains and a concluding couplet.[25] Altogether, in the sonnets, he is strikingly less casual, careless, disrespectful towards the chosen form than he is, when it suits him, in the very varied poems of the *Domestic Breviary*. His contradiction lies more in tone and register, in the mixing of tones and registers, and in subject and cast of mind;

and this sort of contradiction is actually enhanced by his conform-
ing to the sonnet's traditional requirements. Often the words are so
packed into the prosody, in a way so sovereign, forceful and knowing, the lines seem on the verge of detonating: 'Wenn sie dies läs, sie
wüßt nicht, wer es ist' [Nor would she see herself when reading
this];[26] 'Gab's wenig Lust, ist auch der Gram gering' [Where lust
was slight the grief is trivial too], 'Gekonnt ist gut, doch allzu
schlimm: gemußt' [Good if one can; but too bad if one must].[27]
Fitting the words into iambic pentameters unleashes their energy.
That energy, released by form, is also its contradiction.

Obscenity is a more obvious contradiction. There was plenty of
pornography in sonnets before Brecht – in the German baroque
and in the Italian Renaissance (notably Pietro Aretino) – but usually
of a rather polished kind. Obscenity itself is 'enhanced' by being
fitted into an elegant, demanding and highly respected traditional
form. Brecht – very self-consciously – pitches it low, as if to offend
against the decorum, or pseudo-decorum, of the genre. Examples
abound, but 'Sonett über einen durchschnittlichen Beischlaf'/
'Sonnet on a middling sort of copulation', 'On seducing angels' and
'Sauna and copulation' all seem particularly to revel in making
obscenities of thinking, tone and language rhyme and scan.[28] In the
case of the latter two, the last in his sonnet œuvre, written in Zürich
in 1948, Brecht's offensive intention is further indicated by his
having signed them 'Thomas Mann'. Brecht's obscenity is complex
and interesting and I shall say more about it with reference to the
Augsburg Sonnets and those to Margarete Steffin. But first a word on
another aspect of Brecht's contradictory relationship with the
sonnet form.

The sonnet is suitable for great clarity. It has a pleasingly lucid,
intelligent procedure. It is a good medium for clear exposition, fine
discriminations, development, turn and a point. Quite often, adopting and adhering to that form – quatrains and tercets, quatrains and
a couplet, in regular metre, with full euphonious rhymes – Brecht
gives you something of considerable intellectual and moral difficulty. He leaves you perplexed. Clear form is belied by what is being
done in it. For example in 'Sonett Nr.1. Über Mangel an
Bösem'/'On the lack of wickedness'.[29] In the language of sport

('rounds', 'final spurt'), as though it were a matter of stamina, the poem laments our inability to bring forth decisively wicked people. The human race and the earth go on whatever we do. The opinion is very self-assured (line 2: 'as we know'), and its utterance laconic and throwaway, but our difficulty as readers lies more in our having to adjust to a bizarre opinion formally articulated. The regularity and clarity of the first line are very disorientating.[30]

The *Augsburg Sonnets* (the above poem is the first of them) over-lapped in their composition with the poems of the *Reader for Those who Live in Cities*. Unlike them in form, they often resemble them closely in tone and in their mode or procedure. The *Reader*, in its lovelessness, pitilessness, treachery and alienation and in the flat brutality and the sarcasm of the language and in the impoverish-ment of its poetic forms, cries out to be contradicted. That is what I mean by its procedure. It demonstrates through the negative the need for radical humanising change. Humane dealings are actually fetched to the imagination, as a desperate need, through their very absence. Several of the *Augsburg Sonnets* work like that. A man pres-ents himself living badly, his relations with his fellow human beings are contemptuous and loveless. The tone of voice is sardonic. In the poems of the *Reader* free verse, stripped of ornament, minimal and cryptic, is a highly appropriate medium. But so is the sonnet, as a contradiction. Its urbane form is insulted in the urban jungle. Its shapeliness, its harmonies, are denied by the tone and by the mate-rial; but they answer back, and perhaps help the reader do the same. 'Sonett Nr.6. Ein Mann bringt sich zu Bett'/ 'A man gets himself to bed', 'Sonett Nr.12. Vom Liebhaber'/ 'The lover' and 'Sonett über schlechtes Leben'/ 'Sonnet on the subject of living badly' are good examples.[31] We see people living badly, in shapely form, in rhyme, in steady metre, in foul language, in a cynical bearing. The sonnet has been in use in many different societies in seven centuries. This is how it looks, this is what it does (says Brecht) in our own time and place.

A particularly bad thing in the sonnets of 1925–7, as in the poems of the *Reader*, is how men and women deal with one another. There is a moment of pity (or is it only fear?) in 'Entdeckung an einer jungen Frau'/'Discovery about a young woman'.[32] The lover, or client, notices grey in the woman's hair when, like lovers in the traditional 'morning song', they separate after the night together. But the usual tone of the male persona is brutally, sardonically, reductively exploitative. These poems are quite loveless. They have to do with sex, and the best to be hoped for there is improved technique. Thus: 'Forderung nach Kunst' / 'Need for art' and 'Sonnet on a middling sort of copulation'.[33] It is not, I think, prudery that is offended by these sonnets, but humanity. And the offence is calculated and deliberate, in the spirit of Baudelaire's 'Hypocrite lecteur, – mon semblable, – mon frère!'[34] and of Brecht's own almost gleeful insistence on the details in 'On the infanticide Marie Farrar': 'so men may see what I am and you are'.[35]

The moral of the poems (their politics) is this: Life in the cities under capitalism is alienated and deformed. No life worthy the name can survive. They say: See how we live in the social order we have created. They excite revulsion, which is a strong form of contradiction. We are required to answer back, with a better idea of man and a better practice.

Of course, the specific disgust (at what capitalism does to human relations) may verge on or become an absolute cynicism and disgust at the nature and state of humanity under whatever system. The artist George Grosz went that far, I should say, in his *Ecce Homo*, and his friend Brecht, in the 1920s, seems quite near it.

Brecht in real life, especially in his dealings with women, seems not to have been any nicer than the male persona in his *Augsburg Sonnets*. He was, by many accounts, exploitative, sexist, boorish, faithless, ruthless, devious, selfish, cruel and mercenary. He seems quite often to have acted as the living proof of his thesis that true human relations under capitalism are impossible. He said once – or is said to have said – that he was not a poet or a dramatist but 'a teacher of behaviour'.[36] His method, in this endeavour at least, seems to have been more Stanislavsky than Epic. I mean he lived the part. That is one way of understanding him: as the conscious embodiment of the contradictions wrought in humanity by capitalism.

Another possibility is that he and Baal are one flesh.

Of *Baal*, Brecht said (looking back on it) that the play might present all sorts of difficulties to people who had not learned to think dialectically.[37] He meant (I think) that just as the play itself came out of contradiction – the contradiction of the 'soft' play by Hanns Johst – so too Baal's behaviour is to be understood as countering other people's: Mech's for example, who wants, figuratively speaking, to turn him into matchsticks. But should Johanna, Sophie and Eckart have been countered just as ruthlessly? Baal was, Brecht noted in 1938, 'der Sichausleber', the man who lives himself out; but also 'der Andreausleber', the man who lives other people out.[38] His behaviour asks for their antagonism, in very self-defence. He requires them to answer with a countering, self-asserting energy. His way of being in the world must conjure up in others the means of their own equal engagement with him. You might say, putting the best possible slant on it, that he incites them into a robust self-realisation, against him or by means of him. In practice, they cannot answer back with sufficient force. Taking the phrase seriously, we may say *they cannot live up to him*. The perpetual provocation, challenge, threat of Baal's way of living (and of Brecht's perhaps) is, appropriately enough, how the poems work too. We are required to answer back, in defence of a more humane behaviour. Brecht, then, is the teacher of behaviour, dialectically. Poetry is very often an experimenting with possible ways of being in the world and of dealing with one another. Those ways don't have to be pleasant or agreeable. You might even say that it takes courage to try out what is offensive. Brecht is unusually thorough and pitiless (on himself and on us) in trying out attitudes and personae, so that he seems at times to be conducting experiments in the worst possible self. Most people, even the writers among them, are rather more concerned about how they look. Perhaps in his living, certainly in much of his poetry, Brecht shows off himself as badly as he could; and does two things in doing so: asks us are we very much better and cries out for contradiction.

Brecht's sonnets to Margarete Steffin, written between 1932–3 and 1939, are particularly interesting, first because she did answer back, and secondly because, though some are as brutal as any from Augsburg, others are very different – even, indeed, loving.

When Steffin died, of tuberculosis, in a Moscow clinic in June 1941, Brecht mourned her as his collaborator and comrade in the struggle against Hitler and for Communism:

> My general has fallen
> My soldier has fallen
>
> My pupil has gone away
> My teacher has gone away
>
> My nurse has gone
> My nursling has gone.[39]

Later, in America, where she was to have joined him, he wrote that without her he felt quite at a loss; as though his guide had been taken from him just as the desert began.[40] But of the sonnets only one, 'Und nun ist Krieg und unser Weg wird schwerer' / 'And now it's war; our path is growing steeper',[41] addresses her purely in that spirit and in those terms. Two others – 'Sonnet No. 19' and 'The 21st sonnet'[42] – allude strongly to a difficult way that has to be travelled together, and one other, 'The tenth sonnet',[43] presents her as fellow-worker in the cause *and* as lover, resisting and complying in both capacities. But in all the rest, nearly twenty, there is scarcely a mention of work or any public purpose, and the sonnet serves as it very often has, for utterance between two lovers, personal and peculiar to them and accessible and valuable to other readers by virtue of poetic form.

Brecht, as is well known, liked poetry to be useful, and he liked friends to be useful too. He viewed them as bridges and graded them according to their load-bearing capacity. He wrote:

> bridges can bear more or less weight. there are friends you can drive a thousand-ton goods train over, others can carry a bus and most a pram. but bridges that can bear a pram are still bridges (just so long as you don't drive over them in a small motor car because then they collapse and you get Weltschmerz).[44]

He expounded this theory or principle in a discussion concerning Margarete Steffin. She was a bridge over which a thousand-ton goods train might pass. Very candidly, that is how he mourned her in 1941:

Once the stage was reached where a not unkindly Death
Shrugged his shoulders and showed me her lungs' five ravaged lobes
Unable to imagine her surviving on the sixth alone
I rapidly assembled 500 jobs
Things that must be dealt with at once and tomorrow, next year
And in seven years' time from now
Asked endless questions, decisive ones
Unanswerable except by her
And thus needed
She died easier.[45]

We could say he used her; but anyone meaning that wholly critically should remember the urgency of their personal circumstances 'in Year Nine of the flight from Hitler',[46] and the value, incontrovertible as they saw it, of the cause they were both serving. Also acknowledge that being used in such a cause, being called upon, needed ('beansprucht'), might be enobling and empowering rather than demeaning. It might be that through which a self is made authentic. Naturally, people needed and used in that way forfeit their freedom. Brecht said so, as something they both understood, in 'Sonnet No. 19', a poem admitting their need for one another: 'Du weißt es: wer gebraucht wird, ist nicht frei' [You know whoever's needed can't go free].

Still, using people, particularly women, is the fault Brecht is most often accused of, and it runs through the sonnets to Margarete Steffin as it does through the *Augsburg Sonnets*; the vital difference being that in those to her it is challenged and countered by the writer himself, and by her replies. 'To use a woman' is an obsolete English locution meaning to have sex with her. It bears about as much contempt and misogyny as any locution could be made to bear. That tone and attitude prevail in the *Augsburg Sonnets* – 'Daß ich stets höre, wenn er sie gebraucht' / 'That I always hear it when he uses her'[47] – and he tries them in some of the Steffin sonnets too. Possession and commodification in the fifth and seventh sonnets,[48] for example. Then in the ninth,[49] reducing his own involvement to the bare minimum ('Ich geb nicht mich, ich geb dir einen Schwanz' [I don't give me, what I give you's a cock]), he becomes fearful she might learn the lesson and cease caring who she is with. In

'The sixth sonnet' he shows himself as typical of his sex and the sex at its worst:

> Und besser ist: kein Gram als: viele Lust
> Und besser als verlieren: sich bescheiden.
> Der Männer Wollust ist es: nicht zu leiden.
> Gekonnt ist gut, doch allzu schlimm: gemußt.
>
> [Better to feel no grief than too much lust.
> And better than to lose, to be resigned.
> There's pleasure in not being hurt, men find.
> Good if one can; but too bad if one must.]

But admits 'Natürlich ist das eine schäbige Lehre' [Of course that is a pretty shabby moral], and the sonnet ends rather lamely but also more humanely:

> Ich meine nur: wenn einer an nichts hinge
> Dem stünd auch keine schlimme Zeit bevor.
> Indessen sind wir nicht die Herrn der Dinge.
>
> [I only mean that unattached and free
> One may avoid a lot of suffering.
> Meanwhile we can't command what is to be.] [50]

Several of the sonnets adopt the very Brechtian structure of teacher and pupil. The ninth again: 'Als du das Vögeln lerntest, lehrt ich dich/So vögeln, daß du mich dabei vergaßest' [When you learned how to fuck I taught you to/Fuck so that you forgot me doing it].[51] Steffin was sexually experienced but not, by her own account, sexually awakened.[52] So the man in these sonnets thinks of himself as the woman's teacher in the art of love. In that teaching there is an edge of extra pleasure (for him) when what he teaches her comes as a shock. Thus in his calling the thing by its common name:

> Als ich schon dachte, daß wir einig wären
> Gebrauchte ich, fast ohne drauf zu achten
> Die Wörter, welche meinten, was wir machten
> Und zwar die allgemeinsten, ganz vulgären.
>
> Da war's, als ob von neuem du erschrakst
> Als sähst du jetzt erst, was das, was wir machten, sei
> In vielen Wochen, die du bei mir lagst
> Lehrt ich von diesen Wörtern dich kaum zwei.

Mit solchen Wörtern rufe ich den Schrecken
Von einst zurück, als ich dich frisch begattet
Es läßt sich länger nunmehr nicht verdecken:
Das Allerletzte hast du da gestattet!
Wie konntest du dich nur in so was schicken:
Das Wort für das, was du da tatst, war

[Already thinking we were of a mind
I used – and it was almost without knowing –
The words whose meaning was what we were doing
The commonest such words, the vulgarest kind.

All over again it shocked you through as though
Till now you had not seen what thing we did.
In many weeks of you with me in bed
Of words like that I scarcely taught you two.

But with these words I summon up the shock
Afresh of my first fleshly knowing you.
It can't be hidden any longer now:
Of all a lady's favours you kept not one back.
How could you make yourself common as muck?
The word for what it was you did was] [53]

The shock of the word revives the first shock and pleasure of the thing itself. It may be difficult to imagine any such shock in the words nowadays, but Lawrence, in 1927–8, in *Lady Chatterley's Lover*, knowing full well their power to offend, tried to recover them for the language of tenderness between a man and a woman in love. He wrote: 'I always labour at the same thing, to make the sex relation valid and precious, instead of shameful. And this novel is the furthest I've gone. To me it is beautiful and tender and frail as the naked self is'.[54] So Mellors instructs Connie in the use of the taboo words, in a tone very different from Brecht's in the sonnets to Steffin. There is more than a touch of vindictiveness in Brecht, as though he were forcing her to see that she is no better than he is, that he and she are companions in something base. Henry Miller's male characaters, in his *Tropic of Cancer* (1934) and *Tropic of Capricorn* (1939), take a similarly vengeful pleasure in ascertaining that sexual feelings are keen in women too. As though women lived in hypocrisy, and must be made to own up to their sexuality, and so humiliated. Steffin responded to some such triumphant experiment in a poem remarkable for its candour and generosity. It begins:

> Als er mich zum ersten Male fragte
> Ob ich naß sei, dacht ich: Was ist das?
> Als er fragte, ob er nachsehn sollte
> Schämte ich mich sehr. Ich war ja naß.
>
> [When he asked me for the first time
> Was I wet, I thought to myself: What's that?
> When he asked should he look
> I was very ashamed. Because I was wet.] [55]

That poem is one in an ongoing dialogue. Brecht actually altered the third person to the second on his copy, so: 'When you asked me for the first time…' Indeed, he seems to have written in the hope that she would always answer his sonnets with sonnets of her own, thus inviting their qualification or contradiction. [56] Only one such definite pairing has survived (see above, pp. 152–3). His poem is affectionate enough, but her greater dependence (using his words, appropriating his characteristic longer line) and her vulnerability are evident. As she said in her sonnet 'Als der Klassiker am Montag dem siebenten Oktober 1935 es verließ, weinte Dänemark' / 'When the Classic Poet left Denmark on Monday 7 October 1935, Denmark wept': 'I shall be very alone and I shall love you'. [57] What she suffered, she expressed in several of her prose writings too. And noted with a terrible resignation: 'Naturally he is not to blame. He's always told me that he has the conscience of a lump of ice.' That comes in a piece beginning, like the fifth of Brecht's poems from the *Reader for Those who Live in Cities*, [58] with the words 'Ich bin ein Dreck' [I'm dirt]. [59]

But in fairness, and to finish more encouragingly, it must also be said that among Brecht's sonnets to Margarete Steffin there are half a dozen in which tenderness and unselfish concern prevail and the man is shown as quite unable to live by the 'shabby moral' he offered in 'The sixth sonnet'; that is, he suffers from her absence, wants her near. Those two elements jostle in 'Fragen' / 'Questions', and in 'The eleventh sonnet' [60] thoughts of his dressing her warmly against the cold winter mix naturally with thoughts of undressing her, so 'mit sehr kalten Wintern' [with very cold winters] rhymes fitly with 'für den (geliebten) Hintern' [for your (beloved) bottom]. Sex then – as in 'Liebesgewohnheiten' / 'Love habits'[61] – is a shared and equal enjoyment and their secret and incongruous way of alluding to it (the secret word, oddly enough, was the south German greeting 'Grüß Gott', in letters between them abbreviated to GG) gives them, even in the company of strangers, a peculiarly charged intimacy in a place apart. Sonnets very often have that privacy, and reading them is like being let into secrets. Then the details become legendary. The little wooden and ivory elephants Brecht sent Steffin from cities he was in without her have that status. Thus in the lovingly anxious '21st sonnet' (they are 'our guardian beasts'), and in the '19th',[62] when they reprove him for not writing her a letter. To them, as to others among the emigrant's few belongings – the mask, the scroll, the little radio – an unbearable poignancy soon attaches. After she was dead, he wrote:

I often see GRETE with her things that she was forever packing into her suitcases. The portrait on silk, painted by Cas; the wooden and ivory elephants from the different cities I was in…[63]

In 'Sonnet No. 19', urging her not to abandon him (at times he seems to have thought of her illness as a rival, to whom she might give in), Brecht wrote: 'Remember we're surrounded yet by night'.[64] (His sonnet 'Der Orangenkauf' / 'Buying oranges', one of the three *English Sonnets*, is a luminous moment in that darkness (see below, pp. 173). Much poetry, writing it and reading it, is an act of realisation. Something dawns, is made concretely clear. That happens here. The man comes through a pea-souper in Covent Garden into a luminous space, the cart, the lamp, the shining oranges. And that sight is a realisation of what he was unconsciously looking for or wanting. Focusing then so suddenly on that concrete presence, he focuses on her, the absent woman. Oranges are her usual and characteristic treat, and so the best bearer now of his love for her. He does what he always would do, in a loving habit: fishes for the money to buy them. Then comes another dawning: 'Du bist ja gar nicht da in dieser Stadt' [Of course you are not anywhere in this town]. In a regular iambic pentameter, in ordinary language, comes a realisation of pathos at the moment of disillusioning and disappointment (*Enttäuschung*). The love-gift cannot be the oranges, but is the poem instead, luminous as the oranges, standing in for them, *pis-aller* and recompense; and lasting beyond the lovers it first went between. The poem is in its own way concretely effective, stands to the oranges as 'Coal for Mike' stands to the lump of coal, for the lover and comrade Margarete Steffin.

Brecht, so often using the sonnet to experiment with the worst in himself (and in his readers, and in the citizens of any dehumanising social order), in these few at least shows a better possibility. But showing one face or the other, all his sonnets have a Utopian potential. They may conjure up their own contradiction, or realise it themselves in love and self-forgetting, man and woman equal as lovers and comrades. The moral power of poems lies in that agility.

Der Orangenkauf

Bei gelbem Nebel in Southamptonstreet
Plötzlich ein Karren Obst mit einer Lampe
An Tüten zupfend eine alte Schlampe
Ich blieb stumm stehn wie einer, der was sieht
Nach was er lief: nun wurd's ihm hingestellt.

Orangen mußten es doch immer sein!
Ich haucht in meine Hand mir Wärme ein
Und fischte in der Tasche schnell nach Geld

Doch zwischen dem, daß ich die Pennies griff
Und nach dem Preis sah, der auf Zeitungsblatt
Mit schmieriger Kohle aufgeschrieben war
Bemerkte ich, daß ich schon leise pfiff
Mit einem wurd's mir nämlich bitter klar:
Du bist ja gar nicht da in dieser Stadt.[65]

Buying oranges

In a yellow fog along Southampton Street
Suddenly a barrow, a slattern plucking at
Her paper bags, and fruit in lamplight.
I stopped struck dumb like one who has seen what
He was running after: there put in his way.

Oranges! No thing else could it ever be!
I blew some warmth into my hands and quickly
Fished in my pockets after cash to pay

But then between the pence being in my grip
And glancing at the price there written up
In smudged charcoal on newspaper
I caught my own wry whistling undertone
For at that moment bitterly this came clear:
Of course you are not anywhere in this town.

Translated by David Constantine [66]

8

Heißer Tag

Heißer Tag. Auf den Knien die Schreibmappe
Sitze ich im Pavillon. Ein grüner Kahn
Kommt durch die Weide in Sicht. Im Heck
Eine dicke Nonne, dick gekleidet. Vor ihr
Ein ältlicher Mann im Schwimmanzug, wahrscheinlich ein Priester.
An der Ruderbank, aus vollen Kräften rudernd
Ein Kind. Wie in alten Zeiten! denke ich
Wie in alten Zeiten!

Rudern, Gespräche

Es ist Abend. Vorbei gleiten
Zwei Faltboote, darinnen
Zwei nackte junge Männer. Nebeneinander rudernd
Sprechen sie. Sprechend
Rudern sie nebeneinander.

Hot day

Hot day. My writing-case on my knee
I sit in the summer-house. A green boat
Appears through the willow. In the stern
A stout nun, stoutly clad. In front of her
An elderly person in a bathing-costume, probably a priest.
At the oars, rowing for all he's worth
A child. Just like old times, I think
Just like old times.

Translated by Derek Bowman[1]

Paddling, talking

It's evening. Two canoes
Glide past, inside them
Two naked young men: paddling abreast
They talk. Talking
They paddle abreast.

Translated by Michael Hamburger[2]

Empedocles in Buckow:
a sketch-map of misreading in Brecht's poetry

Ray Ockenden

1   Introduction

When, after Brecht's death, his poetry became better known[3] and it became apparent that it was to be taken as seriously as his drama, attempts began to determine whether that principle which had already become inseparably associated with his name, namely *Verfremdung* [defamiliarisation], could similarly be applied to his poetry. A paper by Clemens Heselhaus provides a very early example of this, and concludes that the use of wit and parody, the disappointing of readers' expectations, the trivialising and degrading metaphor and the simplified, epigrammatic style are evidence of *Verfremdung* at work.[4] Heselhaus has a view of the poet–reader relationship that seems at odds with Brecht's, and his use of examples from the early poetry overlooks the important fact that, as with the drama, the notion of *Verfremdung* was not consciously used until Brecht's exile period. Very different is Philip Brady's investigation of how Brecht presents a 'defamiliarised war' in his poetry – though the essay ranges more widely than that and includes, for example, reference to the Breughel 'commentaries', which will be discussed below.[5] Brady notes the deployment of various voices, and of different lines of argument, in the poetry, and he is aware of the crucial interaction between it and the reader. Where I would take issue with him is in his underplaying of what I see as a constant and major theme of Brecht's poetry about the Second World War, that is the view that it will be, and is when it comes, the 'wrong' war. However, Brady does recognise this element[6] in the well-known epigrammatic poem 'Auf der Mauer stand mit Kreide'/'On the wall was chalked'.[7] The graffito writer has already 'fallen' honourably in the *real* war, that between those 'above' and those 'below', in punishment for warning of the *unreal* war being planned by the Nazis. This common theme in Brecht[8] occurs in many of the poems in the 'Deutsche Kriegsfibel'/'German War Primer' section of the *Svendborg Poems* to which Brady refers. For example, the open question dangling at the end of the poem 'Die Arbeiter schreien nach Brot'/'The workers cry out for bread'[9] is why the starving munitions workers do not use the results of their labours against their actual oppressors, instead of allowing them to be stored for use against their potential allies, the dispossessed of other nations. In this essay I want to explore a particular kind of 'voicing' and 'interaction with the reader', starting from the position that Brecht, at least from the exile period onwards, is writing poetry as a form of communication closely akin to teaching or instruction. And I want to suggest parallels between the two periods of writing indicated by the title of the essay.[10]

One of the dominant concerns of Brecht's writing during the exile period, especially in the early years, is learning and teaching – now conceived on a much broader scale than was implied in the term *Lehrstücke* [didactic plays] for the plays of the pre-exile period.[11] Learning remains a vital part of the theatrical experience,[12] but we find also the idea of poetry as teaching, which goes far beyond the unfinished neo-Lucretian project of the *Lehrgedicht* [didactic poem][13] and informs a great deal of Brecht's later poetry – including poems that might appear to be rather dialogic (for example, love poems) or even monologic. The link between writing and teaching/learning is made explicit in 'Der Insasse'/'The passenger'[14] and among other poems dated as 'circa 1935' in the commentated edition are, for example, 'Über das Lehren ohne Schüler'/'On teaching without pupils', 'Der Lernende'/'The learner' and a fragment which concludes: 'In a situation like this/It's as well to know that learning is necessary'.[15] Learning is essential for the child, who is present in several of the exile poems as an evident sign of hope for future.[16] Political figures and writers are presented as teachers, for example Lenin, Gorky and Dimitroff;[17] the last two exemplify the important notion of the teacher as learner, which is expressed with regard to Brecht himself in the motto to the *Svendborg Poems*: 'I will gladly go back to learning'.[18] Learning is an essential quality in being human: only those who are dying no longer seek to learn – indeed they seem almost to define themselves as the dying thereby.[19] By contrast, we are given the picture of 'one who has failed', who none the less continues learning (and, as the context makes clear, teaching) right up to the moment of his death,[20] recalling those centenarians celebrated by Galilei: 'Men of a hundred, even, are getting the young people to bawl the latest example into their ears'.[21]

Verfremdung, as I noted above, is another idea which only begins to concern Brecht consciously from his time of exile; much of the impetus for that concern derives from his Moscow experience of Chinese theatre in March–April 1935, and after the term itself is first used in the second half of 1936,[22] Brecht explores the idea in several writings of 1936 and 1937 especially. At a relatively early stage,[23] Brecht presents the idea of the *Verfremdungseffekt* [defamiliarising effect] being present in the novel, cinema and painting[24] and goes on to comment on paintings by Breughel under the challenging heading 'V-effects in some paintings of Breughel the Elder'.[25] Brecht here suggests that these effects are part of Breughel's intended artistic strategy, rather than being unearthed by his own subtle reinterpretations.

The reasons why Brecht pursues this new strategy are clearly complex; to some extent, it is no more than an extension and reinforcement of his ideas about epic theatre. However, it seems reasonable to take this insistence on a method, which demands reflection and engagement from its receivers, as at least in part a response to the changed circumstances of exile, which also explain the urgent interest in teaching and learning. Some of Brecht's anti-Fascist writing of the early exile years seems almost to imply that the new regime in Germany might be brought down by ridicule, or indignation, and reflects Brecht's sheer astonishment at the gullibility of the German people. The poem which most clearly registers a change of heart, the poignant 'Gedanken über die Dauer des Exils' / 'Thoughts on the duration of exile', is not apparently written until 1937, but the change itself comes much earlier.[26] In the poem the writer's work to liberate Germany (and himself) appears to be negated by his acceptance of exile as likely to be of long duration.[27] On the other hand, the measure of that acceptance, the care for the young tree (which we presume he has himself planted) provides a strong index of hope for the future, recalling the *little* apricot tree in the first 'Frühling 1938' / 'Spring 1938' poem[28] and its clear link to a human figure, 'my *young* son' [my italics], a parallel figure of hope for the not so immediate future.

New circumstances demand new strategies. The often-quoted letter to Tretiakoff, dated in the commentated edition at the end of December 1933 or early January 1934, indicates Brecht's state of mind and is clear evidence of the new direction: 'The time for spectacular proclamations, protests, etc. is over for the moment. What is needed now is patient, persistent, painstaking educational work as well as study.'[29]

One aspect of this new approach is Brecht's hostility to dogmatism, which finds expression in his attack on 'formalism' and his comments regarding the controversy over Realism and Expressionism. Brecht is now opposed to limitations of all kinds, and for him formalism can be equated both with political and with aesthetic dogmatism.[30] The times require not petty-mindedness or narrow orthodoxy, but rather broad alliances. As early as December 1934, searching for allies, he is talking of involving Gide, Shaw and Wells in his efforts.[31] Later comes the fancy of a Diderot society, in which figures such as Auden, Isherwood and Jean Renoir are to be enrolled.[32] Writing to Becher around the same time as he is trying to organise this 'Diderot-Society', he recalls Dimitroff's idea of the Trojan Horse, and the meeting at which the 'Einheitsfront' [United Front] policy was agreed.[33] All these plans are expressive of the long view Brecht is now taking: 'Our goal / Lay far in the distance', as he wrote. Small wonder that from Moscow he was charged with 'defeatism'.[34]

As well as inveighing against the narrow definition of 'socialist realism' offered by Lukács and others in the 'Moscow clique',[35] Brecht, in pursuing the idea and implications of *Verfremdung*, is setting himself apart from the theatrical approach which had become canonised in Moscow, Stanislavsky's 'Method'; nothing further from his own ideas of theatre could be imagined.[36] At the same time, his sense of isolation is clearly heightened by his disastrous experiences with *Die Mutter / The Mother* in America in 1935; in vain does he urge American comrades to accept what is 'new' and 'difficult' about his theatre.[37] However, that his place of ultimate refuge would be America rather than the Soviet Union is clear at a relatively early moment of exile, and from the latter country, despite the fact that in late 1938 he can still describe himself as 'an unshakeable friend of the Soviet Union', the shocks, at a personal level, keep coming.[38]

2 *Verfremdung*

Directness and obviousness are not, in Brecht's view, the desiderata of the day. It is interesting to see him suggesting that plays should be so acted as to yield up their true message only after repeated viewings;[39] the idea of 'repeated viewing' is of course easily transferable to the idea of repeated readings of poems. In this connection, we may note Brecht's poem about his scroll painting of 'Der Zweifler' / 'The doubter',[40] with its hesitation between emphasis on form and on content (lines 11–13), and between being 'viel-deutig' [having numerous meanings] and 'zu eindeutig' [too unambiguous] (lines 14–17): to remove contradictions from things is to render them useless. Doubt, of course, is to become a crucial concept, as shown in 'Lob des Zweifels' / 'In praise of doubt'.[41] There is room too for the cultivation of older classical forms such as Brecht was to pursue both in the 'Tui-Epos' / 'Tui Epic' and the later 'Lehrgedicht'; at the same time as Brecht is attacking the new formalism of the 'Moscow clique' he is alert to the equal and opposite danger of 'focusing purely on content'.[42] The use of classical forms is particularly touched on in the important essay of December 1934, which anticipates a number of the changes in Brecht's approach during the exile period: 'Fünf Schwierigkeiten beim Schreiben der Wahrheit'/'Five Difficulties in Writing the Truth'.[43] Especially relevant to the present context is the most substantial part of that piece, concerning 'the cunning needed to disseminate truth widely'.[44] Brecht cites Lucretius on the advantages of good writing for propaganda, and goes on to say, 'In fact, its high literary register can serve to protect a statement'.[45] The essay also highlights the relationship between writer and public; for reader response and the relationship with the reader also become most important to Brecht at this time: 'It [the truth] has to be written *to* somebody'.[46] One of the consequences of Brecht's contact with Chinese theatre was the realisation that in its tradition clever, allusive theatre is accessible to the simplest people; in consequence, Brecht writes (in April–May 1935) a piece 'Über die Zuschaukunst'/'On the art of being in the audience'.[47]

Many of the poetical devices Brecht employs in his exile and post-exile poetry can, I think, be usefully regarded as types of *Verfremdung*: the jolting of the reader out of familiarity, prompting thought and the seeing of things in a new light. Many of these poetic devices of *Verfremdung* are not in themselves new.[48] From Heine, Brecht borrows the technique of switching abruptly from one mood to another (*Stimmungsbrechung*) and uses it in several exile poems. 'Finnische Landschaft'/'Finnish landscape' portrays a lush scene, before asking about the freighted timber: 'Is that the way that wooden legs are made?'[49] The poem remembers, and reminds us, that there is a murderous war on. Similarly, the poem which begins with neo-romantic echoes, 'Spring is coming. The gentle winds', then reveals what *this* fresh springtime means, namely the arrival of Hitler's warships.[50] *Praeteritio* – not so much a case of 'the poem speaks of that about which it is silent', as Enzensberger said of Nelly Sachs, as 'the poem speaks of that about which it pretends to be silent' – also finds employment.[51] 'Ausschließlich wegen der zunehmenden Unordnung'/'Solely because of the increasing disorder' is an obvious example, a poem that actually lists the things which 'some of us' have decided no longer to mention.[52] The notion recurs famously in 'Schlechte Zeit für Lyrik' / 'Bad time for poetry': 'The green boats and the dancing sails on the Sound / Go unseen' proclaims the poetic voice.[53] But the poem sees them, and we as readers see them, as part of that world which is under threat from war and tyranny, but which it is worth waiting for and hoping for and working for. The use of *praeteritio* is a kind of misdirection, a category I shall come back to later.

A simpler device to prompt response and reflection is of course the question.[54] Questions are the centre and the topic of 'Fragen eines lesenden Arbeiters' / 'Questions from a worker who reads', form the thrust of 'Kantate erster Mai' / 'Cantata for 1st May', and creep into and finally dominate 'Der Zweifler' / 'The doubter';[55] they are to be found in many poems. Sometimes they may masquerade as rhetorical questions, but the effect of looking more closely, of registering the *Verfremdungseffekt*, is the uncovering of more real underlying oppositions. The concluding lines of the poem which begins 'Once I thought: in distant times'[56] might appear vacuous; in view of the accumulated logic of the poem the question 'Why / Should my name be mentioned?' must surely expect the answer 'It will not be mentioned'. But no: the poem implies that we should find other answers.[57]

Sometimes there is a correction within the poem itself. The poem which begins 'To-day, Easter Sunday morning'[58] delivers a breathlessly long catalogue of why, at this historical juncture, there is absolutely no point in caring for a wretched little apricot tree caught in an unseasonal snowstorm. But then, after a pause indicated by the end of the long sentence, we read: 'In silence / We put a sack / Over the freezing tree.' The gesture of responding to the appeal of 'my young son' to care for the (now personalised) tree, to hope in a future, needs no rhetoric, no words at all; but the poem, having poured out its cascade of anxiety in free verse, embodies the silent rescue in a classical pentameter: 'Legten wir einen Sack / Über den frierenden Baum' [We put a sack / Over the freezing tree]. Still more clearly, because of the employment of an empty line to mark the moment of reflection, we see a self-correction in 'Mein junger Sohn fragt mich' / 'My young son asks me'.[59] The reader is asked to fill out that gap by rehearsing what makes the speaker change his mind about education for the future, at a time when, logically, it seems there cannot be any value in it.

Brecht's comments on Breughel's paintings are instructive variants on these techniques of *Verfremdung*. In one case, presenting the 'Landscape with the fall of Icarus',[60] he holds the two aspects of the painting apart (as the title itself does), and shows Breughel saying to us: don't look over there, look here; hence instead of talking about the fall of the famous person, Brecht brings out the 'attention which ploughing demands'.[61] In another case, Brecht brilliantly brings together the two paintings of *The Census at Bethlehem* and *The Massacre of the Innocents*, tersely suggesting that the latter action could only be so effective because of the former.[62] This is an idea Brecht was to make use of in his drama: in the opening scene of *Mother Courage and her Children* the sergeant praises the bureaucratic order brought by the war, with 'man and beast properly numbered and carted off'.[63] In the light of what the Nazi bureaucratic machine was to achieve, that final verb – 'weggebracht' [carted off] – illogical in its immediate context, has gained rather than lost in its power to shock.

The process of demystification, which we can see at work in the reading of Breughel's Icarus painting, is carried out in other ways. At the most intimate level, it involves the cutting of big words down to size, or the replacing of obfuscating words with more real ones. Brecht refers to this technique in 'Five Difficulties in Writing the Truth', discussing how Confucius was able to expose concealed truth. Brecht goes on to refer to the 'bogus mysticism' of the present times, in obvious reference to the Nazi use of certain words, such as 'Volk' [people].[64] The suggestion that the word 'discipline' be replaced by 'obedience' and 'honour' by 'human dignity' also refers directly to Nazi rhetoric, as well as anticipating Wang's complaints to the gods in *The Good Person of Szechwan*.[65] Brecht offers a concrete example of the process of demystifying in his essay;[66] in similar vein, and close to Confucius's procedure, is the piece 'Durch bestimmte Weglassungen werden Geschichten merkwürdig' / 'By dint of certain omissions, stories become remarkable'.[67] In the same month as writing 'Five Difficulties in Writing the Truth',

Brecht composes 'marginal glosses' on speeches by Goering and Hess.[68]

A more extended tackling of myth and legend was evidently planned by Brecht: we have an unfinished sequence of reinterpretations of old myths dating from an early stage in his exile period.[69] The first of these concerns Odysseus and the sirens.[70] Odysseus, the enforced wanderer, the cleverest of the Greeks, is a figure with whom Brecht may well have felt some affinity; the poem 'Heimkehr des Odysseus'/'Odysseus' return home'[71] sounds a personal, as well as a general note, and the reference to the ship suggests it could have been prompted by Brecht's return from America in 1936.[72] It is true that in 1937 the by now negative figure of André Gide is also described as an Odysseus,[73] but as one whose ship and goal are alike uncertain. However, the initial impulse for the retelling of the siren episode is not Brecht's exile or travels, but a reading of Kafka, thanks to Walter Benjamin.[74] The difference from Kafka's 'The Silence of the Sirens' is significant: Kafka's hero is an individual sailor, the members of his crew are present only by implication, as fasteners of ropes, and he himself has wax in his ears as well as chains that bind him to the mast. Brecht's hero (like Homer's) has a crew who are different from Odysseus and important to the story. Brecht borrows the effortful grimaces of the sirens (not in Homer) from Kafka, and reinterprets them, making this light-hearted piece seem more a rewriting of Kafka than of Homer. We shall come back to this episode in another context.

3 Empedocles

Reinterpreting myths is also one aspect of the 'Chronicles' section of the *Svendborg Poems*: questions about history are questions about the facts behind figures who have been accorded mythical status by the processes of historiography. The desire to show that those in power are no more than ordinary people, that princes and prelates have the same legs as ours under their fine robes, is always a part of Brecht's programme.[75] However, figures such as Empedocles, Lao-Tsû and Buddha are presented not as people with power, but as teachers. 'The Shoe of Empedocles' of 1935 is plainly a poem about a teacher and his pupils.[76] Empedocles takes some, not all, on an excursion, climbs Etna with them, then slips away unnoticed to die; before he throws himself into the volcano's crater, he takes off and hides one of his shoes. For him, his dying begins at the moment when he becomes cut off from the conversation with his pupils; but his death, i.e. a public matter, is different. That only begins when he fails to turn up, and weeks, then months, pass. What he achieves by his behaviour is not just that he avoids for himself the painfulness of a deathbed scene with his pupils, and for them an over-exaggerated emphasis on the moment of death. He also continues to teach. His last lesson is one that extends beyond his death, so that on the one hand he can continue to be useful, on the other, once the riddle has been solved, he will have receded – died, so to speak, gradually and peacefully from their memories, so they will have come to terms with their loss. This last lesson is spelt out in the poem. Empedocles has left room for misreadings, precisely to enable those misreadings to be built into a better reading later. Making mistakes is fruitful; you can learn from them; they are a part of you in a way that answers provided from outside by someone else cannot be. So it is altogether beneficial for his pupils that some should wait, and some should think him dead; some should puzzle over his death, while others, dependent on him still, wait for the teacher to provide the answers.

At last, when he has faded from the front of their minds, the rumour arises that he has been snatched up to heaven; and that is only scotched when his discarded and all too earthly sandal is discovered. Of course, that might give rise to a different thought: he has been punished for wanting to appear immortal by the volcano which has thrown his shoe back; but that is only a different kind of metaphysics, as though the volcano had moral force. At this point, Brecht wonderfully questions the argument of his own poem by suggesting that maybe Empedocles, having forgotten about human stupidity, *didn't* leave his shoe behind – but that of course would make Empedocles himself less shrewd and less effective as a teacher. That hypothesis is in itself an example of the misreading that the poem is all about. Brecht's Empedocles, then, has set up a final lesson in and through his death; and that lesson, as the slyly placed sandal indicates, precisely counts in and counts on the misreadings. When the pupils have recognised the subtlety of that lesson, and the wild goose chases it includes, they will be the wiser for the journey, for 'you learn anew when you find out what you have learnt'.[77] They will both have come to terms with their teacher's death and realise that they can do without him; as Brecht noted in another context: 'Once knowledge has been conferred on him/The pupil must set out on his own'.[78]

In his sensitive reading of this poem, Klaus-Detlef Müller makes the interesting suggestion that the opening of part 2 of the poem with its evident narrative distance: 'Others might have described the foregoing/Differently' followed by the explicit perspective of 'But we would rather believe'[79] has the effect of turning the narrative of part 1 into just one among many, rather than the authoritative account we took it to be. This is clearly a valid reading; but might the reverse not equally be urged, namely that the use of 'we' suggests an identification of the narrating voice with the Empedoclean disciples of the original, so that 'our stupidity'[80] refers not only to a universal failing but also to a specific weakness of his followers?[81] But then again, are not both readings possible simultaneously? We realise that Brecht is already applying here a technique that becomes much used in the later poetry, where the bringing together of past and present is achieved by mapping the two on to one another rather than juxtaposing them.[82] In this way, Brecht manages to affirm the reality of the historic past, while acknowledging that the real value of our concern with it lies in its being made freshly relevant for the present.

The poem, from the title onwards, insists that the shoe is central. Brecht boldly borrows two details from the version of the legend hostile to Empedocles – the death in the volcano, and the shoe – and then alters them. The dramatic mode of death is given a new interpretation. The iron or bronze shoe, which belongs to the story of Empedocles the deceiver who is revealed by the shoe which the volcano did not consume, is replaced by a leather shoe, which would surely not have survived a fall into the crater. At no point, incidentally, does part 2 suggest that Empedocles might really have attempted to secure divine honours for himself.[83] If mountains *could* have beliefs, the volcano *might* have supposed Empedocles to be a swindler – but it would, on the evidence we have been given, have been mistaken; such malicious notions are precisely the province of those who indulge in mystifications (such as credulous volcanoes). Our choice is between seeing Empedocles as a more, or as a less, far-sighted teacher; either way his death is to be the gentlest of non-leave-takings, either way the disciples go through a period on a false trail and are the richer for those blind alleys. However, the poem encourages us to believe in a deliberate act, the concealing of the shoe as a piece of creative misdirection.

I want to argue that such misdirection is an element in Brecht's poetry after this time, and I would like to illustrate what I mean by turning to an even better known poem, its immediate neighbour in the 'Chronicles' section of the *Svendborg Poems*, the 'legend' about Lao-Tsû. But before leaving the Empedocles poem, one fact about its legendary hero that is mostly overlooked may be mentioned. The commentated edition of Brecht's works notes Empedocles' fame as 'orator, engineer, doctor, natural scientist and priest',[84] a list that overlaps with that given in the Pauly *Realenzyklopädie* article on Empedocles, but omits (as well as 'politician') one vital element: 'poet'. And while the edition is surely correct to trace the source of the poem back to the main source of all information about Empedocles, Diogenes Laertius,[85] it makes no mention of the references to Empedocles in Horace and Lucretius, where Empedocles' stature as a poet is made clear; and Brecht's knowledge of both these writers is well attested.

The former's *Ars Poetica* (lines 466 ff) presents Empedocles quite simply as a poet; for Horace (at his most satirical here), he appears to be an example of the mad poet, desperate for fame; hence he includes the legend about his casting himself into Etna in order to become one of the immortals. More significant – and this is a more plausible source for Brecht's interest in Empedocles – is the reference in the first book of Lucretius' *De rerum natura*.[86] Although Lucretius goes on to dispute Empedocles' cosmological ideas, he is full of praise for his poetic achievement: 'The poems of his divine mind utter a loud voice and declare illustrious discoveries, so that he seems hardly to be born of mortal stock'.[87] Lucretius does not adduce the Etna legend or discuss the poet's death at all; instead, he presents him as the tutelary spirit of an idealised landscape, mentioning Etna simply as a feature of the 'mighty region' of Sicily (though that inessential mention, coupled with the phrase quoted above, seems to hint that Lucretius is aware of, and determined to ignore, the legend). Empedocles, then, is to be understood not only as a type of the teacher–leader, but also as a type of the poet.

'Legende von der Entstehung des Buches Taoteking auf dem Weg des Laotse in die Emigration'/'Legend of the origin of the Book Tao-Tê-Ching on Lao-Tsû's road into exile'[88] has always been recognised as one of Brecht's major poetic achievements; it prompted a sensitive interpretation by his friend Benjamin, and Brecht allowed himself to propose it (with 'Der Schneider von Ulm'/'The tailor of Ulm' as an alternative) as a text for teaching at primary school level in the new German Democratic Republic.[89] It is at the same time a measure of his impatience with Moscow orthodoxy, as represented by Lukács, that he should have withdrawn it from publication there in 1938, feeling himself out of tune with the current narrow interpretation of socialist realism.[90] I do not wish to rehearse the work's poetic merits here, but simply to draw attention to a problem raised by the final stanza, which commentators have invariably (and understandably) praised as an admirable coda, a succinct summary of the poem's message. However, I think it is a piece of misdirection:

> But the honour should not be restricted
> To the sage whose name is clearly writ.
> For a wise man's wisdom needs to be extracted.
> So the customs man deserves his bit.
> It was he who called for it.[91]

We owe to Walter Benjamin the idea that this concluding celebration of *both* the emigrating sage *and* the downtrodden customs official leaves out of account a 'third thing', the thing that brings these two very different men together, namely the spirit of 'Freundlichkeit' [friendliness].[92]

However, we do not have to scrutinise the poem too closely to see that the meeting between the two depressed men, which produces a book for posterity, is brought about very largely by the mediating agency of the third character in the poem, the boy, representing hope, the future and freedom from conventions. He slips almost unnoticed into the story in stanza 4 as a mere ox-goad, but then at once brings a human note into the frontier formalities by interjecting his explanation of what it is Lao-Tsû has done for a (modest) living. When the customs man asks a (clearly sarcastic) question, the boy takes it seriously and proclaims an essential (and from a Marxist point of view, the most interesting) aspect of Lao-Tsû's wisdom: 'He learnt how quite soft water, by attrition/Over years will grind strong rocks away./D'you follow? That hardness must lose the day'.[93] The disgruntled, world-weary Lao-Tsû has given up teaching, and grants the customs man only a single word; not so the boy, who himself has teacher-like mannerisms, as we see from that last phrase. It is the boy who offers the clinching argument for staying the night – 'It's turning cold'.[94] It is the boy who then writes the book, at the philosopher's dictation (the poem's suggestion that the boy and the sage 'write together'[95] is itself a little piece of misdirection which at the same time emphasises the essential contribution of the former) and he who hands the book to the official.[96] What the effect of the transmitted wisdom on the customs man may be remains unknown (though *we* can still enjoy the consequence, Lao-Tsû's book of wisdom), but we notice that the human touch which the boy is responsible for bringing into the encounter seems to have rubbed off on him, since during the composition period he 'just quietly cursed the whole time with the smugglers'.[97] Or is that a sign of the radicalism implied in the boy's summary of Lao-Tsû's wisdom, causing the customs man to reflect that he and the smugglers are basically on the same side? At all events, the meaningful encounter and the composition of the great work could not occur without the boy's active input.[98]

The wilful misrepresentation of facts as offered in the last stanza of the poem produces, in my view, a fruitful misreading.[99] To what does it lead us? I recall with gratitude a discussion of this poem centred on the role of the boy, which prompted the question from my pupil: 'Would you say that the boy is a figure of the poet?' to which I could only reply, 'Well, I haven't, but I will!' For indeed who else, in Brecht's view, might be able to mediate between the abstractions of philosophy or political theory on the one hand and the realistic problems of life with all its injustices on the other, if not the poet?[100] The great teaching poem Brecht was later to embark upon, the 'Lehrgedicht (von der Natur der Menschen)' / 'Didactic poem (on human nature)', with its versification of *The Communist Manifesto*, remained unfinished; but the role it implies is one that remains central to his later work. We hear it expressed again, in negative form, in the *Buckow Elegy* 'Böser Morgen' / 'Nasty morning',[101] with its concluding couplet, after the empty line: 'You don't know! I shrieked / Conscience-stricken.' If the workers are ignorant, the poet knows who is to blame. The poet, like the boy in the 'Legend', must be a ready communicator; he must not give up hope; yet he can only accord to himself a secondary place in the scheme of things by contrast with the 'classics' on the one hand and the proletarians on the other.

These two 'Chronicle' poems of 1935 and 1938 are, then, interestingly linked, by their presentation or use of misdirection, and by the fact that their central figures are teachers and poets.[102] There is also, of course, a link through the idea of exile, Lao-Tsû's destiny and the probable *historical* fate of Empedocles, although in the latter case Brecht's poem presents the more final cut-off that is death.[103] Hinck, who takes a negative view of Empedocles, and then a distinctly positive view of Lao-Tsû, sees them as linked by contrast.[104] However, while the role of poet, intermediary and teacher is one that Lao-Tsû may formerly have fulfilled, Brecht's poem shows that role sustained rather by the boy. Hinck, in taking the Chinese sage to be the ideal figure, by contrast with the uncertain figure of Empedocles, is thus, in my view, reversing the judgements the poems seem to imply.

4   Later Poems

I want to turn now to Brecht's poems of a later period; but first I
should like to come back to a poem already cited, 'Bad time for
poetry', to recall the misdirection in its final section:

> Inside me contend
> Delight at the apple tree in blossom
> And horror at the house-painter's speeches.
> But only the second
> Drives me to my desk.[105]

The implication that the poet only writes about Hitler's speeches is
misleading, on the evidence of the very poem we have in front of
us: the poem is about 'things contending', not about 'horror'. Or
are we then to conclude that only his political awareness *drives* the
writer to his desk? Does the apple-blossom draw him there more
freely? As often, Brecht leaves us with questions.

   An example of a poem employing misdirection as a kind of 'defamiliarising effect' is 'Glückliche Begegnung'/'Happy encounter' of
1952:

> On Sundays in June among the saplings
> Villagers looking for raspberries hear
> Studious girls and women from the technical college
> Pick out phrases from their textbooks
> About dialectics and the care of children.
>
> Looking up from their textbooks
> The students see the villagers
> Pick berries from the canes.
>
> *Translated by* Michael Hamburger [106]

At first sight, certainly on the basis of the title, we might suppose a
socialist idyll. Klaus Schuhmann in 1973, delicately tracing balances
and finding examples of chiasmus, indicates how ideal is this meeting between the intellectuals and the villagers.[107] Philip Thomson,
losing patience after dealing very even-handedly with the later
Brecht, finds this a poem which 'nosedives into the unintentionally
comical in the fourth and fifth lines...Brecht makes this gaffe
because he is trying too hard...He overdoes the socialist Utopia and

immediately strikes false notes.' Thomson sees that line 4 evokes 'rote learning and mechanical repetition as pedagogical methods' but merely finds it 'unpleasant'; he does not allow for a moment that Brecht, with all his concern for the practicalities of learning, could be exercising irony here. He also spots the incongruity (zeugma, he might have said) of 'dialectics' and 'the care of children' and decides it is a 'juxtaposition of words that is sadly comic'.[108] But those incongruities are resoundingly obvious, and alert us to the fact that the 'happy encounter' is not about two equal parties meeting and sharing. The technical college students are simply going over their homework for Monday morning, and all the villagers hear are unconnected snatches, not coherent text: the word 'lesen' [to pick, to read], which the poem puns on, indicates that they are picking off odd sentences. The two unequal parts of the poem reinforce the sense of a lack of balance; the *Verfremdungseffekt* lies in what does not happen. The fruit-pickers do not interrupt their work to listen to the students; but the students look up to see the villagers. The happy meeting is not an encounter of two balanced groups; it only comes when the students look up from their books and see the villagers spending their Sunday leisure more meaningfully: people whose lives include presumably the bringing up of children. If the students are being trained as children's nurses, do they need dialectics? If they are being trained for parenthood, do they need to memorise sentences? The poem is a (typical) veiled attack on theory for its own sake, and on uncreative teaching.

Glücklicher Vorgang

Das Kind kommt gelaufen
Mutter, binde mir die Schürze!
Die Schürze wird gebunden.

Unglücklicher Vorgang

Hier ist ein Haus, das für euch gebaut ist.
Es ist weit. Es ist dicht.
Es ist gut für euch, tretet ein.
Zögernd nähern sich

Zimmerleute und Maurer
Klempner und Glaser.[109]

[*Happy incident*

The child comes running
Mother, tie my apron!
The apron is tied.

Unhappy incident

Here is a house built for you.
It is spacious. It is weatherproof.
It is good for you, go on in.
Hesitantly there approach
Carpenters and bricklayers,
Plumbers and glaziers.]

Translated by Ray Ockenden

These two poems, which have generally been placed together, also contain an evident notion of contrast.[110] They are not poems that have attracted much attention; the first, indeed, appears to be of remarkable nullity. It is instructive therefore to go back to one of the earliest serious commentators on Brecht's poetry: in his 1973 book, Klaus Schuhmann had no doubt that these poems give us encoded pictures of life in contemporary East Germany and his comments can, I think, be taken as a fair measure of how Brecht might have expected his poems to be understood at an official level.[111] In Schuhmann's view, the first shows a trusting girl getting her mother to tie her apron for her; the second shows a group of workers hesitant about taking up residence in new flats. That is to say, poem 1 represents the good attitude of the new GDR citizens who know they can rely on the state – it's there, like a good mother, for them to presume on it; whereas in poem 2, workers who have been used to building houses for other people to live in, in the bad old days, are unused to living in them themselves, and cannot get used to socialism. The commentated Brecht edition suggests that the second poem relates to the new buildings along the Stalinallee, of which it reports: 'According to the propaganda of the time, the workers are building houses for themselves'.[112] It is clear that

Schuhmann reads line 3 of the first poem as: 'the mother ties the apron' – a possible reading, though not actually what Brecht wrote; similarly, he (and possibly Knopf and Bergheim in the commentated edition) reads line 1 of poem 2 as: 'here is a house which you have built'. Brecht was, we know, aware of the building on the Stalinallee, and a fragmentary poem, addressed to a worker on the project which started in December 1952,[113] lends him a significant voice that typifies Brecht's attitude at this time.

But I do not think the second of our poems has anything to do with the Stalinallee, any more than the first describes a domestic scene witnessed by Brecht. We are looking at attitudes to the young GDR state, and the attitudes of a leadership which is on a collision course, before 17 June 1953, with its rank and file. The happy incident of poem 1 at once looks different if we presume that the tying of the apron is *not* an instant response by an indulgent Mama, thereby prolonging the daughter's dependence on her. Rather, 'the apron is tied' by a joint effort; by helping her daughter to do it, the mother endows her with a measure of independence and makes a start on a learning process, which has practical advantages for both sides. The unhappy incident of poem 2 is not about buildings or flats, but 'ein Haus', a habitation constructed *by others* for the workers – in short, the state.[114] It has been made without the help of those best able to construct it – carpenters, bricklayers, plumbers, glaziers – these are the workers chosen for the poem because of the basic image of the house. They are reluctant to take over something that has been constructed without their input. In each case, our second readings of these poems are enriched by passing through the first and recognising exactly what Brecht *might* have been intending to say.[115]

This use of two linked poems to reflect, to enhance or to question each other is a device which Brecht uses elsewhere, and we have seen poems divided up into two parts ('Thoughts on the duration of exile', 'The shoe of Empedocles') for similar effect. In his later poems Brecht employs this device in even more concentrated form, by using a 'hinge' word at the centre of a short poem, which reflects back and forward.

The voice of the October storm
Around the little house by the reeds
Strikes me as quite like my voice.
Comfortably
I lie on my bed and hear
Above the lake and above the city
My voice.

Translated by Humphrey Milnes [116]

Given the significance of October, the month of revolution, it is easy to read this poem of October 1952, evoking the landscape of Buckow, as self-congratulation: the poet, after years of exile in capitalist countries, comes home to hear the whole of his surroundings playing, as it were, his revolutionary tune. But the highlighted hinge word 'bequem' [comfortably] warns us that something else is going on here – self-satisfied relaxation is hardly an appropriate response to the times, and we recall Brecht's comment of two months earlier which rounded off a description of idyllic aspects of the Buckow retreat: 'But I have grown increasingly unhappy with Horace's contentment'.[117] He is not in harmony with what is going on around him politically, as June 1953 will spell out. This poem is spoken by a 'voice' – and if it is Brecht's, then it comes with irony attached. Another example of 'voicing' in the later poetry is the little poem:

'Hier ist die Karte, da ist die Straße
Sieh hier die Biegung, sieh da das Gefäll!'
'Gib mir die Karte, da will ich gehen.
Nach der Karte
Geht es sich schnell'

['Here is the map, there's the road
Look at the bend here, look at the gradient there!'
'Give me the map, that's the way I'll go.
Going by the map
It won't take long'] [118]

Translated by Ray Ockenden

Again, this is not a poem that has attracted much attention.[119] It appears to be saying no more than 'Thanks for the map, from the map it looks like an easy walk'. However the central hinge line (not a single word here) and the break between lines 4 and 5 help us to reread it as a jaunty, surreal clownish piece, as it might be Karl

Valentin saying, 'Don't think I'll bother to make the journey, it's easier to walk along the map'. So, who are these voices? We are surely still in political territory here.[120] The parties to the conversation are, first, those who have the plan and are recommending others to go by it, and second, those who say, whether disingenuously or earnestly, 'Fine, let's go by the plan, it looks easy that way'. The poem implies, indirectly, that reality is harder to cope with than theory.

Turning to the *Buckow Elegies* themselves, we can find a typical 'hinge' in 'Der Rauch' / 'The smoke';[121] the central line stresses how the lack of a human element would render an apparently idyllic landscape dismal. In the light of Helmut Koopmann's spirited and stimulating attempt to 'liberate' the *Buckow Elegies* from their presumed political context, and to link them, not, as I have sought to do, to Brecht's Scandinavian exile situation but to the *Hollywood-Elegien/ Hollywood Elegies*, it might seem old-fashioned to want to put them back into that context. However, it is hard to ignore the well-known comment in Brecht's journal, 'Buckow. Turandot. Alongside it, the Buckow elegies. June 17th has disconnected my whole existence'[122] – not least because of that final verb, 'verfremdet'. Given the insistence on the motif of building in Brecht's GDR poetry, it seems feasible to take the house here as symbolic of the new socialist state.[123] Brecht's constant concern has been that the leaders, now themselves envisaged as 'teachers', are not listening to the people: this comes out in the poem 'Frage' / 'Question' written in the year before the *Buckow Elegies*.[124]

In the poem 'Tannen' / 'Firs' from the *Buckow Elegies* the 'hinge' is the third line, which is the ambiguous part of the poem:

In the early hours
The fir-trees are copper.
That's how I saw them
Half a century ago
Two world wars ago
With young eyes.

Translated by Derek Bowman [125]

What Brecht does here, once again, is to map two different historical moments on to one another. That brightness of new-day beginnings: can he still believe in it? By taking the first two lines as a timeless statement of fact and the next words, 'that's how', as implying 'goodness, they're just the same', Philip Brady sees two world wars as being relativised by the consistent copper colour of fir-trees.[126] But, *pace* Koopmann, these are elegies, not idylls. Surely we must rather read the 'that's how' as meaning 'ah, but that was then'? But there again, the poem can hold both readings, and perhaps the speaker is himself uncertain whether the opening statement is present reality or distant memory.

With great regularity the Buckow elegy 'Der Blumengarten'/ 'The flower garden' has been understood as a splendid poem of harmony within nature, a poem that might therefore seem to contradict the notion that these poems are elegies.[127]

The flower garden

By the lake, deep amid fir and silver poplar
Sheltered by wall and hedge, a garden
So wisely plotted with monthly flowers
That it blooms from March until October.

Here, in the morning, not too frequently, I sit
And wish I too might always
In all weathers, good or bad,
Show one pleasant aspect or another.

Translated by Edith Anderson [128]

Our mild disquiet is aroused by the fifth line – if this garden is such a wonderful place, why does the speaker wish to emphasise that he sits there 'not too frequently'? To be sure, Brecht the man of the theatre was a busy person, but within the poem itself that is not relevant; perhaps he is avoiding that stance of 'comfortably' mentioned in 'The voice of the October storm'. Our doubts about the garden are then reinforced by the blatant misdirection the poem contains. The two stanzas here imply a tidy mirroring construction – but the suggested parallel between speaker and garden is, when we look more closely, not sustained. The garden only blooms from

March to October, whereas the speaker wants to produce attractive things 'always', even when the weather is bad. Once our doubts have been aroused, we begin to wonder about other things. That 'so wisely plotted' suddenly sounds rather *dirigiste*; the shelter of walls and shrubs seems more a confinement than a protection; and 'monthly'- isn't that an ugly word with bureaucratic overtones of payment?[129] The word 'wall' could not, in summer 1953, have anticipated August 1961; yet our suspicion grows that what is being shown to us here is an over-controlled, artificially guarded show-piece. The abbreviated blooming season suggests that when the winter storms come, the bareness of the beautiful garden will be evident. Again, echoes of the political situation of 1953 are not hard to hear.

As will be clear, I read the *Buckow Elegies* as *elegies* about a hopeful start that was not to be fulfilled, a lament for the socialist idyll that might have been, but by summer 1953 was already revealed to be hollow, because the *nomenklatura* were not prepared to consult the wishes, the interests, the aspirations of the citizens. Brecht's vision is, then, a long one, as it had been under different circumstances in the Scandinavian exile.

I would like finally to turn to another pair of poems within the *Buckow Elegies*; while they are not juxtaposed within any versions of the text we have, they have almost invariably been read together, as contrast, by commentators: 'Heißer Tag' / 'Hot day' and 'Rudern, Gespräche' / 'Paddling, talking' – *see* above, pp. 176–7. Common to these poems is a scene registered by an observer, and the use of per-spective is part of the richness of Brecht's poems that I have wanted to draw attention to. The perspective of the speaker in the summer-house is a removed and possibly heat-befuddled one – the writing-case idle on the knees suggests someone resting from work, perhaps dozing in the summer heat. We are struck by the slightly mysterious, almost dreamlike way in which the boat makes its appearance, and the unreality of the scene is heightened by the fact that after the boat's appearance everything else is reported in par-ticipial form.[130] Critics have noted with some surprise the old-fashioned (pre-war) swimsuit worn by the male passenger, and the unseasonable heavy clothes of the female one. Much more remarkable, it seems to me, is the presence of the nun at all, and the immediate presumption that the man is a priest, as though the Schermützelsee in 1953 was a well-known haunt of Catholic clergy. The last words of the poem offer an explanation: a (much less uncommon) scene from Brecht's Augsburg childhood has been grafted on to the present, another example of *Überblendung* [super-imposing], reminding us of the distancing effect of anachronism. The two exclamations at the end of the poem are not repetition; the first exclamation reflects the direct link with the past, as it were of Brecht's childhood, the second registers (dismayed) astonishment at the similarity with what the speaker sees in the present. What it is that the observer now sees, the poem does not tell us, and we can only guess at what has prompted the evidently allegorical picture we are given in which an unemancipated worker toils to propel a ship of state made heavy by privileged party top-brass.[131] The alienation of the worker is stressed by the fact that his back is turned to the other two whom he is ferrying, and he cannot see where he is going; we presume that the 'priest', the only one who is facing forwards, must be doing the steering.[132] The powerful sense of hierarchy involved is introduced in the first line by the phrase 'on my knee'; in context it underlines the (reprehensible?) passivity of the speaker, but taken by itself it is evocative both of servility and of religious authority. [133]

In contrast to the dream-spectacle of effort in the heat of the day is the calm evening scene of 'Paddling, talking': perhaps the most beautiful of these poems and one which contains, through its elegiac mood, a picture of an ideal. The opening words set a calm mood and perhaps explain how the men have the free time to take exercise; but they also imply that a moment has passed, something is declining. Built into this little poem are several fruitful misreadings. I have often, having given it to students to read for the first time and asked for an account of it, been told that 'there are two men in a boat'. Since it seems to be a poem about mutuality, that is not an unreasonable suggestion, but in fact most solutions of that kind would not be conducive to good rowing and good talking simultaneously; more importantly, the young men retain their independence this way. Now, if it were just conversation they want, they could do it on the bank; alternatively, if it's the exercise they want, why bother with the chat? The fact is, they have chosen to do something quite difficult, demanding a high level of skill, in order to combine physical exercise and intellectual exchange.

The existence of two separate boats brings us back to the matter of perspective. Whereas the green boat in 'Hot day' seemed to loom up through overhanging greenery, possibly making a frontal appearance, here 'past' indicates that the two boats come along the lake, in parallel, past the speaker's viewpoint. If we imagine that first glimpse, what we would naturally presume is a race – indeed, since they are neck and neck, an exciting race. But that's another misreading of the scene; they are not competing, but collaborating. Each is paddling his own canoe – the 'Faltboot' [canoe] in itself a temporary structure redolent of flexibility – which means that they can break away at any moment they choose. They have chosen to stay together, not, like the cranes and the clouds of 'Terzinen über die Liebe' / 'Tercets on love', formerly 'Die Liebenden' / 'The lovers',[134] until fate separates them, for they are in charge. As long as they want to talk, they will row together; for as long as they want to row together, they can talk. There is no cox, they do their own steering. Their nakedness (rather like the clothes in 'Hot day') is surely metaphorical: they have thrown off all outer markings in order to be, for and to each other, just human beings. It is an endorsement of the absolute nature of their harmony.[135] It is a vision of harmony between human beings, collaborating physically and intellectually; individuals, yet absolutely sharing. The extended chiasmus which most commentators mention has the effect, again in contrast to 'Hot day', of breaking down hierarchy. But there is another (unfulfilled) chiastic shape in the poem: 'evening – two canoes – two naked – young men', which brings out an important contrast. There is an elegiac tone in the first sentence, and the next word in the German text, the word meaning 'past', with all its overtones of something lost for ever, strongly reinforces that sense. On the other hand, the rowers are *young* men, and that in itself, as we remember from the Svendborg period, must give grounds for hope.

In a 1956 piece, which both refers to the first criticisms of Stalin at the 20th Party Congress and harks back to the events of 17 June

1953,[136] Brecht is concerned to ally workers and artists – as having been rendered discontent, and as representing a possible joint front against the uncomprehending and exploitative authorities.[137] Both groups are in the business of 'production' and Brecht wants them to do what they do freely, and derive enjoyment from it. His canoeists could be either artists or workers (they have ideally lost any distinguishing marks); either way they are combining physical and intellectual expression in a fully human manner.[138]

The English translation of this poem by Michael Hamburger[139] has 'paddling' for 'rudern' [rowing], which makes more sense with his canoes. Knopf suggests the reason Brecht himself does not use the word 'paddeln' is his wish to link the two poems I have printed together here, which are so obviously a contrast between a bad old world and the hope of a new and better one.[140] Beyond that may lie another text, however, which has links to both poems. The revisions of ancient myths originally under the heading 'Berichtigungen' / 'Corrections', then under 'Zweifel am Mythos' / 'Doubts about Myth', which included Odysseus and the sirens, were sketches that Brecht worked on in 1933, as noted above. It seems that Brecht may have also worked on them during his exile in America,[141] in which case it is at least possible that he discussed them with Adorno, whom he saw fairly frequently at that time, or Horkheimer whom he saw more rarely, during the years 1942–4 when they were working on *Dialectic of Enlightenment*.[142] In the early part of *Dialectic of Enlightenment*, the authors focus on the myth of Odysseus and the sirens to illustrate their ideas about enlightenment: 'Measures such as those taken on Odysseus's ship in regard to the sirens form a presentient allegory of the dialectic of enlightenment'.[143] The picture that is projected touches Brecht's concerns in various ways: the fettered Odysseus becomes a figure of the modern concert-goer (or theatre-goer) – motionless and imprisoned in his seat; his workers, meanwhile, their ears being stopped, have no access to art (the sirens' song) at all. The bosses become nothing but bosses and lose contact with the work process altogether, while the workers are deprived of enjoyment of their work since they do it with their senses shut off.[144] Complex systems mean the loss of real experience; the masses are no longer able to hear new things for themselves.[145]

There are two moments in this detailed discussion of the myth, which I should like to highlight in the present context. One is the simple description of what Odysseus does when confronted with the danger of the sirens: 'He knows only two possible ways to escape. One of them he prescribes for his men. He plugs their ears with wax, and they must row with all their strength'.[146] It is this image of the powerless worker, rowing for all he is worth, that Brecht seems to have picked up in 'Hot day' and, as Knopf points out, the phrase 'An der Ruderbank' [at the oars] has a clear echo of galley slaves.[147] Later in the text we read:

Through the mediation of the total society which embraces all relations and emotions, men are once again made to be that against which the evolutionary law of society, the principle of self, had turned: mere species beings, exactly like one another through isolation in the forcibly united collectivity. The oarsmen, who cannot speak to one another, are each of them yoked in the same rhythm as the modern worker in the factory, movie theater, and collective.[148]

The rower in 'Hot day' is indeed cut off from any contact with his passengers (they are behind him). But things are different in the transfigured vision of 'Paddling, talking', where a common tempo is freely chosen, and conversation flourishes.

If there are echoes of the *Dialectic of Enlightenment* here, it is clear that they are not intended as homage to Adorno and Horkheimer, who (despite some relatively cordial contacts with the former in the USA) came, especially in respect of their work with the 'Institute for social research' to represent for Brecht archetypes of venal intellectualism, that is to say (to give them the term Brecht invented), 'Tuis'.[149] Rather the echoes stress the difference between the over-intellectualised abstractions of the analysis conducted by Adorno and Horkheimer, and the more direct images illustrative of exploitation and equality presented in the *Buckow Elegies*. On the one hand, there is abstruse theory, on the other, accessible pictures of praxis.

I have wanted in this paper to suggest new ways of approaching some of Brecht's poems. I am conscious that to talk of 'misreadings' may controversially presume a hierarchy of understanding, whereas it seems to me a part of the understated nature of the later poetry that it opens itself to a variety of interpretative overtures. Brecht was surely aware that not only the blackbird's song of which he once wrote,[150] but the reactions to poetry, will continue after the singer is dead and the maker buried. He himself, as we have seen, insisted on the contradictions in reality being maintained within poetry: 'Poems become fallow, empty, trite if they remove the contradictions from their subjects, when the things they deal with do not appear in their living, i.e. multi-faceted form, which is incomplete and cannot be completely formulated. If they are about politics, you end up with *bad* partisan literature.'[151]

And we should take heart with regard to our interpretative activity. Just as Brecht insisted that schoolchildren should be acquainted with *kitsch* as well as high art on the grounds that 'Neither political judgements nor judgements of taste can be formed by acquaintance only with what is good',[152] so he recognised the value of apparently unsuccessful explorations. As his Empedocles clearly knew, and Brecht proclaimed: 'In der Nähe der Fehler wachsen die Wirkungen' [Next door to errors is where real effects can flourish].[153]

9

Two German Anthems

Das Lied der Deutschen

Deutschland, Deutschland über alles,
Über alles in der Welt,
Wenn es stets zu Schutz und Trutze
Brüderlich zusammenhält,
Von der Maas bis an die Memel,
Von der Etsch bis an den Belt –
Deutschland, Deutschland über alles,
Über alles in der Welt!

Deutsche Frauen, deutsche Treue,
Deutscher Wein und deutscher Sang
Sollen in der Welt behalten
Ihren alten schönen Klang,
Uns zu edler Tat begeistern
Unser ganzes Leben lang –
Deutsche Frauen, deutsche Treue
Deutscher Wein und deutscher Sang!

Einigkeit und Recht und Freiheit
Für das deutsche Vaterland!
Danach laßt uns all streben
Brüderlich mit Herz und Hand!
Einigkeit und Recht und Freiheit
Sind des Glückes Unterpfand –
Blüh' im Glanze dieses Glückes,
Blühe, deutsches Vaterland!

August Heinrich Hoffmann von Fallersleben (1841)[1]

Song of the Germans

Germany, Germany above all others,
In this world above all things,
If in its defence we brothers
Hold together, whate'er fate brings,
From the Maas and to the Memel
From the Etsch and to the Belt –
Germany, Germany above all others,
In this world above all things!

German women, German honour
German wine and German song
Shall remain, the whole world over,
Beautiful, revered and strong,
Inspiring us to noble exploits
All our days – our whole lives long –
German women, German honour
German wine and German song!

Justice, unity and freedom
For the German Fatherland!
Let us strive for this together
Brotherly, with heart and hand.
Justice, unity and freedom
Are the pledge of happiness –
May you flourish in such fortune
Flourish, German Fatherland!

Translated by Tom Kuhn

Kinderhymne

Anmut sparet nicht noch Mühe
Leidenschaft nicht noch Verstand.
Daß ein gutes Deutschland blühe
Wie ein andres gutes Land.

Daß die Völker nicht erbleichen
Wie vor einer Räuberin
Sondern ihre Hände reichen
Uns wie anderen Völkern hin.

Und nicht über und nicht unter
Andern Völkern wolln wir sein
Von der See bis zu den Alpen
Von der Oder bis zum Rhein.

Und weil wir dies Land verbessern
Lieben und beschirmen wir's
Und das liebste mag's uns scheinen
So wie andern Völkern ihrs.[2]

Bertolt Brecht

Children's Anthem

Spare no grace and spare no effort
Passion nor intelligence
That a decent Germany may
Flourish as do other lands.

That the nations don't turn pale
As confronted by a thug
But might rather reach their hands out
As they do to other folk.

And not over nor yet under
Other nations would we be
From the Rhine and to the Oder
From the Alps and to the sea.

And because we'd make it better
We protect and love our home.
May it seem to us our dearest
Just as others love their own.

Translated by Tom Kuhn[3]

'May it seem to us our dearest ...'

Brecht's 'Children's Anthem'

Erdmut Wizisla

In memoriam Gerhard Seidel (1929–2000)

'Brecht our watchword!' That was how Ernst Bloch greeted the plan in 1975 to ask German authors for a selection of the three Brecht poems which had played the most important part in shaping their ideas and their actions. It is striking that none of those involved took up the 'Kinderhymne'/'Children's Anthem' in this sense – although contributions came from, amongst others, Anna Seghers, Max Frisch, Peter Weiss, Christa Wolf, Friederike Mayröcker, Hans Magnus Enzensberger, Uwe Johnson, and Volker Braun. Why was that? Was this text not important for them? Did they think it 'too unambiguous', as Brecht puts it in the poem-fragment 'Der Zweifler'/'The doubter', had it 'taken the contradictions out of things'? [4]

We know little about the genesis of the 'Children's Anthem', other than that it was first published in November/December 1950 in the journal *Sinn und Form* (vol. 2, no. 6). Brecht had already put together the 'Kinderlieder'/'Children's songs' as a cycle in June of that year. There is a stubborn legend that the anthem was Brecht's submission, or response to an official request for a national anthem for the GDR. It goes something like this: 'Bert Brecht submitted this text in 1950 for a competition to find an anthem for the GDR. But his riposte to the "Deutschlandlied" was not acceptable to a jury led by the Minister for Culture Johannes R. Becher (the author of the song which did then become the GDR anthem "Auferstanden aus Ruinen" – Risen up from out of ruins).' [5] Friedrich Dieckmann writes that, after the foundation of the GDR, Brecht and Becher were asked to provide texts for a national anthem; as his source he mentions Brecht's collaborator Käthe Rülicke.[6] But all these tales are dubious; there is certainly no documentary evidence to support them. In a report by the State President Wilhelm Pieck about the adoption of the national anthem, there is no mention of Brecht's poem. Indeed, the choice that faced the politburo on 5 November 1949 was not between Brecht and Becher, but between Hanns Eisler and the Thuringian composer Ottmar Gerster for a musical accompaniment to Becher's text.[7] A hitherto unnoticed piece of evidence, a note by Ernst Busch dating from the 1960s or 70s, refutes any notion of a direct competition:

The Children's Anthem/to sing along with/was composed in the same night as the provisional national anthem. Writers were generally disappointed that there wasn't a competition for a national anthem – but it seems there was too little time, what's more, it was supposed to be just a provisional anthem, until the unification of Germany. I wasn't to sing the song, Eisler told me, because the coalition parties couldn't be expected to put up with a performance by a proletarian singer. 'But here's something else for you', and he gave me a sheet of music. bb had done his at the same time as Becher.[8]

Busch appears to have got the precise date wrong; the only plausible period for Brecht's composition is some time in the months from November 1949 to June 1950.

All the same, whether it was officially discussed or not, there is no doubt that the poem was a suggestion for a national anthem. Gerhard Seidel puts it nicely: the 'Children's Anthem' was 'a private attempt' to create a national anthem for the GDR.[9] This is even clearer in the first draft than it is in the published version. The poem was originally entitled simply 'Hymne'; in the fourth line, it cites Hoffmann von Fallersleben's 'Song of the Germans', 'Auf dass deutschland, deutschland blühe' [So that Germany may flourish] – albeit with an almost opposite meaning. This first version consisted of only three strophes, and it was the third, in which Brecht deals more directly with the 'Deutschlandlied', that was added later.[10] Also noteworthy is the correction of the first word: originally Brecht had 'Arbeit' [work] instead of 'Anmut' [grace]. The important change of title, from 'Hymne/Festlied' to 'Kinderhymne', is in Brecht's hand on a sheet with the finished, four-strophe version of the poem.[11] The editors of the new Berlin and Frankfurt edition would have done well to document such stages of the genesis of one of the most important of Brecht's poems. Instead, the edition gives us a quite superfluous additional version of the poem with a simple error (which is significant both for the rhythm and for the interpretation). It is, however, perfectly clear that the beginning of the fourth strophe should read 'Und weil wir dies Land verbessern' [literally: And because we'd improve this country], not 'dieses Land'.[12]

A hymn for Germany after 1945, all the more if it was by Brecht, simply had to be a riposte to Hoffmann von Fallersleben's 'Deutschlandlied'. One might feel tempted to ask whether 'that foolish phrase of a loudmouthed poem', as Kurt Tucholsky referred to the line 'Deutschland, Deutschland über alles', had indeed been politically abused, or whether it had not rather, in the fullness of time, achieved its true meaning. Certainly after the Nazis had attempted to make a bloody political reality of it, the liberal roots of the song, which Reichspräsident Friedrich Ebert had elevated to be the national anthem in 1922, were buried for ever. It is true, in 1842 Hoffmann von Fallersleben was dismissed for his political opinions from his post as professor of German language and literature at Breslau university, yet the man was equally no stranger to anti-Semitic and nationalist sentiment, and he could not have cared less how his song, written in 1841, was received internationally: the 'Deutschlandlied' should, he remarked, 'now, more than ever, be sung as a song for all Germans, however much it irritates the rest of the world'[13] – which is of course exactly what it did. Friedrich Nietzsche soberly described the terrible consequences: '"Deutschland, Deutschland über alles", I fear that was the end of German philosophy ...'[14] To this day, people seem keen to forget, on certain national (or sporting) occasions, that it is officially only the third strophe which is now the national anthem ('Justice, unity and freedom').

The components of Brecht's response are clear enough. He contradicts Hoffmann von Fallersleben's opening with the lines 'And not over nor yet under/Other nations would we be', and he draws the boundaries of a unified Germany in keeping with the Potsdam Agreement and the contemporary politics of the GDR:

not 'From the Maas and to the Memel/From the Etsch and to the Belt', but rather 'From the Rhine and to the Oder/From the Alps and to the sea'. Whereas von Fallersleben invokes tradition ('German women, German honour/German wine and German song/Shall remain, the whole world over,/Beautiful, revered and strong'), Brecht's image of Germany looks towards the future. Like von Fallersleben he employs the optative (subjunctive of desire/ wish) 'blühe', but not in imitation of the pathos of 'Flourish, German Fatherland'; instead the tone is emphatic: 'That a decent Germany may/Flourish'. The decisive difference is achieved by the epithet 'gut' ['decent', literally just 'good']. This is no description of 'my-country-right-or-wrong' sentiment, but rather of an interventionist patriotism which seeks to 'make better' the homeland. To be more precise: it is the activity by which the country is to be made better which provides a reason to love and to protect it (Brecht uses a poetic, biblical term for to protect, 'beschirmen'). Emotion and action are not to be separated. The causal construction is one of the poem's most felicitous turns: 'And because we'd make it better/ We protect and love our home'. Love becomes a keyword of this anthem; it completes, as Friedrich Dieckmann has put it, the ambiguous 'über alles', from which von Fallersleben had omitted the verb (now we know: it is 'to love above all things'). And it is a love which 'is appropriately moderated' by Brecht's careful 'das liebste mag's uns scheinen' [literally: may it seem to us the most loved].[15]

The matter is more complex, however. Brecht was reacting not only to Hoffmann von Fallersleben; his poem plays also, openly and cryptically, with Becher's composition for the national anthem.[16] So Brecht must already have known Becher's text when he wrote his own poem (that helps to dispel the myth of simultaneous contributions to a kind of public competition). Eisler, too, in his Brecht setting, quotes his own music for the national anthem: in the accompaniment to the lines 'From the Rhine and to the Oder/From the Alps and to the sea' we hear the opening melody of 'Risen up from out of ruins/Faces towards the future turned'. (Wolf Biermann maintained this was a coded message, with which

Eisler sought to promote the 'Children's Anthem' as an alternative to the Becher anthem.)[17]

But the relationship with the Becher poem is problematic. Brecht and Becher were united in their rejection of the 'Deutschlandlied', a rejection they shared with many of those who cared about the fate of the new republic. Becher himself, however, was a colleague and a rival, with whom Brecht already had a somewhat tense relationship. We recall Brecht's comment on the essay 'Deutsche Lehre'/ 'Lessons from German history' of 1943, in which Becher had invoked the 'genius of an eternal Germany': 'Neighbour, pass the sick-bag!'[18] Becher's text 'seems to have been written in a great hurry', and Dieckmann wonders, 'was it a question of getting in first?'[19] 'Risen up from out of ruins' distilled the leading political notions of the SED-leadership in a sort of rhyming creed of consti- tution: national unity, peace politics, anti-Fascism.[20] These are principles which Brecht took up as well, albeit somewhat differently from Becher. There are correspondences, for example, between Becher's invocation of 'German youth' and Brecht's title 'Children's Anthem', Becher's 'let us serve you in the good cause' and Brecht's 'decent Germany', or 'trusting our own energies' and 'because we'd make it better'. And there are signs of a more imme- diate reception and variation in what Brecht makes of Becher's self-assured 'hold your hand out to the nations': the gesture is inverted, and the hope is that other nations 'reach out their hands in friendship' to Germany.

The film-maker Peter Voigt, once Brecht's most junior assistant, remembers a comment by Helene Weigel: that Brecht had dubbed the Becher poem 'that meteorological anthem' ('And the sun, more beautiful than ever/Shines down on Germany'), but that his own attempts to write a German national anthem had never progressed beyond a first line: 'Mir san a Scheißvolk' [Bavarian dialect: We're a crap nation].[21]

As usual, the anecdote is an exaggeration. None the less, the essential difference between Brecht and Becher (and of course between Brecht and Hoffmann von Fallersleben too) is indeed the anti-hymnic posture of Brecht's poem. Hymns and anthems mirror the history of states and of their national self-image, or so the

Brockhaus-Riemann-Musiklexikon of 1979 maintains. They exist as 'royal hymns, patriotic folk-songs, extracts from stage works with national themes, military marches, religious hymns, odes to freedom and revolutionary anthems'.[22]

So how does this 'ironic–parodistic'[23] use of the hymn arise? Brecht begins conventionally enough, with a direct appeal, but he does not stick with the form of second-person address and moves instead to 'we', including himself amongst the ranks of those to whom the appeal is made. He introduces inimitable laconic turns, like the 'may it seem' already quoted. One might almost say his anthem depends upon its casual nonchalance. The repeated relativising comparisons – 'as do other lands', 'As they do to other folk', 'Just as others love their own' – divert attention to other countries, such that the singer can no longer be indifferent to the fate of these 'others'. Hanns Eisler's setting places particular emphasis on these lines: the tune ascends a scale and seems to lose itself. All this lightness is further proof, if it were needed, that it must be 'dies Land' (not 'dieses'): there is no emphasis on what is our own, no exclusion of others. Brecht's patriotic, anti-nationalist attitude to his homeland is expressed in a song which combines courage and grace, wisdom and simplicity in a quite unpathetic way. The paired concepts at the beginning must be unusual for a national anthem: grace and effort, passion and intelligence are opposite and complementary, and they embody in their interplay an attitude which anyone might feel happy to adopt towards their country, at once independent and committed. Brecht's correction of 'Arbeit' [work], in the first draft, to 'Anmut' [grace] seems particularly appropriate. It enabled him not only to avoid tautology (in Middle High German, 'Arbeit' and 'Mühe' are synonyms), but also to enlarge the lexical range of such poems and songs to embrace the incomparable word 'grace'. Surely any song which features this word has turned its face against nationalist bigotry. Finally, Brecht's poem achieves its particular identity by the simple correction from 'Anthem' to 'Children's Anthem'. The political scientist Iring Fetscher has explained the implications. The hymn

can scarcely be sung by those before whom other nations – rightly – once flinched in terror. It is the song of the new generation, of whom Brecht was not alone in hoping that they might make this country better. Not a hymn for children, but the song that children sing (or may sing). And only they. It is they who have rejected the 'über alles', in order to become just one nation amongst the nations. [...] There can be no other anthem which explains love of one's country so beautifully, rationally and critically, and none which ends with such conciliatory lines.[24]

Wolf Biermann, among others, urged insistently that the 'Children's Anthem' be sung as the anthem of both East and West. On his LP *Seelengeld / Soul money* of 1986, he makes the proposal in characteristic terms:

So there you have it, a forgotten treasure, from yesteryear and for tomorrow: the 'Children's Anthem' composed by Brecht and Eisler. Allons enfants! So we've got a new German national anthem. Perhaps one day we'll manage to achieve the country that fits it. [...] Yes, this is a song we should teach our children.[25]

In a similar spirit, before autumn 1989, the members of the 'Alternative List' (an independent political grouping represented in the Berlin Senate and later amalgamated with the Greens) had the poem printed in their green membership cards. What do you have in your cards these days, friends?

The revolutionary changes in the East in 1989–90 lent Brecht's 'Children's Anthem' a quite unexpected relevance. The suggestion that we now, finally, leave the 'Deutschlandlied' behind, and substitute the 'Children's Anthem', kept cropping up in the debates about German unification. Those in favour included the writers Walter Jens, Christa Wolf, Martin Walser, Volker Braun and Christoph Hein, the theologian and Green Party delegate Antje Vollmer, the essayist Peter Bender, trades unions like the IG Medien, members of the SPD, and, just recently, the graphic artist Klaus Staeck.[26] Opinions differed about which music would be best for Brecht's text. Some wanted to keep the tune from Haydn's 'Emperor Quartet', since 'Spare no grace and spare no effort' has the same metre as the 'Deutschlandlied'. A 'project for a new national anthem' introduced a version in 1990 with union workers singing Brecht's words to the tune of Beethoven's setting of Schiller's 'Ode to Joy'.[27] Hanns Eisler's music has sometimes been thought too difficult, above all for choirs. Brecht, it seems, according to Ernst

Busch, was not happy with the first recording of the anthem with a large orchestra and chorus; and at a celebration of revolution in the Berliner Ensemble in 1954 the song was sung, at Brecht's request, just by children, accompanied by the composer at the piano.[28] Kurt Schwaen, who composed new music for the 'Children's Anthem' in 1955, pointed out the range required by Eisler's setting; Eisler's interpretation was 'characteristic, charming and Viennese – but an anthem?'.[29] Eisler's song, never more movingly rendered than by the composer himself, takes up Brecht's unpathetic, unhymnic mode with an almost playful wit. The melody is not simple, admittedly, but once it has established itself, the ear readily recalls it. It makes an essential contribution to the charm of the 'Children's Anthem', and should surely not be usurped. To set Brecht's text with compositions by Haydn or Beethoven would inevitably invoke all the history and the associations of those tunes and their other texts.

In the negotiations between the government of the Federal Republic and the last government of the GDR there appears to have been a secret agreement to retain the West German anthem[30] – of course, it was no proper reunification, but rather the GDR was joined to the pre-existing Federal Republic. An exchange of memos between the Federal President Richard von Weizsäcker and the Chancellor Helmut Kohl on the occasion of the 150th anniversary of the composition of the 'Deutschlandlied' in August 1991 dispels any lingering doubt: 'The third strophe of the Hoffmann– Haydn song has proved itself a powerful symbol', the President wrote. 'It is a compelling expression of the values to which we feel committed, as Germans, as Europeans and as members of the community of nations.'[31] History repeats itself. In 1952, Konrad Adenauer insisted on the 'Deutschlandlied' against the objections of the then President, Theodor Heuss. 'I underestimated the power of tradition and its obstinate inertia,' commented a resigned Heuss at the time.[32] Gerhard Schröder, the Federal Chancellor of the red–green coalition which has been in power since 1998, quoted Brecht's song when the parliament moved into the new Reichstag. He hoped that the 'Children's Anthem' might be 'a symbol of integration for East and West, for the self-image of the "Berlin Republic"'. The

Chancellor's repeated references – he gave one of his books the title *Und weil wir unser Land verbessern/ And because we're making our country better* – have not, however, been enough to provoke a serious debate about changing the national anthem.

And yet: is it not perhaps appropriate that the Germans should have to bear a while longer the burden of the 'Deutschlandlied'? After all, they have still not entirely cast off the delusions of that first verse, which corrupts the whole song, even if today the 'Räuberin' [the 'thug' or 'robber-nation' of Brecht's line 6] is on the trail of profit rather than of foreign territory. Such terms as 'brotherly' and 'Fatherland' will still serve well enough as catchwords for a mentality which glorifies the powerful, spurns the foreign and treasures national interest above the stability of the world. It will be some time before this country can lay claim to such a quality as 'grace'. But let's not lose hope: the 'Children's Anthem' may, at some future date, still become the German national anthem.

Translated by Tom Kuhn

Seven poems after Brecht [1]

Brecht in Svendborg

1.   A Danish Refuge

We have lashed oars on the thatch
To keep it down in everything
Short of a cyclone, and
The sun gilds our garden;
But deadly visions hang
Like rain-clouds in the sound.

A little boat with a patched
Sail skates on the crinkly
Tinfoil of the bay; but we
Are not deceived by scenery.
Ears cocked, we can hear
Screams beyond the frontier.

The owl announces death
From the foliage these spring
Nights while I read *Macbeth*,
Kant, or the Tao Tê Ching;
Twice daily the starlings
Are silenced by a shriek

Of ordnance from the naval
War-games of the Reich.
The whitewash is peeling
From the damp ceiling
As I work at *Galileo*
In the converted stable.

Tacked to the oak beams,
A stage poster from
The old Schiffbauerdamm,
Faded now, proclaims
THE TRUTH IS CONCRETE.
Confucius' scroll portrait,

The ashtrays, cigar boxes
And drawers of microfilm
Make everything familiar.
From here I can watch
Helene gardening,
The children at the swing.

This could be home from home
If things were otherwise.
Twice daily the mails come
Up the sound in a ship.
I notice that the house
Has four doors for escape…

2. *To the Unborn*

Truly, we live in a dark time.
The candid word is suicide;
A clear brow argues
A thick skin. The man
Who laughs is merely someone
Who has not yet heard the terrible news.

What sort of times are these
When idle chat is treated
As wicked nonsense,
Implying as it does
Avoidance of other topics?
And who has a clear conscience?

Eat, drink and be thankful! –
But how can I do this
If my food belongs
To the starving,
My drink to the parched?
At the same time, I eat and drink.

I would so much like to be wise,
To shun strife and live
Quietly, without fear;
To love my enemies.
I can do none of these.
Truly, we live in a dark time.

We know that hatred, even of evil,
Disfigures the face;
That anger, even at cruelty,
Hardens the voice.
We who wished to found
A kind future could not ourselves be kind.

To the unborn who will emerge
From the deluge
In which we drown
I would say only this:
Remember, when you condemn us,
You do not live, like us, in a dark time.

Startled awake at first light
By whistling, I peer out
At the garden, where a young
Fellow in torn denims
Is cheerfully pocketing plums.
He nods to me and returns to his song.

Derek Mahon

The Emigration of the Poets (after Brecht)

Homer belonged nowhere
and Dante he'd to leave home
as for Tu Fu and Li Po
they did a flit through the smoke
– 30 million were no
more in those civil wars
while the high courts
tried to stuff Euripides under the floor
and even Shakespeare got a gagging order
as he lay dying in Stratford
– Villon who wrote 'Les Pendus'
had visits from the Muse
and from the Beast
– i.e. the police
though at least Lucretius
was nicknamed *Le bien aimé*
and slipped away from *Heim*
just like Heine
– now watch me here Bertolt Brecht
I'm a pike
*sh*tuck in this Danish thatch

Tom Paulin

Desert Island Discs (after reading Brecht)

Only those who, waking, ran down to the sand,
Now ship-shape and scrubbed by last night's gales,
Leaping through surf at low tide like castaways
Beached on a dirty little island
Littered with sea-wrack, sun-bathers and dead whales,
Who kept the bonfires dry for clear days
Like this – know how it felt to see a man
Swimming towards them, to feel like Caliban.

Only those who listened to the stranger's speech
While the sea looked the other way,
Saw fabulous cities fall, sacked by the sand.
Who smelt diesel rumors creep up the beach,
And pitied the pity of the castaway,
Whose silence hath cheated us of this island –
Know the cost of Empire, buying and selling
Ourselves for cargo-cults, which first was mine own king.

Only those who breasted the tide and could not swim
And made a religion of the sea
Knew why he spoke of water with such respect,
And how it had almost defeated him,
Embraced the nakedness of the refugee,
And watched all hope of rescue wrecked
In sight of land, the last hopeless chance for years,
Whom he taught language – know now how to curse.

And only those of us who can't say whether
This black tide will fall back at last,
If thunder still blows hoarse or continents will wait
Or if the Flood won't last for ever –
Know the ruin floating past
Is fuel for fires we must create
Again, to keep the world's one hope still burning.
Above high-water. Thus may we too die learning.

Andy Croft

Neighbourhood Watch

The tinkers live beyond the verges
Of town. Under cover of night
Their dogs scavenge from the dustbins,
Knocking the lids off. In broad daylight
They tether their ponies by our hedges.

The shopkeepers live lives of their own.
They pull down the blinds at 9 p.m.
To count their takings behind locked doors.
Their children often die before their parents
While business is creamed off by supermarkets.

The people live in the better parts of town,
With long lawns and variegated borders
Stretching down to the lane. They used to take
The tinkers' children in service by the year,
But now they're warier and make their own beds.

Bernard O'Donoghue

After Brecht

In the end it is Joachim with his maps,
Thora in her garden: roses, lilies,
the scents she desires so she grows them.

It is the sunlight, high
through the tall evergreens, the birdsong,
the afternoon wind in this place, and our voices.

Telling our tales. We grew up on the other side
of a long long war we all lost.
Years have gone by. All our lives have.

With songs, sometimes music, children,
some love in this old cold world,
years of many letters and a few kisses.

It will always be so: this moment,
the sunlight, the long afternoon, the blackbirds,
Joachim with his maps, Thora in her garden.

Ken Smith

Two Photographs

I
At an outdoor table of the Café Heck
In the Munich Hofgarten
Six gentlemen in suits
And stiff white collars
Are sitting over coffee,
Earnestly talking.
The one with a half-moustache
Wears a trilby hat.
The others have hung up theirs,
With their overcoats, on hooks
Clamped to a tree.
The season looks like spring.
The year could be '26.

On a hook otherwise bare
Hangs a dogwhip.

No dog appears in the picture –

An ordinary scene.
Of all the clients
At adjoining tables
None bothers to stare.

2
The year is '33.
The gentleman in a trilby
Is about to board a train.
Behind him stand
Four men in black uniforms.
'For his personal protection'
The Chancellor of the Reich
Carries a dogwhip.

No dog appears in the picture

Michael Hamburger

Housing Shortage

I tried to live small.
I took a narrow bed.
I held my elbows to my sides.
I tried to think carefully
And to think softly
And to breathe shallowly
In my portion of air
And to disturb no one.

But see how I spread out and I cannot help it.
I take to myself more and more, and I take nothing
That I do not need, but my needs grow like weeds,
All over and invading; I clutter this place
With all the apparatus of living.
You stumble over it daily.

And then my lungs take their fill.
And then you gasp for air.

Excuse me for living.
But, since I am living,
Given inches, I take yards,
Taking yards, dream of miles
And a landscape, unbounded
And vast in abandon.

And you dreaming the same.

Naomi Replansky

'After Brecht':

the reception of Brecht's poetry in English

Karen Leeder

In memoriam my father (1935–1998)

Herr Brecht

What, he thought,
Are you still not finished
With all that junk?

And he smiled
His insolent–modest smile
And was content.

Wolf Biermann

In Germany, the reception of Brecht has long been a highly charged political matter. The questions asked of him and his poetry have reflected the changes in the ideological landscape over half a century of writing. After the collapse of the socialist state, of which he was the most famous literary representative, it is inevitable that his legacy should be open to question once again. The poet Günter Kunert comments on the paradoxical state of affairs when history has contradicted the political intention of the poetry but the poetry remains. If Kunert laments what he calls the 'growing minority'[2] who still read the poet in Germany, he is, however, being unduly (and characteristically) pessimistic. There has been a very vigorous dialogue between German writers and Brecht's poetic legacy over the past few years.[3] Since the fall of the Wall, Brecht has been taken up not only by the writers who were sympathetic to his Communist ideal, or lived through the socialist reality it inspired, as one might expect, but also by writers who do not share his political convictions.[4] In English, it has been different. The figure of Brecht exerts a powerful magnetism here, as in Germany; and, whether 'loving Brecht' (the title of Elaine Feinstein's 1992 novel), or hating him – as in the aggressive and damagingly inaccurate 'Brecht-buster', John Fuegi's *Life and Lies of Bertolt Brecht* – the contradictions and personal charisma of the figure still fascinate.[5] Brecht has recently found his way into drama – in the successful revival of Christopher Hampton's *Tales from Hollywood*; film – in Jan Schütte's *The Farewell* (2000); and poetry.[6] As always, it is the details which are the focus: the haircut, the glasses, the silk shirts under the worker's jacket, or the attitude:[7]

> [...] With him went always
> The scroll of the Skeptic, the cloth cap of finest material
> And plebeian cut

However, the work (as opposed to the figure) has been more partially received in English. When the volume of translations, *Bertolt Brecht Poems 1913–1956*, edited by John Willett and Ralph Manheim with the cooperation of Erich Fried, was published in 1976, it was greeted by extraordinary reviews: definitive statements from powerful backers: 'A mind-changing volume, after which, for all but the most parochial critics, the pecking order in the modern pantheon will never be the same' (Kenneth Tynan); 'It is clear that Brecht was that very rare phenomenon: a great poet for whom poetry is an almost everyday visitation and drawing of breath' (George Steiner).[8] However, writing about Brecht's legacy in 1984, John Willett commented that Brecht 'has even now not really broken through to the English speaking audience'. A decade later, reviewing the reception of Brecht's poetry, Willett pointed out that the poetry was translated much later than the drama, and would take time to filter into the public's consciousness.[9] When Tony Davies, in a fine piece on Brecht and Auden, asked more recently 'Is there an English Brecht?', he was forced to acknowledge once again that 'his poetry remains almost unknown'.[10] There are many reasons for this; some of them practical, as Willett suggests, to do with the timing of translations and the power of the Brecht estate. But Davies is right in pointing to something more fundamental. He argues that Brecht 'has been adopted, in this country by a particular type of engaged and politicised critical practice for which lyric poetry [...] remains problematic'.[11] The formulation is careful, focusing as it does on the way Brecht has been read, rather than anything intrinsic to his poetry. I shall come back to why the sense of Brecht's foreignness is so acute in English. In any case, it is clear that he has a reputation as an austere poet, intellectual and fiercely political, with no time for the affect or subjectivity often associated with the roots of the lyric genre. Seamus Heaney even takes Brecht's very name as a representation of all that is difficult and obstinately, awkwardly intellectual in one of the sequence of poems 'Clearances', a series of poems dealing with his great-great-grandmother.

> Fear of affectation made her affect
> Inadequacy whenever it came to
> Pronouncing words 'beyond her'. Bertolt Brek.
> She'd manage something hampered and askew
> Every time, as if she might betray
> The hampered and inadequate by too
> Well-adjusted a vocabulary.
>
> 'So I governed my tongue
> In front of her, a genuinely well-
> adjusted, adequate betrayal
> Of what I knew better.' [12]

Heaney's poem – in a familiar territory for Heaney – is about the gap that can open up between generations and ways of being, because of education, and the guilt that involves. It is really the pronunciation of Brecht's name that is at issue – on the surface at least. But the oppositions are teed up neatly enough. Authentic feeling and simplicity on the one side; an intellectual legacy which sits uncomfortably even in the mouth on the other. Heaney's would not be a poetry one would associate immediately with Brecht's legacy, although his is a political poetry, precisely about 'the government of the tongue' in all its aspects.[13] However, even a writer like Adrian Henri, who has been inspired by Brecht directly in his own work, shares that sense of Brecht's aura, and sends his dossier of poetic reports from America to 'Dr Bertolt Brecht' – awarding him a spurious, but telling, title.[14]

233

Brecht's apparent difficulty and aloofness, and his association with a discredited political regime, both serve to reinforce the fundamental foreignness of his legacy to the English-speaking world. And yet, paradoxically, Brecht has not gone the way of many other Communist monuments. In the 1960s, the dissident GDR singer–songwriter Wolf Biermann, in his poem 'Herr Brecht' (part of which is quoted as a motto to this piece), sketched a marvellous image of Brecht (three years dead) wandering into the Huguenot graveyard along the Chausseestraße, where he was buried, and seeing workers from the adjoining Brecht archive on their way home.[15] Brecht's gleeful satisfaction that his legacy still perplexes and concerns, reflects the poet's own deliberations about his own posterity (to which I shall return). For Biermann, writing from the GDR, Brecht was a self-evident, if not always comfortable, inspiration. However, if Biermann's Brecht is bemused and delighted in the 1960s, Fredric Jameson has him in similar mood some forty years later, in his *Brecht and Method*:

Brecht would have been delighted, I like to think, at an argument, not for his greatness, or his canonicity, nor even for some new and unexpected value of posterity (let alone for his 'postmodernity'), as rather for his *usefulness* – and that not only for some uncertain or merely possible future, but right now, in a post-Cold-War market-rhetorical situation even more anti-communist than the good old days. [16]

Jameson's accent on Brecht's 'usefulness' for a contemporary moment would certainly square with Brecht's own hopes for his posterity. Famously, in his poem 'I need no gravestone',[17] he suggested that future generations might honour his memory, and their own endeavours, with a memorial inscription that commemorated his status as a 'proposer of proposals': 'He made suggestions. We / Carried them out'. Nevertheless, it is characteristic of Brecht's method that no such suggestions were wholly unambiguous (nor indeed is the poem). And 'usefulness' is, for Brecht, not a synonym of an unquestioning reception, but rather a process of learning. Jameson inveighs against the constant attempts to rebrand the writer (the postmodern Brecht, the post-socialist Brecht, the Brecht of queer theory, *et al*), and the repressed conception of posterity which such attempts disguise. However, he simultaneously argues that one does not have to be antiquarian or nostalgic to appreciate the ways in which Brecht is alive for us. Instead, the very plurality of actual and possible 'virtual Brechts' provides a productive challenge to canonical readings of Brecht, in that they focus, not on the monument (or any repackaging of it) but on 'discontinuities and deeper fragmentation' within the work.[18] What Jameson emphasises more than anything else is the contemporaneity of Brecht's critical legacy.

This could be argued another way, however. Brecht's great hymn about, and to, posterity, 'An die Nachgeborenen' / 'To those born later',[19] looked forward to a time when the struggles of those who lived through the dark times of Fascism would be almost incomprehensible to a truly humane (socialist) society of the future. He wrote the poem in the belief that the experiences he reported would one day be seen as an historical anachronism – reprehensible and completely foreign. The poem has nevertheless enjoyed a quite extraordinary afterlife in the work of later writers, a posterity perhaps without equivalent in German literature.[20] From almost the year in which it was written until now, over a century after Brecht's birth, many of the most important poets in the German language have felt the need to measure themselves and their own times against this poem. Erich Fried draws attention to the fact that the immediacy of Brecht's poem for the contemporary world simultaneously illuminates the frustration of Brecht's hopes. In a poem of his own which itself draws on the Brecht text, Fried depicts how the Brecht poem needs no explanation or comment when read to an audience of contemporary listeners ('Nachgeborenen'). They nod in recognition at the curtailments of humanity depicted in the poem, and draw parallels with their own times. Although Brecht was always concerned that he should write accessible poetry, Fried's poem closes with the poet's misery that his poem might be understood all too well.

> This immediate comprehensibility,
> Though he was always trying
> To make himself understood,
> Would have made the poet sad.

The paradox is a moving one. The very comprehensibility of Brecht's poem, its currency even, is a proof, if it were needed, that Brecht's ideal future has not arrived, that it is, to borrow the title of Fried's poem: 'Still too soon'.[21] This is confirmed by Adrian Henri, writing from England in the 1990s about 'B.B. and me', and remembering his American poetry of the 1970s: 'It is no accident that, writing about an unjust and divisive regime, it is again necessary to report to Dr Bertolt Brecht'.[22]

Brecht and the English tradition

Brecht's *œuvre* satisfies a number of preconditions which might be thought to assure its positive reception in English. For example, Brecht always had a lively engagement with English literary traditions. John Willett summarises Brecht's interests, from Shakespeare to Shelley, from the Elizabethan playwrights to detective novels, or Chinese and Japanese poetry in Arthur Waley's translations (much of which he was introduced to by Elisabeth Hauptmann). He also devotes 'case studies' to Auden, Kipling, and what he calls 'Anglo-American forays'. But the affinities go further than such influences, or 'reciprocal relations'.[23] And quite apart from an affinity of humour, which Willett identifies,[24] one could look to the linguistic and stylistic closeness to English, especially of Brecht's poetry. Much of this, it is true, probably came via Latin; but in any case it means that – at a lexical and rhetorical level at least – Brecht's poetry goes much less awkwardly into English than that of many other German poets. In the United States, Brecht even found his German being affected by English and also tried his hand in the foreign tongue.

The problems, however, are more to do with Brecht's relationship to traditions in his own language. Even in German, Brecht was an outsider, and the type of poetry he wrote placed itself consciously outside the two dominant German lyrical traditions – the *Erlebnislyrik* [poetry of experience] of Goethe and the *Stimmungslyrik* [poetry of mood] of the Romantics. On occasions, he formalised that challenge in satire or in theoretical texts, but, more importantly, it is the poetry itself which stakes its claim to new ground. Brecht drew on traditional forms: ballads, song, the 'Moritat' [broadsheet], the hymn, the sonnet, or adapted folk forms – all forms which emphasise a closeness to real life and a simplicity of diction. As Philip Thomson comments, and Brecht himself was to claim in a later poem, he threw in his lot with the vagabond outsider Villon's 'earthly' verse, instead of the self-indulgence or abstruseness he saw in German traditions.[25] His language reflected that choice. Almost from the beginning, he eschewed sentimentality and displays of emotion, and worked towards a spare and matter-of-fact diction, a syntax close to normal spoken style, and a basic vocabulary. To this he added elements of Luther's Bible, Southern German speech forms, and his own idiosyncratic renderings to create a new poetry: rhythmically concentrated but understated. It was also expressly a poetry of the everyday and of communication with his audience. His impatience with German poetry was bluntly expressed when he was judging a poetry competition in 1927 and dismissed all the entrants (and several of his contemporaries) as guilty of 'sentimentality, untruth and lack of worldliness', their poems as 'neither useful nor beautiful', awarding the prize instead to a poem of his own choice from a cycling magazine.[26] He was attempting to set up an abrasive 'countertradition' to the central development of German poetry, one which Michael Hamburger sums up as 'aesthetic self-sufficiency'.[27] Moreover, this set him outside the dominant mode of nineteenth and early twentieth-century poetry which was to become associated with the 'modern'. Hugo Friedrich's influential work, *Die Struktur der modernen Lyrik / The Structure of Modern Poetry* of 1956, posited a trajectory for modern poetry from Baudelaire, Rimbaud, Mallarmé, Benn, Trakl, Eliot, Pound, towards Ungaretti and Montale.[28] Characteristic of the modern for him was the irrational and obsessive imagination, the poet as part technician and magician, and the poetry itself as hermetic and monological. Brecht's poetry was, of course, far from this model. Crucially, Brecht rejected the notion of a straightforward and intimate relationship between the experience of the poet and the work, and at the same time insisted fundamentally on a communicative gesture which is foreign to the high modernist poetic. It is not my purpose here to reassess what may be defined as modern – and what not (though Friedrich was surely mistaken to have such a narrow focus in his definition); but this is important because the same sense of modern poetry is central to English culture. The English poetic tradition rests on a deep-seated distinction between the private and the public, which leads to a disavowal of what are seen as the abstract and rhetorical aspects of politics in favour of the authenticity and immediacy of the felt, the human.[29] Tony Davies points out the dilemma. On the one hand, the 'English Brecht' is a fully paid-up Modern, he argues, but, on the other hand, he lacks the programmatic experimentalism and the ideological apocalypticism of the 'make it new' modernists.[30] The result is that, for all his affinities with a writer like Auden, for example, Brecht remained curiously adrift in the English-speaking poetic tradition.

Brecht and style

It is here, perhaps, that one begins to attempt something very difficult: to define what it is – not only about Brecht's premise, but also about his style – that makes him so foreign to that tradition. Defining a single style which would give an accurate sense of the flavour of Brecht is impossible. Brecht was a protean writer, constantly experimenting with new forms and voices and, what is more, adjusting his aesthetics to maximise the potential for communication at any given moment. The mode which has perhaps come to be most closely associated with Brecht, and which commentators turn to when attempting to define his 'style', is that of the middle and later years. Paradoxically enough, however, it is Brecht's early work with music, his use of song forms, and particularly the *Threepenny Opera*, that provides the starting-point for his reception among many non-German speakers.[31] Walter Benjamin famously found in Brecht's poetry both the immediacy of the chalked wall-slogan and the chiselled terseness of commemorative marble, and called it, punningly, 'lapidary'. Almost all those who attempt to define something of his style, or to identify what it is that drew them to his poetry, comment upon the 'crafted simplicity, directness and accessibility of his political verse' (Andy Croft), 'his reduction, spareness and plainness of diction' (Michael Hamburger).[32] When Hamburger goes on to say that Brecht was 'almost alone in writing a large body of poetry that was clearly intended to convey a single meaning in language as plain and unfigurative as the best prose',[33] however, one is already tempted to object. For although the political imperatives of clarity and strength during exile drew Brecht away from the extended forms and narrative or elegiac tone of his earlier work and towards the force and precision of aphorism and fable, this is very different, for example, from the almost cryptic and intensely lyrical reduction of the late work in the GDR. And almost all of it is ambiguous in some sense. In the late GDR years, in particular, Brecht's poetry – modelled perhaps on Horace, whom he read repeatedly at this time – insisted on a minimal language and an apparently straightforward lexical meaning. Yet there is no sacrifice of complexity. For although the poems operate apparently without design on the reader, on the surface at least, it is in their movement, their metaphorical suggestion, and especially in their rhythmical and syntactic patterning, that they reveal their 'cunning'.[34] They entice us to read allegorically, especially perhaps in political or historical context, but simultaneously they thwart easy readings. Brecht makes stringent demands on his reader: seeking an attitude more actively dialogical, and 'alert'[35] than otherwise. But he also offers a unique angle on reality. John Willett calls it a 'subversive, plebeian angle on things', although perhaps Darko Suvin comes closer when he tries to define the Brechtian 'structure of feeling' or 'Haltung' [attitude] and reflects on 'seeing the general in the particular, and especially seeing a possible new and better generality instead of the automatically accepted and current one'.[36] In any case, Brecht was at work on creating a new kind of political poetry: one authentically, and not merely rhetorically, engaged with the transactions between life and language. His goal was an intricate play with the public and personal – very far from the divergent interests these are commonly thought to represent. An aesthetic was for him functional rather than intrinsic. Perhaps, however, as Jameson points out, the present with its 'new found taste for impure aesthetics of all kinds' might find it much easier than earlier generations, who were more focused on a modernist mandate, to feel kinship with this kind of practice.[37]

Brecht and the poets

This cannot be the place for a detailed and comprehensive survey of Brecht's reception in English. It must function rather as a snapshot of how poets writing in English have read Brecht and how he has influenced their work. The idea comes out of an event held in Oxford in 1998, as part of the celebrations to mark the centenary of Brecht's birth, and some of the poems were read on that occasion, or indeed commissioned especially for it. Of course it is difficult, in any case, to speak of a global reception. Different generations have different contact with Brecht himself, and many of the ideas he represents, and they respond differently. Brecht's poetry has many facets (as Tom Kuhn outlines in the Introduction). Similarly, at different moments, it has been the exuberant ballad and song tradition of his early years, the bald, politically explicit verse of the middle period, or the more allusive and epigrammatic late poetry which has struck a particular chord. But the notion of reception can also entail very different things. Some of the poets cited below knew Brecht or worked with him. Some have translated his work or engaged with it critically in a sustained way. Some have little German, and know him only through the translated *Poems*. The forms that the reception takes, therefore, are also very different. Some have translated him, some cite directly, some develop images or motifs, some write 'versions' of particular poems, and some have simply been inspired by the tone or style of his work. In 1995, in an edition of the *Brecht Yearbook*, John Willett collected responses and poems from thirteen poets. I intend to draw on these but also to show how the reception has developed more recently.

Many of those who knew or worked closely with Brecht, have been marked by his critical legacy. Naomi Replansky explains how she worked on Brecht's poetry in California, translating the poems that were later published under the title *Kriegsfibel / War Primer*. She had little German, but her engagement with the bleak quatrains which were to accompany pictures collected from European and American magazines,[38] and her intense translation sessions with Brecht himself, resulted in a direct influence on her own work. She had become intrigued by the epigrammatic form, and herself had written some epigrams, mostly epitaphs, in the past, but attributes 'Epitaph 1945' to Brecht's influence.[39]

Epitaph: 1945

My spoon was lifted when the bomb came down
That left no face, no hand, no spoon to hold.
A hundred thousand died in my home town.
This came to pass before my soup was cold.

Immediately recognisable are the four-line form, with a/b rhyme, the attitude of looking up at the heavens, the focus on the detail (especially eating), and the final turn from the individual incident to the larger picture. In fact, Replansky speaks of an 'affinity of influence'[40] with Brecht, in their shared liking for Shakespeare, or Chinese and Japanese poetry in translation, especially in translations by Arthur Waley. This kind of shared background perhaps prepares the way for a productive meeting of styles. Replansky also translated the city poems of *Aus einem Lesebuch für Städtebewohner/ From a Reader for Those who Live in Cities*. There again it was the 'direct, stripped almost conversational diction, their use of homely metaphor'[41] that attracted her and that can be clearly seen in her later poem 'Housing Shortage' (see p. 229):

I tried to live small
I took a narrow bed
I held my elbows to my sides.
I tried to step carefully
And to think softly
And to breathe shallowly
In my portion of air
And to disturb no one.

This poem is perhaps more sentimental than Brecht would have allowed, particularly in the turn where the self-hood of the lyric subject asserts itself against the reduction and anonymity of city-life: 'I clutter this place / With all the apparatus of living'. However, a 1957 'Factory poem' captures well the sympathy for the drudgery of work in capitalism, but also the matter-of-fact tone, familiar from Brecht.

> The tool-bit cut, the metal curled,
> The oil soaked through her clothing.
> She made six-hundred parts a day
> And timed herself by breathing.[42]

Many others who have turned to Brecht also had a personal connection with him or with his work. Willett's anthology, for example, includes Christopher Logue, who sat in on rehearsals at the Schiffbauerdamm Theatre and watched Brecht at work, and Michael Hamburger, Christopher Middleton and Darko Suvin, who have translated and published criticism on Brecht. But just as Replansky also cited some of her poetry from the 1990s as having been influenced by Brecht,[43] the legacy still proves powerful to those at a greater distance, in time or proximity. Keith Armstrong, for example, a contemporary writer from the UK, finds kinship and inspiration in the 'crafted simplicity, directness and accessibility of his political verse'[44] and demonstrates how Brecht can become immediately accessible in an entirely contemporary moment. Into 'Senefelderstraße 19, East Berlin', a long poem set after the fall of the Berlin Wall and detailing the nostalgia and bewilderment of a 'Berlin sizzling / in a panful of history', he inserts a counterweight:

> And Me?
> I am walking in blistered hours,
> Sick of the sight of money
> And what it does to people I love.
> 'A tip for your trip!
> Instead of a brick from the Wall to take home,
> Bring back a Bertolt Brecht poem':
>
> 'And I always thought; the very simplest words
> Must be enough. When I say what things are like
> Everyone's heart must be torn to shreds

That you'll go down if you don't stand up for yourself
Surely you see that.'[45]

On then leaving, this is the poem the lyric subject posts back to his friends into the letterbox of 'Senefelderstraße 19'. It is a bold poet who includes a Brecht poem within his own, especially one as moving and as tautly constructed as this one (compare the Introduction for Tom Kuhn's comments). However, Brecht's hugely ambivalent lament for the mistakes of the past, and the present of the GDR, is re-functioned here to become a lament for past ideals, and an indictment of the grasping reality of post-Communist Germany.

Brecht has long been an inspiration for a certain kind of explicitly left-wing political poetry. Writers like Christopher Middleton, Christopher Logue, Michael Hamburger, Adrian Mitchell, Adrian Henri (and, following on more recently, Ken Smith and Sean O'Brien) draw on the possibilities which Brecht has developed in poetry. The extent to which Brecht functions as a model in this of course varies greatly. Christopher Middleton, the poet, scholar and translator, writes persuasively about how it was the language more than anything that inspired him. He explains how the way Brecht had developed gestic rhythms as a direct reflection of social dissonance led him to seek cadences of direct, moment-to-moment speech, pervasive rhythmic patterning and a language both 'casual and profane' in his own work.[46] Certainly the familiar economy of patterning is evident in his work, as is the use of traditional forms, such as the ballad.[47] For Michael Hamburger, the poet, critic and translator, the spare diction is also central, and is again to be found in his own poems.[48] One might also turn especially to his so-called 'Unpleasantries', poems from the 1960s and early 1970s, and mostly written on an American theme, which seem to echo many of Brecht's sentiments. Ironically enough, the blistering satire 'Big Deal',[49] in which the US President has the 'brainwave' of putting 'the whole great country up for sale' reminds the reader of Brecht's Buckow poem, 'Die Lösung' / 'The solution'.[50] In this poem, Brecht responds to a comment by a GDR official after the 1953 Workers'

Uprising that the people had forfeited the confidence of the government, with the ironic rejoinder: ' Would it not be easier / In that case for the government / To dissolve the people / And elect another?' Hamburger's conclusion is less slyly elliptical, but equally incisive.

> Strange, though the moon was thrown in,
> And the means of getting there, it was not
> That nobody could afford it –
> Long-term credit was offered,
> With no down-payment at all –
> But that nobody wanted to buy.[51]

Like many of those mentioned, Adrian Henri, the Liverpool-based poet, also came to Brecht late, and was particularly inspired by the songs, setting of poems to music, and the use of songs in the theatre. His *AMERICA* of 1972 emerged from a tour of the United States with a Liverpool-scene poetry rock group in 1969. On the tour, he had a book of Brecht poems with him and interspersed quotations from Brecht's 'Vanished Glory of New York the Giant City'.[52] Against Brecht's exuberant (if ironic) poem comes a bleaker and slightly more surreal take on the American dream, powered by the rhythms of music. But Henri's interest is ongoing: he explains how, in 1987, commissioned to produce a modern version of the Wakefield mystery plays, he again turned to Brecht. And again, when Altered States theatre company proposed staging Brecht's *Fear and Misery of the Third Reich* using the Brecht piece as a model and also commenting upon modern Britain, Henri was involved. The performance, *Thatcher's Britain, Fear and Misery of the Third Term* involved episodes written by eleven playwrights, and Henri's own short narrative poems linking the scenes. In one, a single mother throws her baby from a high-rise flat:

> Rockabye baby on the tenth floor
> Mummy will hold you nice and secure
> When Mummy breaks the cradle will fall
> Down will come baby, Mummy and all. [53]

Adrian Mitchell, whom Kenneth Tynan called 'the British Mayakovsky', also draws on the Brecht of social sympathy. Like Brecht, his poetry espouses a simple and clear diction and a very powerful communicative gesture. Many poems have an explicit addressee. His passion and humour (and he is certainly much more explicitly humorous than Brecht) engage, however, with a wide variety of influences, all within a vital popular tradition – embracing Blake, the Border ballads and the Blues. His most nakedly political poems – about nuclear war, Vietnam, prisons and racism – have become part of the folklore of the left, sung and recited at demonstrations and rallies. He also looked to Brecht in his use of traditional forms, particularly the ballad and the song form, even maybe in the many poems 'for my son'.[54] In their titles, a number of the poems are also reminiscent of a Brechtian tone or conviction: 'From Rich Uneasy America to My Friend Christopher Logue', 'Flag Day – But Not for the Revolution' and 'The Dichotomy Between the Collapse of Civilisation and Making Money', for example.[55] Nevertheless, all these things are broadly characteristic of 'a heart on the Left', to borrow the title of his *Collected Poems*, and it would be difficult to pin down a direct influence. In a note on his poem, 'Saw it in the papers',[56] Mitchell comments more specifically: 'Brecht. He gave me courage. I wouldn't have dared to tackle such a bleak documentary subject if I hadn't read Brecht's poem about Marie Farrar, the infanticide. It's a great poem which I've read aloud often.'[57] Mitchell's own narrative poem was written in response to an article in the *Guardian* about a mother whose baby died of neglect, and who was sentenced to imprisonment.

> Her baby was two years old.
> She left him, strapped in his pram, in the kitchen.
> She went out.
> She stayed with friends.
> She went out drinking.
>
> The baby was hungry.
> Nobody came.
> The baby cried.
> Nobody came.
> The baby tore at the upholstery of his pram.
> Nobody came.

The bald tone of reporting and the repetition have a model in Brecht, but it is particularly in the sympathetic treatment of the young mother (rather than the cadence or tone) that this poem points back to its inspiration. The mantra of the poem, 'There was no evidence of mental instability', and the loneliness of the young woman both contribute to the criticism of a society which seems little more advanced than when Brecht wrote his poem. But there is a further aspect to this poem which also testifies to Brecht's practice. Mitchell reports how after reading the poem in Gloucester prison, he was inspired by one of the inmates to write two new verses, which deal precisely with the state of life in prisons, and the ways people find of surviving:

> There is love in prisons.
> There is great love in prisons.
> A man in Gloucester Prison told me:
> 'Some of us care for each other.
> Some of us don't.
> Some of us are gentle,
> Some are brutal.
> All kinds.'
>
> I said: 'Just the same as people outside.'
> He nodded twice,
> and stared me in the eyes.

The communicative gesture and the reported speech are familiar enough, but also the sense of a poem responding to its time and being 'changeable' according to its relevance at a particular moment and in a particular place. Mitchell comments: 'It's a piece which I've rewritten many times since it was published. Poetry doesn't have to be a one-man band.'[58] The sense of the poem being part of a collaborative effort, and also of its changing to earn its place in the here and now, are very much in the spirit of his precursor. The final injunction: to think beyond the individual case and to act – 'Cry if you like. / Do something if you can. You can' – also takes up Brecht's conviction that poetry could make things happen – even if the language here is more abrupt than one might associate with the often downbeat endings of Brecht's poems.

Poetry in dark times

The general adaptation of a mood or diction for the contemporary moment, outlined above, is widespread, if sometimes difficult to pin down precisely. But there is another aspect of the reception of Brecht's work which has not been commented upon. I have spoken about the reception in different generations, and also about the reception of a particular style or theme. However, it is also worth saying something about which of Brecht's poems consistently inspire posterity. One very striking feature of the work surveyed is how often poets take up Brecht's exile poems, especially those of the *Svendborger Gedichte / Svendborg Poems*. This is interesting for several reasons: These poems, 'frightened into existence' in the 'dark times'[59] of Fascism are the poems in which Brecht was most concerned with posterity. While inevitably preoccupied with his own situation, he also reflected on the value of, and possibilities for, art more generally; tapping into myths and models of exile throughout history.[60] Paradoxically, however, this was also the poetry which Brecht himself saw as most reduced by circumstance. He recognised in his *Journal* the literary price he had paid for political consciousness in the *Svendborg Poems*. Political necessity had, he claimed, made his voice hoarse and his verses raw; the need to eliminate ambiguity of thought worked, of necessity, against the multi-valency of bold metaphors.[61] If the times are out of joint, he argued, the forms of poetry must respond: harmony and musicality must give way to rationality, critical distance, argumentative logic, contradiction and aesthetic rupture. He summed it up in a poem, 'Solely because of the increasing disorder'.

> Solely because of the increasing disorder
> In our cities of class struggle
> Some of us have now decided
> To speak no more of cities by the sea, snow on roofs, women
> The smell of ripe apples in cellars, the sense of the flesh, all
> That makes a man round and human
> But to speak in future only about the disorder
> And so become one-sided, reduced, enmeshed in the business
> Of politics and the dry indecorous vocabulary
> Of dialectical economics.[62]

Translated by Frank Jones

Of course, Brecht does nothing of the sort, as the poem itself demonstrates. And this is part of his cunning. The constellation, however – exile, survival and an apparent impoverishment of language – is intriguing, and I shall conclude by examining a number of poems which take up Brecht's preoccupations and poems of exile.

Throughout his life, Brecht pondered what would survive of him and his work. From very early on, he liked to think of himself as a 'classic' and speculated on how his legacy would be received. However, in exile, these questions became more urgent and acute. There was the real possibility that he – and even possibly his work – might not survive the 'flood'. His *Svendborg Poems* constantly come back to the themes of exile and posterity in a whole matrix of issues surrounding survival and forgetting, memorialisation and inscription.

If any number of poems from this collection worry at the notions of 'emigration', 'exile', and 'banishment', the Ulster poet Tom Paulin offers an intriguing contemporary response to one of the most interesting: Brecht's 'Besuch bei den verbannten Dichtern' / 'Visit to the banished poets'.[63] Brecht's dark poem about the tradition of exile and possibility of extinction inspires a demotic take on the 'Emigration of the Poets'. Dante, Shakespeare and Villon make an appearance (along with Euripides and Heine) – all of them pursued by forces of order (if not justice): 'the Beast / i.e. the police'. They all manage to escape, but Brecht catches at the end of the poem: ' – now watch me here Bertolt Brecht / I'm a pike / *sh*tuck in this Danish thatch.' The poem fixes the image of Brecht's Svendborg house, which appears so often in the Svendborg collection, along with all its doors for escape, but it also turns to remind the reader of the pikes stashed away in the thatch during the Irish Wars. Brecht's subversive voice itself becomes subversive in the context of the new poem. But Paulin's own role as an Irish poet and critic writing from England, and explicitly concerned with questions of political identity, comes into play. The history of repression and ongoing questions about a poet's poetic and political identity are revoiced in a modern context.

But it is perhaps in his great hymn to posterity 'To those born later',[64] that Brecht addresses the question of survival, and responsibility for one's times, most memorably. And it is this poem which seems to have inspired more responses than any other.[65] At root, the poem is an impassioned complaint about perverse times: 'Truly, I live in dark times'. These are times when simplicity and innocence and everyday positive values have been fundamentally put into doubt. Even laughter (line 3) reminds you only of the bad news which will inevitably come to silence it. The programme of quietist wisdom prescribed in the 'old books' (line 22) has become impossible. To follow such advice would now denote a lack of compassion and awareness – an unfurrowed brow argues a thick skin (lines 2–3). In a world thus out of joint, survival is random and the speaker bares his bad conscience. This feeling, familiar in its most extreme form from the survivors of the holocaust, is here also a part of a rhetorical strategy with which the speaker hopes to engage the reader's sympathy and justify his continued actions. The conversational interjections and questions which structure the piece imply that it is one half of a dialogue. The present-tense verbs and exemplary sufferings also suggest that this is a mixture of confession and strategic argument. All urgently seek the reader's assent that these are conditions in which humankind cannot live humanely: 'All this I cannot do'. The second part of the poem shifts in tone; the dark times are situated in the historical context as 'a time of disorder'. But it is also a 'time of revolt' and the poem works to enlist us in the partisan struggle in the 'war of the classes'. Engagement in that struggle has its costs. It is not just the values of the first part that are rendered suspect, but the individual is lessened too: the relation to nature is disrupted, love withers, but, worst of all, the struggle forces those who fight for humanity to become inhumane themselves:

> Hatred, even of meanness
> contorts the features.
> Anger, even against injustice
> Makes the voice hoarse.

The elegiac mood is transformed, however, in that last section, which switches into the future tense and looks to a time which will succeed the flood. This cathartic catastrophe of biblical proportions will eventually issue into a world of 'friendliness' that does not know the divisions of the present. That time will only come, however, when the condition of *homo homini lupus* which exists under capitalism is overthrown and the class war is over. The possibility of this future illuminates all the struggles in retrospect, and the poem ends with the speaker entreating his future readers to consider his cause with forbearance. For he is conscious that those who have fought for mankind have been excluded from full humanity by dint of the struggle. It is unsurprising, perhaps, that this poem, more than any other, has prompted responses from those born after.

Christopher Logue has a powerful reputation as a political poet who mobilised the left-wing intelligentsia around issues like 1968 and the Vietnam War. He met Brecht and has translated many poems. Many versions of, and quotations from, Brecht's work appear in his own poems.[66] 'A Singing Prayer'[67] is a five-part text, written in the 1960s. The poem is set at the turning of the year and opens with a feeling of relief and anxiety.

> By mutual fear
> we have come in peace
> to the end of the year.

It is tempting to see this as a poem about living under the threat of nuclear war, and the phrase 'mutual fear' seems to reinforce that. The poem, however, moves backwards to question the origin of war more generally and urges the reader to see through the words of those who claim that disaster is somehow natural.

> Why imagine
> if a thing happens often it is natural?
> Rather
> ask after its kind, and where it started.

The demystification of the status quo, and the interrogation of those in whose interest it lies is familiar from Brecht – as in the simple diction and the rhetorical inversion. But the poem also questions the 'small acts of malice', cowardice and compromise of everyday life, in a tone very reminiscent of Brecht's 'To those born later'. Beyond that, it questions the sins of omission, when one did not do wrong exactly, but failed to do what was right. In a direct reference to the Brecht text ('But those in power / Sat safer without me: that was my hope'),[68] however, the poem insists that the questions, at least, are right:

> Yet ask yourself questions, once.
> It is little enough; but something; and
> be sure they sleep less tight because you asked

The third part of the poem is a condensed version of 'To those born later':

> It is hard – I know.
> Cold comfort – I know.
> And if you came to see me you would find
> a man needing much forgiveness.
>
> Indeed I would like to change; to be wise.
> And I have been told that wisdom consists
> of avoiding strife.
> To dig my own square inch till it bears
> apples in March, is held to be wise.
> 'Be still', such wisdom says, 'and when
> your neighbour's beard goes up in flames
> moisten your own. Make no attempt
> to actualise your dreams; but call them vanity,
> and lose your shame in compromise.'
> Alas, I can do none of these things.
> It cannot be said that I am wise.

Phrases from Brecht's poem jostle with details from a different reality – the neighbour's beard, the apples in March – to echo the lyric subject's helplessness in a contemporary dark time. And the poem moves to a close in distinctly elegiac mode, condemning the inadequacies of the present, but also looking, like Brecht, to future judgement.

> We were three generations possessing money and time
> who were too much possessed by them.
>
> Infinitely careful of each self,
> we stood for liars in public places;
> and called it freedom,
> because we did not have to hear them.
>
> When you ask after us and find
> weakness, falsehood, malice, pride,

and the complex excuses we made about them,
judge us – but with forbearance.

For if we did not seek out
the evil among us too carefully,
nor did we rest in peace.

Logue's poem does not use the vision of a luminous socialist future to set against the darkness of the present as Brecht had done. It is more an elegy for old age ('more than half our time is gone'), and it looks also to a more intimate future. But finally, it is a testament to the hopeful, but flawed, present.

I wrote this song
for those who will be born
in the time we call New Year

The song is given away
like a man's top-coat when he dies,
who knew it cost too much
for him not meant to last,
and knowing this would make
the same mistake again.

In this, it is like his 'To my Fellow Artists',[69] which again is a version of a Brecht poem from the Svendborg collection: this time, 'Rat an die bildenden Künstler, das Schicksal ihrer Kunstwerke in den kommenden Kriegen betreffend' / 'Advice to artists concerning the fate of their art-works in the wars to come'.[70] Logue's poem again looks to the unborn future, and translates Brecht's anxieties and his advice forward to the negative silos of a more contemporary threat. His injunction, though, carries the same force and hope (against hope).

But let us remember to leave behind
permanent signs. Signs that are easily read.[71]

Andy Croft has picked up such signs. His recourse to Brecht was born out of the urgent need, as a Communist, to address political reality and to find a voice to write politically in contemporary Britain. For him, the tradition of English poetry 'long ago learned to inoculate itself against writing like Brecht's – too ideological, too propagandist, too much like hard work'. But 1989 brought a further layer of difficulty: 'The end of the Cold War has of course only legitimised prejudice against Brecht's writings, easy to dismiss now as period pieces, dated, dull and *so obvious*.[72] But there is also another aspect. English poetry, he claims is 'still terribly constricted by irony, unable to say things directly, embarrassed by plain speaking'.[73] Brecht represents for him a model of 'simple, brutal unironic verse', undiminished by 1989.[74] One could argue about the question of irony in Brecht, though the exile poems are certainly those in which the urgency of the struggle militates against such ambiguities. Nevertheless, one poem by Croft tries to draw on Brecht's 1938 poem and Hans Magnus Enzensberger's epic poem, *The Sinking of the Titanic* (1978), to capture a 'sensibility of apocalyptic defeat'. It is written in memory of Margot Heinemann – Communist, critic, novelist, poet and Brecht scholar:

After the Deluge

'You who will emerge from the flood
In which we have gone under
Remember when you speak of our failings
The dark time too which you have escaped?'
(Brecht)

Margot is dead, and the sun is out,
And the wet London streets from the train
Are lovely, dazzling rivers of brass
Bursting their banks in the rain –
A submarine city, a mirage, a drought,
An ocean of sand in this hour's empty glass.

History's an iceberg, a desert of snow,
And the future's a hole in the ice,
Then cities of sand are all raining down,
And glaciers float in the skies,
And swimming in sand, down we all go,
Still dreaming of water, together we drown.

Nothing is constant but change, but this weather,
But sinks to the bottom one day.
The nearest we get to the Land of Cockaygne
Is a vision of clouds, up, up and away
And over the mountains, still wheeling for ever
Like ashes and dust, still falling like rain.[75]

This poem speaks from the perspective of a generation who should have 'emerged from the flood', but here still threaten to drown. It works with motifs from Brecht's poems but also looks to the threat of global destruction in the present age. It can be read alongside his poem 'Desert Island Discs (after reading Brecht)' (see p. 226), which takes up Brecht's 1938 poem 'Bericht über einen Gescheiterten'/ 'Report on a Castaway'[76] about a Viennese doctor, an anti-Fascist exile whom Brecht met in Denmark. He calls it a 're-tread' of the Brecht, playing on two senses of 'gescheitert' [to fail and to wreck]. The castaway becomes Brecht (and a version of Prospero) stranded in a contemporary present. The poem works closely with Brecht's original and, at first sight, like the one quoted above, gives a negative response from those born after. On closer inspection, both, however, preserve something of Brecht's ideal. 'After the Deluge' still courts that vision of the 'Land of Cockaygne'. And this poem too, for all that one sees 'all hope of rescue wrecked/In sight of land', concludes with an alternative vision, but also the hope of a productive and continuing engagement – and usefulness.

> Or if the Flood won't last for ever –
> Know the ruin floating past
> Is fuel for fires we must create
> Again, to keep the world's one hope burning,
> Above high-water. Thus may we too die learning.

Derek Mahon's 'Brecht in Svendborg' (compare pp. 222–4) is also about learning of a sort.[77] It is a complex response to Brecht's exile, and 'To those born later' in particular, which links together many phrases from many of the *Svendborg Poems*. The first part is a role poem in the voice of Brecht which borrows details of Brecht's Danish refuge and works them together to make a coherent picture. Overwhelming is the sense of threat, from the owls in the garden to the sound of the ships, or the four doors for escape. The potential domesticity ('if things were otherwise') is set against the perversions of the moment. The second part of the poem, entitled 'To the Unborn', begins as a translation of 'An die Nachgeborenen'. It is a very good one – smoothing some of the awkwardness of the version in *Poems* into a taut and familiar idiom. But as it goes, it begins to condense and intensify into a series of urgent questions.

Commenting on this poem, Craig Raine suggests that Mahon simply seems to have got bored or impatient.[78] In fact, there is more at stake. Three things are particularly striking. The first is that the lyric 'I' of Brecht's poem has become 'we' in Mahon. The biographical details which pin the first part of the poem to a particular person and a historical moment are gone in this second part. Mahon speaks for a 'we' which could be speaking at any time and in any place. The 'I' comes in only towards the end:

> To the unborn who will emerge
> From the deluge
> In which we drown
> I would say only this:
> Remember, when you condemn us,
> You do not live, like us, in a dark time.

Instead of the plea for forbearance, there is a more colloquial and personal demand to a future which once again is posited as better than the present. The end of the poem is most interesting, however. A final strophe is added, which is a condensed version of Brecht's 'Der Kirschdieb' / 'The cherry thief'.[79]

> Startled awake at first light
> By whistling, I peer out
> At the garden, where a young
> Fellow in torn denims
> Is cheerfully pocketing plums.
> He nods to me and returns to his song.

The effect is interesting. It brings the poem back to the more intimate tone of the first part, but although not timeless (the young man wears torn jeans), it is curiously placeless. In any case, it offers a hopeful potential. The poet figure is surprised by a cheerful act of appropriation, quite different in tone from the earlier menace. The positioning of the piece suggests that although at one level he belongs to the time and place that the poem conjures, Svendborg 1938, this young man is also one of those born after, here seen cheerful and availing himself unselfconsciously of what he needs. Mahon's poem becomes an ironic comment on its own procedures. For if the young man finds what he wants and takes it, so too does the lyric subject, writing about the anecdote, and so too, of course, do Brecht and Mahon. The poem enacts a kind of learning appropriation, but also demonstrates an urgent solidarity – both in the figure of the poet, but also in the 'we' who (still) live in a dark time. And yet it is hopeful, finishing on a song.

Andy Croft comments that, for those 'cast away on this poor little island',[80] there is scarcely any more fitting companion than Brecht's *Poems*. It certainly seems as if Brecht's poetry is being read, more than ever, by poets who find themselves in that position. It is interesting to reflect that it is often those who are somehow marginal to the mainstream English traditions – either politically or by national identity – who have turned to Brecht. The number of poets of Irish extraction who have taken up Brecht's poems about exile is noteworthy, for example. That this engagement continues is evidenced by poems which gesture towards Brecht, perhaps more distantly than those cited above, but nevertheless present themselves as 'after Brecht'. (Compare the poems by Bernard O'Donoghue and Ken Smith, p. 227.) Brecht's poetic legacy still seems 'useful', then, even after the collapse of Communism and so far from the circumstances that gave rise to Brecht's aesthetic. For all of these poets, Brecht provides a model, an inspiration or an interlocutor to help them work on perhaps the most important task of poetry (Brecht would certainly have thought so): to forge the connection between responsibility to the word and responsibility for the kind of society in which we live, to be useful, to learn.

NOTES

Foreword

1. BFA 12, p. 95.

Introduction

1. BFA 12, pp. 30–2.
2. Empedocles, *The Extant Fragments*, edited by M. R. Wright (Yale and London, 1981, 1995) has been my source for much of this detail.
3. Ruth Berlau, *Brechts Lai-Tu. Erinnerungen und Notate*, ed. Hans Bunge (Berlin, 1987), p. 275.
4. BFA 12, pp. 35–6.
5. For translations from the Greek and Latin sources I have drawn on the Penguin Classics volume, Jonathan Barnes, *Early Greek Philosophy* (London, 1987), here pp. 193–4, as well as M. R. Wright (as above), here pp. 270–5.
6. Wright, p. 166; *see also* Barnes, p. 166.
7. 'Kurzer Bericht über 400 (vierhundert) junge Lyriker' (Short report on 400 young poets), BFA 21, p. 191.
8. BFA 12, p. 37; *Poems*, p. 175.
9. Spender and Steiner are quoted from the jacket of later editions of Bertolt Brecht, *Poems 1913–1956*.
10. 30 vols, edited by Werner Hecht, Jan Knopf, Werner Mittenzwei, Klaus-Detlef Müller and others (Berlin, Weimar, Frankfurt am Main, 1988–2000), cited elsewhere in the form: BFA +volume (11–15 for the poems), +page numbers.
11. 'Of landscape and all that it formerly offered the poet all that is left today is one leaf. And perhaps one would have to be a great poet to try to reach for more.' Benjamin, *Versuche über Brecht* (Frankfurt am Main, 1966), p. 78.
12. BFA 12, p. 21; *Poems*, p. 243.
13. BFA 12, p. 26; *Poems*, p. 229.
14. Compare my article, '"Ja, damals waren wir Dichter": Hanns Otto Münsterer, Bertolt Brecht and the dynamics of literary friendship', *The Brecht Yearbook* 21, pp. 49–66.
15. BBA 800/01 and /04.
16. BFA 11, p. 9; *see also Poems and Songs*, p. 11.
17. BFA 11, p. 46; *Poems*, p. 92.
18. BFA 22.1, pp. 357–64; *Brecht on Theatre*, pp. 115–20.
19. 'Und was bekam des Soldaten Weib?' / 'Song of the Nazi soldier's wife', *see* Ulla C. Lerg-Kill, *Dichterwort und Parteiparole: Propagandistische Gedichte und Lieder Bertolt Brechts* (Bad Homburg v. d. Höhe, 1968), pp. 196–7 (+note 67).

20. BFA 14, p. 119.
21. Edited by Ronald Speirs (Cambridge, 2000). It contains essays by some of the same contributors as the present volume.
22. BFA 26, *Journals*, 10.9.38.
23. BFA 14, p. 432; *Poems*, pp. 330–1.
24. BFA 12, pp. 47–8.
25. BFA 12, p. 12; *Poems*, p. 288.
26. Letter to Wieland Herzfelde, May 1950 (BFA 30, p. 26).
27. BFA 22.1, pp.188–90.
28. BFA 27, *Journals*, 5.4.1942.
29. One friend commented that the *Elegies* were so alienated and depersonal in tone 'as if they were written from Mars' (BFA 27, p. 125).
30. BFA 12, p. 85; *Poems*, p. 318; and *see* Derek Mahon's free variation, discussed in Karen Leeder's essay, pp. 254–5.
31. The reference is to Adorno's later remark about poetry after Auschwitz being 'barbaric'. Jan Knopf, *Gelegentlich Poesie. Ein Essay über die Lyrik Bertolt Brechts* (Frankfurt am Main, 1996), p. 23.
32. Max Frisch, *Tagebuch 1946–1949* (Frankfurt am Main, 1950), pp. 224–6.
33. BFA 15, p. 185.
34. BFA 15, p. 205; *Poems*, p. 416.
35. BFA 12, p. 315; *Poems*, p. 442.
36. One thinks of Stalin, 'the steel one'.
37. BFA 12, p. 310; *Poems*, p. 439.
38. Peter Handke, who came to prominence in the 1960s and struggled against the Brechtian legacy, calls them, in a memorable diatribe, 'seine letzten abgeklärten chinoiden Teekannensprüche' [his last serene chinoid teapot-sayings], in *Ich bin ein Bewohner des Elfenbeinturms* (Frankfurt am Main, 1972), p. 63.
39. For example, BFA 23, pp. 316–18; *Brecht on Theatre*, pp. 272–3. This book is an encouragement likewise to sweep off any dust that has gathered on Brecht.
40. BFA 11, p. 72; *Poems*, p. 29.
41. Compare also the water and trees discussed by Speirs, Müller and Brown.
42. BFA 12, p. 307; *Poems*, p. 439.
43. For example, Günter Häntzschel, in Hans-Jörg Knobloch and Helmut Koopmann (eds), *Hundert Jahre Brecht – Brechts Jahrhundert?* (Tübingen, 1998), p. 78.
44. Letter to Herzfelde, as note 26.
45. His notes in 1931 on the legal proceedings over the ownership of copyright in a dispute with a film company, BFA 21, p. 448; *Bertolt Brecht on Film and Radio*, edited and translated by Marc Silberman (London, 2000), p. 148.
46. BFA 12, p. 87; *Poems*, p. 320.
47. BFA 15, p. 295; *Poems*, p. 452.
48. BFA 14, pp. 320–1; *Poems*, pp. 264–5.
49. BFA 27, *Journals*, 5.4.1942.

1. 'Of poor B. B.' – and others

1. BFA 11, pp. 119–20; *Poems* pp. 107–8.
2. 'Ich, Bertolt Brecht, bin aus den schwarzen Wäldern' (BFA 13, pp. 241–2).
3. Wulf Segebrecht, 'Vom armen B. B.', in *Ausgewählte Gedichte Brechts mit Interpretationen*, ed. Walter Hinck (Frankfurt am Main, 1978), pp. 18–23.
4. The standard translation is to be found in the second edition of Brecht's *Poems*, pp. 107–8, where the first line is rendered slightly more freely as 'I, Bertolt Brecht, came out of the black forests'.
5. *Complete Poems of François Villon* , ed. J. Fox (London, 1968), p. 153 and ibid., pp. 2–20.
6. BFA 21, p. 248.
7. Thomas Mann, *Werke in dreizehn Bänden* (Frankfurt am Main, 1974), vol. 11, p. 393.
8. *See* Philip Thomson, *The Poetry of Brecht* (Chapel Hill and London, 1989), in particular the chapter 'Nihilism, Anarchism and Role-Playing', pp. 45–74.
9. A version of the poem appears in *Poems and Songs* as 'Lucifer's Evening Song', p. 3.
10. BFA 11, p. 116.
11. The motif occurs in the earlier version of 'Of poor B. B.': 'ich aber liege und spüre im Rücken noch einen Stein' [but I lie and still feel in my back a stone] (BFA 13, p. 242).
12. In his analysis of another of Brecht's early poems, 'Von der Freundlichkeit der Welt', Carl Pietzcker reaches a similar conclusion: 'The poem does indeed offer a polemical parody of Christian ideas, yet remains indebted to those very ideas and uses them to convey its own point of view', *Die Lyrik des jungen Brecht* (Frankfurt am Main, 1974), pp. 39–40.
13. *Poems*, p. 107.
14. Brecht's close friend, the artist Caspar Neher, provided an illustration for the appendix of the *Domestic Breviary* depicting the 'hydatopyranthropos' ('fire and water man'), a symbol of the type of person (presumably Brecht), whose contradictory experiences and attitudes are articulated by the poems and whom the legend characterises as 'semper aequam servans mentem', a stoic who remains unperturbed in all circumstances.
15. BFA 13, p. 292. In Brecht's early poetry, rocking, whether in a chair or on the swings at the fair, connotes intercourse.
16. The desire for apocalyptic revenge on the cities that were fast devouring the world of nature was elaborated more fully by Brecht in the dramatic fragment *Die Geschichte der Sintflut* (1926) (BFA 10, pp. 535–45).
17. BFA 12, p. 26; *Poems*, p. 229.
18. BFA 13, p. 251.
19. BFA 13, p. 71.
20. BFA, 13, p. 89.

2. Love – Not – Memory. An interpretation of 'Remembering Marie A.'

1. BFA 11, p. 92.

2. *Poems*, pp. 35–6.

3. Hanns Otto Münsterer, *The Young Brecht*, translated and introduced by Tom Kuhn and Karen Leeder (London, 1992, orig. Zürich, 1963), p. 58.

4. Albrecht Weber, 'Zu Liebesgedichten Bert Brechts', in *Interpretationen zur Lyrik Brechts*, ed. Rupert Hirschenauer and Albrecht Weber (2nd ed., Munich, 1973), pp. 57–87 (p. 64).

5. Jan Knopf, 'Amor lieblos. Brechts *Terzinen über die Liebe* mit einem Ausblick auf die *Marie A.*', in *Der Deutschunterricht*, 6 (1994), pp. 32–43 (p. 42).

6. *See* Hans-Harald Müller, 'Brechts *Ballade von des Cortez Leuten*. Struktur, Quelle, Interpretation (samt Anmerkungen zur Theorie und Methodologie)', in *Zeitschrift für deutsche Philologie*, 112 (1993), pp. 569–94.

7. *See* Albrecht Schöne, 'Erinnerung an die Marie A.', in *Die deutsche Lyrik. Form und Geschichte. Interpretationen. Von der Spätromantik bis zur Gegenwart*, ed. Benno von Wiese (Düsseldorf, 1957), pp. 485–94.

8. *See* Jan Knopf, *Brecht-Handbuch. Lyrik, Prosa, Schriften. Eine Ästhetik der Widersprüche* (Stuttgart, 1986), pp. 35–6 and 'Gewölke, ungeheuer oben. "Erinnerung an die Marie A."', in Jan Knopf, *Gelegentlich: Poesie. Ein Essay über die Lyrik Bertolt Brechts* (Frankfurt am Main, 1996), pp. 71–82; Klaus Schuhmann, *Der Lyriker Bertolt Brecht. 1913–1933* (München, 1971), pp. 103–9; Herbert Frenken, *Das Frauenbild in Brechts Lyrik* (Frankfurt am Main etc., 1993), pp. 91–4.

9. *See* Schuhmann, *Der Lyriker Bertolt Brecht*, p. 493 and Andreas Hapkemeyer, 'Bertolt Brecht: Formale Aspekte der *Hauspostille*. Am Beispiel von "Erinnerung an die Marie A."', in *Sprachkunst*, 17 (1986), pp. 38–45 (p. 39).

10. Schöne, 'Erinnerung an die Marie A.', pp. 494, 491, 487 and 493.

11. *See* Jan Knopf, 'Sehr weiß und ungeheuer oben', in *Interpretationen. Gedichte von Bertolt Brecht*, ed. Jan Knopf (Stuttgart, 1995), pp. 32–41 and the essays in notes 5 and 8 above.

12. Knopf, *Brecht-Handbuch. Lyrik, Prosa, Schriften*, p. 35.

13. *See* section 4, below.

14. Knopf, 'Amor lieblos', p. 76.

15. Gerhard Neumann, 'Geschlechterrollen und Autorschaft: Brechts Konzeption der lyrischen Konfiguration', in *Der andere Brecht 1. Das Brecht-Jahrbuch*, 17 (1992), pp. 101–23 (pp. 103–4).

16. Wilhelm von Humboldt, 'Latium und Hellas oder Betrachtungen über das classische Alterthum', in *Werke in fünf Bänden*, ed. Andreas Flitner (Darmstadt, 1979), vol.2, pp. 25–64 (p. 62).

17. *See* Daniel Müller Nielaba, 'Vergessen und Erinnern im Text. Noch einmal Bert Brechts "Erinnerung an die Marie A."', in *Poetica*, 29 (1997), pp. 234–54, who restricts his discussion to a deconstructive interpretation which contains some similarities to our part 3; and Dorothee Ostmeier, 'The Rhetorics of Erasure: Cloud and Moon in Brecht's Poetic and Political Texts of the Twenties and Early Thirties', in *German Studies Review* 23 (2000), pp. 275–95.

18. Marcel Reich-Ranicki, *Ungeheuer oben. Über Bertolt Brecht* (Berlin, 1996), pp. 27–8.

19. *See* Jacques Derrida, *Of Grammatology*, trans. Gayatri Chakravorty Spivak (Baltimore and London, 1976), pp. 9–10.

20. Jacques Derrida, 'Différance', in *Margins of Philosophy* (Brighton, 1982), pp. 1–27.

21. *See* Jacques Derrida, 'Structure, Sign, and Play in the Discourse of the Human Sciences', in *Writing and Difference*, tr. Alan Bass (London and Henley, 1978), pp. 278–93 (pp. 292–3).

22. *See* Derrida, *Of Grammatology*, p. 12.

23. *See* Werner Frisch, K. W. Obermeier, *Brecht in Augsburg. Erinnerungen, Texte, Fotos. Eine Dokumentation* (Frankfurt am Main, 1976), p. 91.

24. *See* letters nos 21, 24, 28, 32 (pp. 35–6, 38–40, 42–3, 47) in BFA 28.

25. *See* Arnold Stadler, *Das Buch der Psalmen und die deutschsprachige Lyrik des 20. Jahrhunderts. Zu den Psalmen im Werk Bertolt Brechts und Paul Celans* (Köln and Wien, 1989), p. 50.

26. BFA 1, p. 48.

27. Schuhmann, *Der Lyriker Bertolt Brecht*, pp. 107–8.

28. *Poems*, pp. 30–2 ; BFA 13, p. 484.

29. *See also* Bertolt Brecht-Archiv, Folder and sheet no. 1087/66–7.

30. *See* Knopf, 'Gewölke, ungeheuer oben', pp. 78–9.

31. *See* Goethe, *Faust 1*, V. 2603–4: 'Du siehst mit diesem Trank im Leibe / Bald Helenen in jedem Weibe.'

32. According to the Brecht-Archiv, Brecht changed the title in the spring of 1922; *see* BBA E 21/37 and BBA E 21/54.

3. Reading 'The drowned girl': a Brecht poem and its contexts

1. BFA 11, p. 109.

2. *Poems and Songs*, p. 14.

3. *See* the previous essay, 'Love – Not – Memory. An interpretation of "Remembering Marie. A."'.

4. There is a sense of progression in the way in which the 'Ophelia' motif, signifying an intact beauty (*see* Millais's famous picture entitled 'Ophélie', illustration 6), metamorphoses into the water-logged corpse, in which decay and decomposition become the focal point. *See* Bernhard Blume, 'Das ertrunkene Mädchen. Rimbauds "Ophélie" und die deutsche Literatur', *Germanisch-Romanische Monatsschrift*, Neue Folge vol. 4 (1954), p. 116.

5. For instance, Hans-Thies Lehmann, 'Text und Erfahrung ("Vom ertrunkenen Mädchen")' in H.-T. Lehmann and Helmut Lethen (eds), *Bertolt Brechts 'Hauspostille'. Text und kollektives Lesen* (Stuttgart, 1978), pp. 122–45 (p. 143). For a different reading, *see* Stefan Bodo Würffel, *Ophelia. Figur und Entfremdung* (Bern, 1985): 'an image of transience and fleetingness, it is, wherever it is mentioned, also a sign of the life of which it is a trace' (p. 108). Würffel links the 'smoke' motif to that of the 'cloud' (*see* p. 108).

6. Peter Paul Schwarz, *Brechts frühe Lyrik 1914–22. Nihilismus als Werkzusammenhang der frühen Lyrik Brechts* (Bonn, 1971), p. 49, sees a link between 'sky' and 'God', finding in this a 'fiction of transcendence'.

7. *See*, for example, Georg Trakl, 'Drei Blicke in einen Opal', *Historisch-kritische Ausgabe*, ed. Walter Killy and Hans Szklenar (Salzburg, 1969), vol.1, pp. 66–7.

8. *See* Würffel, p. 107.

9. The young Brecht frequently uses planetary imagery to express this idea, cf. *Baal*: 'Es ist einer von den kleineren Sternen'; *Im Dickicht der Städte*: 'Worte auf einem Planeten, der nicht in der Mitte ist' (BFA 1, pp. 66 and 594). On Brecht's use of this motif, *see* H. M. Brown, *Leitmotiv and Drama: Wagner, Brecht and the limits of 'epic' theatre* (Oxford, 1991), pp. 121–2.

10. S. Steffensen, 'Brecht's "Himmel" and Rimbaud's "L'Infini terrible" (Ophélie) is the heaven of nihilistic outrage, without God and without a message', in *Bertolt Brechts Gedichte* (Copenhagen, 1972; originally in Danish, Copenhagen, 1965), p. 55. Würffel, op. cit., puts it rather differently: 'God . . . has become a mere motif, the memory of which is motivated by the traditional association with the theme of death' (p. 110).

11. For information about the poem's complicated genesis, *see* BFA 11, p. 322.

12. 'The murdered girl' and 'Ballad of red Rosa'. See Hanns Otto Münsterer, *The Young Brecht*, translated and introduced by Tom Kuhn and Karen Leeder (London, 1992, orig. Zürich, 1963) p. 59.

13. *Baal*, 1919, BFA 1, pp. 36 and 76 (*Plays 1*, p. 54). *See also* Dieter Schmidt, *'Baal' und der junge Brecht* (Stuttgart, 1966), p. 112.

14. Peter Paul Schwarz calls it 'an ironic companion', *Brechts frühe Lyrik*, p. 2.

15. *See* 'Bei Durchsicht meiner ersten Stücke', BFA 23, pp. 239–45.

16. The most thorough investigation of the Ophelia motif and its tradition can be found in Würffel, op.cit.

17. Arthur Rimbaud, 'Ophélie' (1870), for example, in *Collected Poems* (Penguin Classics), ed. Oliver Bernard (London, 1962, this ed. 1997), p. 81.

18. *See* H. M. Brown, 'Between Plagiarism and Parody: the function of the Rimbaud quotations in Brecht's *Im Dickicht der Städte*', *The Modern Language Review* (82) 1987, pp. 662–74.

4.   The poet in Berlin: Brecht's city poetry of the 1920s

1. BFA 11, p. 157; *Poems*, pp. 131–3.

2. Georg Simmel, 'Die Großstädte und das Geistesleben', reprinted in *Das Individuum und die Freiheit* (Frankfurt am Main, 1993), pp. 192–204.

3. BFA 26, p. 236.

4. *See* Werner Mittenzwei, *Das Leben des Bertolt Brecht* (Frankfurt am Main, 1987), vol. i, p.165; Peter Jelavich, *Berlin Cabaret* (Cambridge, Mass., 1993), p. 150.

5. *See* Walter Mehring, *Großes Ketzerbrevier* (Munich, 1975), pp. 146–8. For a fuller account of Mehring's contribution to German poetic writing in the 1920s, *see* Hans-Peter Bayerdörfer, 'Weimarer Republik', in *Geschichte der deutschen Lyrik vom Mittelalter bis zur Gegenwart*, ed. Walter Hinderer (Stuttgart, 1983), pp. 439–76.

6. GW, p. 277; *Poems*, p. 141. Page references in this paragraph are to Bertolt Brecht, *Gesammelte Werke* (Frankfurt am Main, 1967), in which the arrangement of the poems by Elisabeth Hauptmann gives a more immediate sense of the range of Brecht's city poetry than the new BFA edition, which recognises only those poems as 'belonging' to the *Reader* project which Brecht himself expressly assigned to it.

7. GW, p. 282; *Poems*, p. 144.

8. GW, p. 281; *Poems*, p. 143.

9. GW, p. 288; *Poems*, pp. 146–7.

10. GW, p. 277; *Poems*, p. 141.

11. GW, pp. 293ff; *Poems*, pp. 127–8.

12. Helmut Lethen, *Verhaltenslehren der Kälte. Lebensversuche zwischen den Kriegen*, (Frankfurt am Main, 1994).

13. Lethen, *Verhaltenslehren*, pp. 175–8. For a full account of my reservations about Lethen's argument, *see* my article 'Vom Lebenswandel in der mechanisierten Gesellschaft. Zu neueren Tendenzen in der Theoretisierung der kulturellen Entwicklung im Zeitraum der Weimarer Republik', in *Schwellen. Exkursionen der Literaturwissenschaft*, ed. F. Möbius, N. Saul und D. Steuer (Würzburg, 1999), pp. 177–84.

14. *See* Gert Ueding and Bernd Steinbrink, *Grundriß der Rhetorik: Geschichte, Technik, Methode* (Stuttgart, 1986), pp. 291ff.

15. I am following the 1938 version of this text, which I interpret as a clarification of intentions on Brecht's part, as I explain below.

16. For fuller discussion of the rhetorical effects in these poems, *see* Franz Norbert Mennemeier, *Bertolt Brechts Lyrik: Aspekte Tendenzen* (Düsseldorf, 1982), p. 97; P. V. Brady, '*Aus einem Lesebuch für Städtebewohner*: On a Brecht Essay in Obliqueness', *German Life & Letters*, 26 (1972), pp. 160–72; Peter Whitaker, *Brecht's Poetry* (Oxford, 1985), p. 53.

17. BFA 11, p. 165; *Poems*, p. 140.

18. Brady, loc. cit.

19. Walter Benjamin, *Versuche über Brecht* (Frankfurt am Main, 1981), pp. 80ff.

20. BFA 9, p. 350.

21. BFA 11, pp. 107–8; BFA 11, pp. 84–5.

22. *See* Mennemeier, *Bertolt Brechts Lyrik*, p. 97; Whitaker, *Brecht's Poetry*, pp. 42ff.

23. *See* Hans-Thies Lehmann, 'Schlaglichter auf den anderen Brecht', *Das Brecht-Jahrbuch*, 17 (1992), 1–13 (p. 10).

24. BFA 3, p. 26.

25. *See* Horst Jesse, *Die Lyrik Bertolt Brechts von 1914–1956 unter besonderer Berücksichtigung der 'ars vivendi' angesichts der Todesbedrohungen* (Frankfurt am Main, 1994), p. 15.

26. Lethen, op. cit., p. 173.

27. *Poems*, p. 136.

5.   The eulogistic mode in Brecht's poetry

1. BFA 11, p. 234. *Poems and Songs*, p. 110.

2. BFA 14, pp. 459–61; *Poems*, pp. 333–4.

3. BFA 14, pp. 34–6.

4. *Poems*, p.195. The version of the poem in Bertolt Brecht, *Gesammelte Werke*, viii (Frankfurt am Main, 1967), pp. 387–90 amalgamates two versions of the poem, BFA 14, pp. 34–6 and BFA 14, pp. 36–8. The translation, however, follows the second of the two versions.

5. BFA 11, p. 234; BFA 11, p. 234; BFA 11, p. 237; mostly in *Poems and Songs*, pp. 97–117.

6. The title *Die Maßnahme* , also sometimes translated as *The Measures Taken*, is translated as *The Decision* in *Poems and Songs*.

7. Franz Norbert Mennemeier, *Bertolt Brechts Lyrik. Aspekte Tendenzen* (Düsseldorf, 1982) treats some of these in a chapter on the didactic mode. His chapter 'Brechts Preisgedichte' (pp. 151–61) takes a sample of eulogies from several periods of Brecht's production, rightly arguing that, in the context of a historical poetics, they form an important category of experimental risk-taking.

8. BFA 15, pp. 260–1.

9. BFA 11, pp. 229–30.

10. BFA 12, pp. 57–60; p. 59.

11. BFA 12, pp. 45–6.

12. *See* Klaus Schuhmann, *Untersuchungen zur Lyrik Brechts* (Berlin and Weimar, 1977), pp. 62–7, on the October Revolution as a recurrent motif in Brecht's work.

13. BFA 12, pp. 37–9; BFA 12, pp. 39–40; BFA 12, pp. 43–5.

14. BFA 12, p. 50.

15. BFA 14, p. 41; BFA 14, p. 48. A third poem, 'Die Verlustliste'/'List of losses' (BFA 15, p. 43) includes Walter Benjamin in a list of those whose loss the poet mourns, along with Margarete Steffin, Karl Koch and Caspar Neher.

16. BFA 14, p. 48; *Poems*, p. 363.

17. Peter Whitaker, *Brecht's Poetry: A Critical Study* (Oxford, 1985), p. 89.

18. Roger Fowler, 'Ode', in *Modern Critical Terms*, ed. Roger Fowler (London and New York, 1987), pp. 166–8.

19. Fowler, 'Ode', p. 167.

20. Fowler, 'Ode', p. 167.

21. See Whitaker, *Poems*, p. 91, where he cites Ulla Lerg-Kill on echoes of Horace and Klopstock in the opening lines of 'Praise of illegal work'.

22. BFA 14, pp. 459–61; BFA 11, pp. 237–8; BFA 14, pp. 521–2.

23. The term 'Dolchstoß' [stab in the back] was used of the supposed betrayal of the army and the German people by leaders who, so the claim ran, robbed Germany of victory in the First World War, by capitulating prematurely.

24. 'Die Klassiker' is translated as 'its [the Party's] philosophers' in 'Praise of the Party'.

25. BFA 11, p. 233.

26. The critical method of deconstruction seeks to undermine such generalising categories by uncovering the differences, which are suppressed to establish collective identity, while postmodern discourse values difference or heterogeneity over identity. Both tendencies can have a depoliticising or disempowering effect, however, if deployed to undermine the collective terms necessary to political alliances.

27. For a discussion of the position of intellectuals speaking for silenced masses, *see* Gayatri Chakravorty Spivak, 'Can the Subaltern Speak?', in *Marxism and the Interpretation of Culture*, ed. C. Nelson and L. Grossberg (Basingstoke, 1988), pp. 271–313. Spivak is discussing colonialism, but raises theoretical issues relevant to representation generally.

28. BFA 11, pp. 231–2; BFA 11, pp. 232–3. In *Poems and Songs*, 'Song of the soup' has the title 'As the raven'.

29. The sequence comes in BFA 11, pp. 231–8; for an analysis of the whole collection, this 'meticulously organised series of poems', *see* Whitaker, *Brecht's Poetry*, pp. 80–97.

30. *See*, for example, *Der gute Mensch von Sezuan, The Good Person of Szechwan* and *Mutter Courage / Mother Courage*. In *Der kaukasische Kreidekreis / The Caucasian Chalk Circle* that the maternal woman is not the biological mother makes a similar point, but is less repressive in allowing love for a particular baby to exemplify the social instinct.

31. BFA 11, p. 234; *Poems and Songs*, p. 103.

32. The drily mechanical plot justifying self-obliteration, in answer to a punitive political super-ego, is very different in mood from 'On the suicide of the refugee W.B.' with its pitiful evocation of the 'torturable bodies'.

33. Klaus-Detlev Müller, ed., *Bertolt Brecht. Epoche – Werk – Wirkung* (Munich, 1985), p. 160.

34. BFA 14, pp. 122–4.

35. Such ambiguity eludes translation into English, which must plump either for 'it', and so lose the personification, or for 'he' and so overdo it.

36. BFA 11, p. 234; *Poems and Songs*, p. 110.

37. BFA 11, p. 237.

38. At his first press conference appealing to the GDR government, following his expulsion in 1976, Wolf Biermann quoted 'Praise of the revolutionary'. For a wry commentary on the poem at a time of authoritarianism in the GDR and repressive state measures against terrorism in the liberal FRG, *see* Silvia Volckmann, 'Lob des Revolutionärs', in *Ausgewählte Gedichte Brechts mit Interpretationen*, ed. Walter Hinck (Frankfurt am Main, 1978), pp. 35–40.

39. BFA 11, p. 237; *Poems and Songs*, p. 112.

40. BFA 11, p. 237; *Poems and Songs*, p. 112.

41. Katharine Hodgson, 'Exiled in "Danish Siberia": the Soviet Union in the Svendborg Poems', in *Brecht's Poetry of Political Exile*, ed. Ronald Speirs (Cambridge, 2000), pp. 66–85, argues that in contrast to the doubts expressed in the work of Soviet poets despite their exposed position, Brecht kept his doubts out of his poetry. Hodgson attributes this to wish-fulfillment, but also to the need to sustain a credible alternative to Fascism.

42. David Constantine, 'The Usefulness of Poetry', in *Brecht's Poetry*, ed. Speirs, pp. 29–46 (p. 38).

43. BFA 11, pp. 234–5.

44. 'Praise of the Party' in English translation retains the order in the play and includes both sections together under the one title.

45. BFA 11, p. 235.

46. BFA 11, p. 235.

47. BFA 11, p. 235.

48. BFA 11, p. 238; *Poems and Songs*, p. 117. These lines, which form the beginning of the poem in *The Mother*, are preceded in *Songs Poems Choruses* by a preliminary section setting the immediate context of the Third Reich.

49. BFA 11, pp. 235–6.

50. As Peter Brooks suggests, from its inception during the French Revolution, melodrama offers the assurance of a morally legible universe in a post-sacred age and 'celebrates the sign of the right'. *See* Peter Brooks, *The Melodramatic Imagination: Balzac, Henry James, Melodrama and the Mode of Excess* (New York, 1985), p. 43.

51. BFA 12, pp. 85–7.

52. BFA 14, p. 461; *Poems*, p. 336.

53. BFA 14, p. 461; *Poems*, p. 336.

6. Returning generals: Brecht's 'The Manifesto' and its contexts

1. BFA 15, pp. 120–57. The most significant material dealing with the genesis of 'Das Manifest' (The Manifesto) was published in Hans Bunge, '"Das Manifest" von Bertolt Brecht. Notizen zur Entstehungsgeschichte', *Sinn und Form*, 15 (1967), pp. 183–203. English versions are my own unless otherwise stated.

2. BFA 15, p. 387.

3. *See* BFA 15, p. 386. The fragment 'Das Wachsen des "Nichts" durch den Gebrauch' (BFA 14, p. 171) paraphrases Lucretius' 'Nullam rem e nilo', *De rerum natura* (Loeb Classical Library), ed. W. H. D. Rouse, revised by Martin Ferguson Smith (London, 1982), I, 150, and *see* Lucretius, *On the Nature of the Universe*, translated by R. E. Latham (Harmondsworth, 1994).

4. BFA 15, pp. 120–35; BFA 15, pp. 135–48; BFA 15, pp. 148–56.

5. BFA 27, p. 226.

6. Ruth Berlau, *Brechts Lai-Tu: Erinnerungen und Notate*, ed. Hans Bunge (Berlin, 1987), p.182.

7. BFA 27, pp. 219–20.

8. BFA 15, p. 120.

9. BFA 15, p. 120; BFA 15, p. 136.

10. Karl Marx and Frederick Engels, *The Communist Manifesto. A Modern Edition*, with an Introduction by Eric Hobsbawm (London, 1998), p. 34. *Manifest der kommunistischen Partei* is quoted from Karl Marx, Friedrich Engels, *Studienausgabe*, III, ed. Iring Fetscher (Frankfurt am Main, 1966), pp. 59–87.

11. BFA 12, p. 29.

12. On Brecht and peasants, *see* Fredric Jameson, *Brecht and Method* (London, 1998), pp. 16ff., pp. 131–40, and *passim*.

13. BFA 15, p. 121.

14. BFA 15, p. 136.

15. BFA 15, p. 136.

16. BFA 27, p. 221.

17. *See also* Marion Lauser, 'Brechts Lyrik und die Antike', in *Brechts Lyrik – neue Deutungen*, ed. Helmut Koopmann (Würzburg, 1999), pp. 163–98; on Lucretius, pp. 168–74.

18. BFA 19, pp. 425–33. Brecht, 'Über das Begreifen des Vorhandenen', 'Das Wachsen des "Nichts" durch den Gebrauch', 'Da sie nun glauben' (BFA 14, p. 171) and 'Über den Frieden' (p. 172) certainly continues the hexameter

experiment, and appears to be an early version of 'Viele sprachen vom Krieg' (BFA 14, pp. 453ff.).

19. BFA 19, p. 430. Bertolt Brecht, *Collected Short Stories*, ed. and intr. by John Willett and Ralph Manheim (London, 1983), p. 175.

20. BFA 14, p. 431; *Short Stories*, p. 177.

21. BFA 15, p. 138.

22. BFA 14, p. 453.

23. Lucretius, *On the Nature of the Universe*, p. 77. Edmund Licher, 'Nichts ist also der Tod...', *Neophilologus*, 82 (1998), pp. 435–62, identifies impulses from Lucretius and Epicurus as early as 1924 in *Man Equals Man. See* p. 452.

24. Lucretius says of a statue of Nike, goddess of victory, carved to look like the goddess of peace: 'The statuette must hail from a time in which these peoples had not yet been conquered' (BFA 14, p. 430; *Short Stories*, p. 177).

25. BFA 15, pp. 183ff.

26. *The Communist Manifesto*, p. 38.

27. On 'The Shoe of Empedocles', *see* Jan Knopf's suggestive note BFA 11, p. 366.

28. *See* Werner Mittenzwei, *Brechts Verhältnis zur Tradition* (Berlin, 1972), p. 121.

29. Reported to Hans Bunge 17.5.1958 (BFA 15, p. 393).

30. Lucretius, *De rerum natura* I: 136–9, *On the Nature of the Universe*, p. 13.

31. Lucretius, *De rerum natura*, I: 66–7, *On the Nature of the Universe*, p. 11. Lucretius names Epicurus in Book III: 1042.

32. *See* Georg Büchner, *Complete Plays, Lenz and Other Writings*, trans. John Reddick (London, 1993), p. 167.

33. M^3, lines 46–8.

34. *Communist Manifesto*, pp. 35–6.

35. M^3, lines 56–66.

36. For another account of such concretisation, *see* Wolfgang Rösler, 'Vom Scheitern eines literarischen Experiments. Brechts "Manifest" und das Lehrgedicht des Lukrez', *Gymnasium*, 82 (1975), 1–25 (pp. 14–15).

37. *Communist Manifesto*, p. 37.

38. BFA 15, p. 151.

39. M^2, line 171; M^3, line 76.

40. BFA 23, pp. 269–70.

41. *Communist Manifesto*, p. 37.

42. BFA 15, p. 123. *See Manifest der kommunistischen Partei*, p. 61.

43. BFA 15, p. 270.

44. *Communist Manifesto*, p. 41.

45. BFA 15, pp. 142ff.

46. *See* Bunge, 'Das Manifest von Bertolt Brecht', p. 183.

47. BFA 15, pp. 151–2.

48. *Communist Manifesto*, p. 38.

49. BFA 15, p. 141.

50. BFA 15, p. 141.

51. Jameson calls this 'the modernity of the machine itself', *Brecht and Method*, p. 165; *see* the subsequent discussion of Brecht's Lindbergh play, which links manned flight with the conquest of the ether by radio, in parallel to their conjunction in 'Das Manifest' (BFA 15, p. 141).

52. *See* 'The Tailor of Ulm' (BFA 12, pp. 19–20). Shen-Te's lover in *The Good Person of Szechwan* also wants to be a postal pilot. In this part of 'Das Manifest' the distribution of news, the introduction of radio, and the invention of manned flight form a crescendo of innovations which overcome geographical space.
53. BFA 15, p. 139.
54. *Manifesto*, p. 47.
55. BFA 15, p. 147.
56. BFA 11, pp. 85–9.
57. BFA 12, pp. 41–3.
58. *See* H. M. Brown, 'Between Plagiarism and Parody: The Function of the Rimbaud Quotations in Brecht's Im Dickicht der Städte', *Modern Language Review*, 82 (1987), pp. 662–74; Steffen Steffensen, 'Brecht und Rimbaud: Zu den Gedichten des jungen Brecht', *Zeitschift für deutsche Philologie*, 84 (1965), pp. 82–9.

7. Brecht's sonnets

1. BFA 11, p. 185.
2. Margarete Steffin, July 1933, *Konfutse versteht nichts von Frauen: Nachgelassene Texte* (Berlin, 1991), p. 201.
3. Compare BFA 15, p. 193, 'Über die Verführung von Engeln'. In an excess of naughtiness, Brecht signed this and another poem, 'Sauna und Beischlaf'/'Sauna and copulation', both of 1948, with the name 'Thomas Mann', but he made no attempt to publish them. The German poem may read rather differently from the above: the word for angel, 'der Engel', is a masculine noun; the use of the masculine pronoun does not necessarily imply a homosexual encounter.
4. Compare BFA 14, p. 417. Brecht's poem is prefaced by an explanation: 'The Augsburger walks with Dante through the hell of the departed. He speaks to the inconsolable souls and reports that on earth some things have changed.' The reference is to the story of the adulterers, Paolo and Francesca, in Dante's *Inferno*.
5. Identifying poems as sonnets or as drafts for sonnets and keeping a tally is difficult through the five volumes of the collected poems. Two sonnets – 'Über das Böse'/'On wickedness' and 'Über die Gedichte des Dante'/'On the poems of Dante' – feature twice (BFA 11, p. 123 and 13, p. 341; 11, pp. 190 and 269) in slightly differing forms. 'Unfinished' may mean wanting half a line ('Sonett vom Erbe'/'Sonnet on the legacy', BFA 14, p. 422) or wanting several lines ('Und als ich dringend fragte'/'And when I urgently enquired', BFA 13, p. 326, or 'Als wir so lang getrennt wie vordem nie'/'Longer apart than ever before', BFA 14, p. 332). It is also likely that Brecht would have altered things before any publication and in that sense several more may be thought unfinished. The fourteen-liners but not strictly sonnets are: 'Der Narr'/'The fool' (BFA 13, p. 50), 'Die Schneetruppe'/'Snow unit' (p. 76), 'Und als sie wegsah'/'And when she looked away' (p. 145) and 'Schlechter Vorgang'/'Bad occurrence' (BFA 14, p. 385). 'Als ich den beiden'/'When I had told them both' (p. 417), though

associated with the *Studies*, is more terza rima than sonnet. 'Schmalhans'/'Slim Jim' (p. 385), unfinished, seems to be heading towards sonnet-form.

Brigitte Bergheim has undertaken a similar general appraisal of Brecht's sonnets, which was drawn to my attention at a late stage in the work for this piece: 'Die Sonette Bertolt Brechts', in Theo Stemmler and Stefan Horlacher (eds), *Erscheinungsformen des Sonetts* (Mannheim, 1999), pp. 245–70. She identifies seventy-two sonnets. In other respects, her conclusions differ notably from mine.

6. He seems to have written none after his return to Germany. Elisabeth Hauptmann noted that he was not the author of 'Lied der neuen Erde'/'Song of the new earth', 1955 (BFA 15, p. 494).

7. BFA 13, p. 409. He was consciously trying out other forms as well. *See* his note on a poem, 'Heimat'/'Homeland', written next day: 'This is an attempt at a ballad. I still haven't mastered the style!'

8. BFA 13, p. 413.

9. BFA 13, p. 9.

10. BFA 13, p. 76.

11. BFA 13, p. 146.

12. The collection contains one poem, 'Lehrstück Nr. 2. Ratschläge einer älteren Fohse an eine jüngere'/'Didactic Piece No. 2. An old whore's advice to a younger whore', which is not a sonnet but which is consonant with its context in subject and tone. The first sonnet in the collection, 'Über Mangel an Bösem'/'On the lack of wickedness', is a reworking of the uncollected sonnet 'On wickedness' (BFA 13, p. 341). The two uncollected sonnets of these years which don't obviously fit with those collected are 'Sonett vom Sieger'/'Sonnet on the victor' (p. 320), whose subject is pointless combat in the manner of *In the Jungle of Cities*, and 'Das zehnte Sonett'/'The tenth sonnet' (p. 394), which, from first drafts in 1927, only evolved into a sonnet for publication in 1929. The fragment 'And when I urgently enquired' (p. 326), perhaps of 1925–6, is unlike the other sonnets of that time. It is, for one thing, more politically engaged.

13. '19. Sonett' (1937; BFA 14, p. 354), 'Das 21. Sonett' (*c*.1938; p. 418), and 'Sonett Nr. 19' (1939; p. 437) are certainly for Steffin; 'Und nun ist Krieg'/'And now it's war' (1939; p. 437), almost certainly; 'Über die Untreue der Weiber'/'On the faithlessness of women' (*c*.1937; p. 384), quite possibly. 'Über induktive Liebe'/'On inductive love' (*c*.1938; p. 425) seems to belong with the *Studies*, but could also be addressed to Steffin. The fragment 'Longer apart than ever before' (1936; p. 332) also looks to be for her and is very likely the beginnings of a sonnet.

14. 'Über die Gedichte des Dante auf die Beatrice'/'On Dante's poems to Beatrice' was written in 1934 and included, as 'Das zwölfte Sonett'/'The twelfth sonnet', in the *Sonnets* for Margarete Steffin. The sonnet on Lenz's *Der Hofmeister*/*The Tutor* was written in 1940. Brecht wrote or worked at half a dozen further sonnets on literary and artistic subjects in or around 1938. All may be associated with the *Studies* but only one of them, 'Über den Tod des Dichters Thomas Otway'/'On the death of the poet Thomas Otway' (BFA 14, p. 424), is both finished and strictly a sonnet. 'When I had told them both'(p. 417) is fourteen lines of terza rima, appropriately since its subject is drawn from Dante. The

others are: 'Du zarter Geist' / 'You gentle spirit' (p. 420), on Nietzsche, unfinished; 'Kritik an Michelangelos "Weltschöpfung"' / 'Criticism of Michelangelo's "Creation"' (p. 420), probably unfinished, and a response to it, '(Vermutliche) Antwort des Malers' / 'The artist's likely reply', doubtless to be in sonnet form, was only sketched out; 'Sonnet on the legacy' (p. 424), an important poem, wanting half a line. 'An einen befreundeten Dichter' / 'To a poet friend' (p. 417), is a sonnet addressed, around 1938, to Johannes Becher. It warns him that his sonnets on the subject of Germany have lost touch with reality.

15. BFA 15, pp. 117–18; p. 193. 'Finnische Landschaft' / 'Finnish Landscape' (1940; BFA 12, p. 110) was taken into the *Steffinsche Sammlung* / *Steffin Collection*). 'Der Erbe' / 'The heir' (unfinished, around 1940; BFA 15, pp. 29–30) and 'Sonett in der Emigration' / 'Sonnet in emigration' (1941; p. 48) deal with survival in exile, the latter straightforwardly, the former cryptically.

16. BFA 14, p. 424.

17. BFA 12, p. 40; *Poems,* p. 123.

18. BFA 14, p. 425.

19. George Seferis, *Days of 1945–51: A Poet's Journal* (Cambridge, Mass., 1974), p. 134.

20. But see also 'Vorschlag, die Architektur mit der Lyrik zu verbinden' / 'Suggestion that architecture should be joined with lyric poetry' (1935; BFA 14, p. 301), a sonnet proposing that the workers in Moscow should decorate their Metro with poems. The formality of the sonnet suits the proposal, and again there is the wish that poetry should have its place in the midst of the more material work of the soldier-builders.

21. BFA 13, pp. 190 and 468.

22. BFA 11, p. 325.

23. Line 6 of the poem 'An Diotima' ('Komm und siehe die Freude um uns . . .').

24. BFA 13, p. 302; *Poems,* pp. 113 and 114.

25. Tercets rhyming eff egg, as in BFA 11, pp. 190 and 196, do, of course, give a concluding couplet, but Brecht sets them out as tercets, as he does also the rhyme scheme efe fgg, for example, at pp. 125 and 189. Thus, he never emphasises the finality of a concluding couplet, but rather conceals it.

26. BFA 13, p. 302; *Poems,* p. 114.

27. BFA 11, p. 187; *Poems,* p. 213.

28. Auden does the same in the poems (five sonnets and a chorale) that he wrote in German in 1930 after his months in Berlin. *See* my 'The German Auden: Six Early Poems', in *Auden Studies* I (Oxford, 1990), pp. 1–15.

29. BFA 11, p. 123.

30. *See also* 'The tenth sonnet' (BFA 13, p. 394) and 'Sonett Nr.14. Von der inneren Leere' / 'On inner emptiness' (BFA 11, p. 127).

31. BFA 11, pp. 125 and 127; *Poems,* p. 151. BFA 13, p. 306.

32. BFA 11, p. 312; *Poems,* p. 114.

33. BFA 13, pp. 312 and 341.

34. The last line of 'Au Lecteur', which is the opening poem of *Les Fleurs du mal*.

35. *Poems,* p. 91.

36. John Fuegi, *The Life and Lies of Bertolt Brecht* (London, 1995), p. 310.

37. BFA 23, p. 241.

38. BFA 26, p. 323.
39. BFA 15, p. 45; *Poems*, p. 364.
40. *Journal*, 1.8.1941.
41. BFA 14, p. 437; *Poems*, p. 345.
42. BFA 14, pp. 437 and 418; *Poems*, p. 330.
43. BFA 11, p. 189.
44. Margarete Steffin, *Konfutse versteht nichts von Frauen. Nachgelassene Texte* (Berlin, 1991), p. 352.
45. BFA 15, p. 45; *Poems*, pp. 364–5.
46. Ibid., p. 364.
47. BFA 11, p. 127.
48. BFA 11, pp. 187 and 188.
49. Ibid., p. 188.
50. BFA 11, p. 187; *Poems*, pp. 213–14.
51. BFA, p. 188.
52. See *Konfutse*, p. 204.
53. 'Das dritte Sonett' (BFA 11, p. 186); here translated by David Constantine. *See also* the thirteenth (p. 190), in which he etymologises on the missing word. The sonnet fragment 'Longer apart than ever before . . .' takes an anxious interest in the woman's vocabulary during an absence.
54. In a letter to Nancy Pearn, 12 April 1927. See *The Collected Letters of D. H. Lawrence*, edited by Harry T. Moore, 2 vols (London, 1962) ii, 972.
55. *Konfutse*, p. 202.
56. *Konfutse*, p. 312.
57. *Konfutse*, p. 206. Properly set out, the initial letters of title and poem read: 'ADE GRÜSS GOTT BIDI' ['Farewell God Greet You Bidi']. 'Grüß Gott' was their 'word' and Bidi was a pet name for Brecht.
58. BFA 11, p. 160.
59. *Konfutse*, p. 181.
60. BFA 11, p. 195; p. 189.
61. Ibid., p. 196.
62. BFA 14, p. 418; p. 354; *Poems*, p. 275.
63. *Journal*, 16.3.1942.
64. BFA 14, p. 437; *Poems*, p. 330.
65. BFA 11, p. 195.
66. See *Poems*, p. 231.

8. Empedocles in Buckow: a sketch-map of misreading in Brecht's poetry

1. BFA 12, p. 308; *Poems*, p. 441.
2. BFA 12, p. 307; *Poems*, p. 443.
3. *See* the introduction to *Bertolt Brecht, Poems 1913-1956*, especially pp. ix–xiv. The delayed impact of Brecht's poetry was recently recalled in the first part of Klaus Schuhmann, ' "Ich brauche [sic] keinen Grabstein." Der Lyriker Bertolt Brecht und seine Nachgeborenen', in *Lyrik des 20. Jahrhunderts*, ed. Heinz Ludwig Arnold (Munich, 1999), pp. 138–54.

4. Clemens Heselhaus, 'Brechts Verfremdung der Lyrik', in *Immanente Ästhetik –*
    Ästhetische Reflexion. Lyrik als Paradigma der Moderne, ed. Wolfgang Iser (Munich,
    1966), pp. 307–26. The conclusions I mention may be found respectively on
    pp. 318–20; pp. 322–3; pp. 323–4.
5. Philip Brady, 'Der verfremdete Krieg in der Lyrik Bertolt Brechts', in *Krieg und*
    Frieden in Gedichten von der Antike bis zum 20. Jahrhundert, ed. Theo Stemmler
    (Mannheim, 1994), pp. 157–73.
6. Loc cit., pp. 169–70.
7. BFA 12, p. 12; *Poems*, p. 288.
8. *See*, for example, BFA 14, pp. 306–7.
9. BFA 12, p. 10; *Poems*, p. 287.
10. A recent commentator who has made this connection is Albrecht Kloepfer,
    ' "Was über allem Schein, trag ich in mir...": zu Brechts Essay "Über reimlose
    Lyrik mit unregelmäßigen Rhythmen"', *Brecht Yearbook*, 24 (1999), 129–39,
    (pp. 138–9). In this piece, Kloepfer demonstrates that Brecht's essay is more a
    response to a particular political situation than an attempt at a timeless aesthetic
    statement. Others have sought to link the *Buckow Elegies* with the *Hollywood*
    Elegies of 1942: Marion Fuhrmann, *Hollywood und Buckow, Politisch-ästhetische*
    Strukturen in den Elegien Brechts (Cologne, 1985) and Helmut Koopmann,
    'Brechts "Buckower Elegien" – ein Alterswerk des Exils?' in *Hundert Jahre Brecht –*
    Brechts Jahrhundert?, ed. Hans-Jörg Knobloch und Helmut Koopmann
    (Tübingen, 1998), pp. 113–34.
11. *See* Silvia Schlenstedt, 'Lyrik im Gesamtplan der Produktion. Ein Arbeitsprinzip
    Brechts und Probleme der Gedichte im Exil', *Weimarer Beiträge*, 24 (1978), 5–29,
    (p. 17). The importance of this theme is also brought out by Helmut Brandt,
    'Funktionswandel und ästhetische Gestalt in der Exillyrik Bertolt Brechts', in
    Schreiben im Exil, Zur Ästhetik der deutschen Exilliteratur 1933–1945, ed. Alexander
    Stephan and Hans Wagener (Bonn, 1985), pp. 123–44, (pp. 132–5).
12. *See* 'Über das Urteilen' / 'On judgement' (BFA 14, pp. 386–7).
13. On this project, *see* BFA 15, pp. 386–94, especially. *See also* the piece by Anthony
    Phelan in this volume.
14. BFA 14, p. 308; *Poems*, p. 257.
15. BFA 14, p. 315; BFA 14, p. 309; BFA 14, p. 312; *Poems*, p. 255 and p. 256.
16. For example, BFA 14, p. 387.
17. BFA 12, p. 60 and 14, pp. 234–6.
18. BFA 12, p. 7; *Poems*, p. 320.
19. BFA 14, pp. 176ff. At the same time, Brecht shows awareness of the fact that in a
    capitalist society learning is a commodity, cf. 'Durch langes Studium' / 'Through
    lengthy study' (BFA 14, pp. 317–18) and 'Alljährlich im September' / 'Annually in
    September' (BFA 14, p. 371; *Poems*, p. 272).
20. BFA 14, p. 439.
21. BFA 5, p. 10; *Plays* 5, p. 7.
22. BFA 22.2, p. 959.
23. *See* BFA 22.2, p. 973, where the date of 1936 is suggested but qualified by 'dating
    uncertain'.
24. BFA 21.1, pp. 223–4.

25. BFA 21.1, pp. 270–3. *See* BFA 22.2, pp. 986–7, which suggests a date of January–February 1937, but 'dating uncertain'.

26. Cf. BFA 12, p. 387 and pp. 405–6.

27. BFA 12, p. 82; *Poems*, p. 301.

28. BFA 12, p. 95; *Poems*, p. 303 and *see* pp. 4 and 184–5.

29. BFA 28, p. 398; *Letters*, p. 152.

30. In the light of this new direction, we may wonder whether a poem such as 'The passenger' (BFA 14, p. 308; *Poems*, p. 257.) with its warning about the dangers of blinkered and single-minded endeavour, should be read as concerning political work generally, not just the work of writing dramas.

31. BFA 28, p. 471.

32. *See* BFA 22.2, p. 988 and the letters of March 1937 to Piscator and Gorelik (BFA 29, pp. 22–4).

33. BFA 29, pp. 20–1 and p. 583. *Poems*, p. 319.

34. For the quotation, 'An die Nachgeborenen' / 'To those born later' (BFA 12, p. 86; *Poems*, p. 319), this part of the poem is dated 1934 (BFA 12, p. 387). Jan Knopf, *Gelegentlich: Poesie* (Frankfurt am Main, 1996), p. 143, quotes the accusation of 'Defaitismus' by Julius Hay in 1936 from the volume *Die Säuberung*. On the feud with Hay in 1937, *see* BFA 29, p. 13 and pp. 19–22; *see* also BFA 29, p. 106.

35. BFA 29, p. 109.

36. On this, *see* Brecht's own comments on Stanislavsky, especially BFA 22.1, pp. 279–85. Brecht was dogged by the shade of Stanislavsky at a later stage in his life, *see* his essays in the 1950s (BFA 23, pp. 167–8, pp. 224–39 and p. 502).

37. BFA 14, p. 293. The poem 'Brief an das Arbeitertheater "Theatre Union" in New York' / 'Letter to the New York Workers' Company "Theatre Union"', may date from August 1935 (BFA 14, p. 611), but reads more like a retrospective reflection on the whole sorry American experience of the winter 1935–6.

38. BFA 29, p. 124. It is a sharp irony that the (unsent) letter with this phrase, asking how to obtain information about people who have 'disappeared' in the Soviet Union, was addressed to someone (Dimitroff) who had already been tried and condemned to death on a trumped-up charge. Brecht's poem on hearing of his death, 'Ist das Volk unfehlbar' / 'If the people are infallible' makes painful reading (BFA 14, pp. 435–6). The development of Brecht's ideas during the years 1933–40, particularly in regard to the Marxist orthodoxy represented by the 'Moscow clique', is discussed, with differing nuances, by Silvia Schlenstedt (as above), and by Jost Hermand, 'Zwischen Tuismus und Tümlichkeit. Brechts Konzept eines "klassischen" Stils', in *Brecht-Jahrbuch 1975*, ed. John Fuegi, Reinhold Grimm and Jost Hermand (Frankfurt am Main, 1975), pp. 9–42. Brecht's reactions to events in the Soviet Union may be traced in the *Schriften* unpublished during his lifetime, e.g. BFA 21.1, pp. 297–8, pp. 365–9.

39. BFA 22.2, p. 669.

40. BFA 14, pp. 376–7; *Poems*, p. 270.

41. BFA 14, pp. 459–61; *Poems*, p. 333.

42. BFA 22.1, pp. 462–3.

43. BFA 22.1, pp. 74–89.

44. BFA 22.1, pp. 81–8.

45. BFA 22.1, p. 83. If the editors of the BFA are right to allot many of Brecht's 1930s poetic fragments in hexameters to the 'Tui-Epos' project, it seems that the 'protection' provided by classical style here is directed against Brecht's left-wing friends, rather than against his fundamental enemies.

46. BFA 22.1, p. 80. There are, of course, earlier poems by Brecht which directly show concern with readers' reactions, such as 'Von der Kindesmörderin Marie Farrar' / 'On the infanticide Marie Farrar' (BFA 11, pp. 44–6; *Poems*, p. 89); closer to the style of the later poetry is the poem about a night's lodgings 'Die Nachtlager' / 'Bed for the night' (BFA 14, pp. 137–8; *Poems*, p. 181).

47. BFA 22.1, pp. 124–5. The word recurs in a note of 1951–2 (BFA 23, p. 191); *see also* the *Messingkauf* note on 'the audience member who not only observes but also actively participates' (BFA 22.2, p. 719).

48. Even something so fundamental to poetry as the use of symbols can be seen as a kind of *Verfremdungseffekt*: see Jürgen Link, 'Klassik als List, oder über die Schwierigkeiten des späten Brecht beim Schreiben der Wahrheit', in *Interpretationen. Gedichte von Bertolt Brecht*, ed. Jan Knopf (Stuttgart, 1995), pp. 161–76, (p. 169).

49. BFA 12, p. 110; *Poems*, p. 353.

50. BFA 12, p. 96; *Poems*, p. 347.

51. In a review of Sachs's poetry entitled 'Die Steine der Freiheit', *Merkur*, 138 (1959), pp. 770–5.

52. BFA 14, p. 388; *Poems*, p. 225.

53. BFA 14, p. 432; *Poems*, p. 331.

54. Silvia Schlenstedt brings out the significance of questions at the end of her essay on Brecht in *Wer schreibt, handelt. Strategien und Verfahren literarischer Arbeit vor und nach 1933*, ed. Silvia Schlenstedt (Berlin and Weimar, 1986), pp. 343–4; note also the section 'Fragen' in the earlier essay (as above), pp. 19–22.

55. BFA 12, p. 29; BFA 14, pp. 294–5; BFA 14, pp. 376–7; *Poems*, p. 252 and p. 270.

56. BFA 14, pp. 320–1; *Poems*, p. 264.

57. *See* the essay on this poem by Gunter Pakendorf, ' "Warum soll mein Name genannt werden?" Überlegungen zu Brechts Gedichten', in *Hundert Jahre Brecht* (as above), pp. 83–98.

58. BFA 12, p. 95; *Poems*, p. 303 and *see* p. 4.

59. BFA 12, pp. 97–8; *Poems*, p. 348.

60. BFA 22.1, p. 270 and pp. 271–2.

61. BFA 22.1, p. 272.

62. BFA 22.1, p. 273.

63. BFA 6, p. 9; *Plays* 5, p. 110.

64. BFA 22.1, p. 81.

65. BFA 6, p. 253; *Plays* 6, p. 84.

66. Loc.cit., pp. 87–8.

67. BFA 19, pp. 342–3.

68. BFA 21.1, pp. 90–6. On the latter, *see* Roland Barthes's essay on 'Brecht and Discourse', trans. Richard Howard, in Barthes, *The Rustle of Language* (California, 1989), pp. 212–22, especially 215–9.

69. BFA 19, pp. 338–41. *See also* the notes in BFA 19, pp. 662–5. Brecht evidently returned to these sketches in 1954, which could also suggest a link between the two periods alluded to in my title.

70. BFA 19, p. 338.

71. BFA 14, p. 339.

72. The motif of smoke links this poem to the Buckow elegy 'Der Rauch'/'The smoke'. *See* p. 198.

73. BFA 22.1, p. 286.

74. BFA 19, p. 663.

75. *See* BFA 5, p. 10; *Plays 5*, p. 7.

76. BFA 12, pp. 30–2; *Poems*, p. 253. Unlike some of the other 'Chronicles', this poem has not received a great deal of critical attention. Note Klaus-Detlef Müller's interpretation in *Geschichte im Gedicht, Texte und Interpretationen*, ed. Walter Hinck (Frankfurt am Main, 1979), pp. 214–21, and that by Franco Fortini in *Poesia Tedesca del Novecento*, ed. Anna Chiarloni and Ursula Isselstein (Turin, 1990), pp. 155–68.

77. BFA 23, p. 267.

78. BFA 14, p. 422.

79. *Poems*, p. 255.

80. Ibid.

81. This point is emphasised by Fortini, p. 162.

82. Fuhrmann, *Hollywood und Buckow* (p. 92) uses the filmic term 'Überblendung' for the superimposing of one image on another in the poem 'Gewohnheiten, noch immer'/'Still at it' (BFA 12, p. 307; *Poems*, p. 441).

83. This is the view strangely taken by Walter Hinck in his interpretation of the poem 'Legende von der Entstehung des Buches Taoteking', in *Interpretationen*, ed. Jan Knopf (as above), p. 141. Fortini, by contrast, notes the similarities between the two parts (p. 163).

84. BFA 12, p. 366.

85. Ibid.

86. I: 716–33 and also less directly in 734–9. The earliest evidence for Brecht's acquaintance with Lucretius (in 1933), as BFA 14, p. 548 suggests, is the line in BFA 14, p. 171, which renders Lucretius, I: 151. The later, much clearer echo (BFA 14, pp. 431–2), comes from Book III of *De rerum natura*; the note in BFA 14, p. 675 needs amending accordingly. See also the piece by Anthony Phelan in this volume.

87. This is the translation given in the Loeb Classical Library edition of Lucretius (Harvard, 1992), p. 61.

88. BFA 12, pp. 32–4; *Poems*, p. 314.

89. BFA 30, pp. 102–3.

90. BFA 29, pp. 109–10. For Brecht's later views on socialist realism, *see* BFA 23, p. 265 and pp. 286–8.

91. *Poems*, p. 316.

92. Walter Benjamin, 'Kommentare zu den Gedichten von Brecht', *Versuche über Brecht* (Frankfurt am Main, 1966), p. 81.

93. BFA 12, p. 33; compare *Poems*, p. 315.

94. *Poems*, p. 316. Not itself simply 'a deeply worldly argument' (Christiane Bohnert, *Brechts Lyrik im Kontext, Zyklen und Exil* (Königstein, 1982, p. 101); given the significance of the idea of 'cold' for Brecht, it clearly refers to the philosopher's isolated state: *see* Schlensted '*Lyrik im Gesamtplan der Produktion*' (as above), pp. 23–7, and Ursula Heukenkamp, 'Kälte bei Brecht 1945. Ein Marxist korrigiert sein Weltbild' in *Wechsel der Orte. Studien zum Wandel des literarischen Geschichtsbewußtseins*, ed. Irmela von der Lühe and Anita Runge (Göttingen, 1997) pp. 39–50.

95. BFA 12, p. 34; *Poems*, p. 316.

96. Brecht's 'misdirection' has been so successful that one commentator sees Lao-Tsû as doing the writing himself, and then, with 'a gesture of relaxed detachment', passing the text to the boy to hand over to the customs man: Franz Norbert Mennemeier, *Bertolt Brechts Lyrik* (Düsseldorf, 1982), p. 172.

97. BFA 12, p. 34; compare *Poems*, p. 316.

98. It should be noted that neither in Brecht's early prose version of this story, 'Die höflichen Chinesen' / 'The polite Chinese' of 1925 (BFA 19, p. 200), nor in the letter to Karl Kraus about the story (BFA 28, p. 369), possibly of summer 1933, is the boy mentioned at all.

99. Bohnert, *Brechts Lyrik im Kontext* does draw some attention to the boy's activities, but immediately after she finds 'the author's comment in the final strophe fully justified' (p. 101).

100. Hermand, 'Zwischen Tuismus und Tümlichkeit' (p. 32) talks about the poet in a similar vein, but sees the clearest fictional embodiment of such a figure as being the singer in *The Caucasian Chalk Circle*: 'This man is really one of those who tries to mediate appropriately between Party doctrine and the wisdom of ordinary people.' For my part, I would see Arkadi Tscheidse as a more unorthodox and independent figure than that.

101. BFA 12, pp. 310–11; *Poems*, p. 440.

102. That at least in the exile situation teachers and poets have much in common has been demonstrated, with reference to another of the 'Chronicles', by Tom Kuhn, 'Politische Vertreibung und poetische Verbannung in einigen Gedichten Bertolt Brechts', in *Deutschsprachige Exillyrik von 1933 bis zur Nachkriegszeit*, ed. Jörg Thunecke (Amsterdam and Atlanta, 1998), pp. 30–1.

103. The most prosaic version of his end suggests that he died in exile in the Peloponnese. I should like at this point to acknowledge the ready help of my Classics colleague at Wadham College, Stephen Heyworth.

104. Hinck, *Interpretationen*, ed. Jan Knopf (as above), p. 142.

105. BFA 14, p. 432; *Poems*, p. 331.

106. BFA 15, p. 60; *Poems*, p. 431.

107. Klaus Schuhmann, *Untersuchungen zur Lyrik Brechts* (Berlin and Weimar, 1973), pp. 122–3.

108. Philip Thomson, *The Poetry of Brecht* (London, 1989), pp. 164–5.

109. BFA 15, p. 262 and p. 263.

110. They are separated in the commentated edition, though the notes assure us that they are closely connected, *see* BFA 15, p. 468. Where translations of whole poems are not credited to a named translator, they are my own.

111. Schuhmann, *Untersuchungen zur Lyrik Brechts*, pp. 109–10.

112. BFA 15, p. 469.
113. Ibid.
114. The image of the state as a house goes back to Brecht's critical comments on the Soviet Union in 1937, *see* BFA 22.1, p. 304; there the 'builders' are evidently the leaders who, having built the 'state', decline to leave.
115. Peter Whitaker, *Brecht's Poetry. A critical study* (Oxford, 1985), pp. 198–9 agrees with Schuhmann's reading of Poem 1, but shares in part my view of Poem 2.
116. BFA 15, p. 259; *Poems*, p. 432.
117. BFA 27, p. 333.
118. BFA 15, p. 286.
119. Antony Tatlow, *The Mask of Evil* (Frankfurt am Main, 1977), p. 43 finds it to be about 'the pleasures of co-operation' and suggests that Brecht 'has cut the last line in two as if embarrassed by the banality of its regularity'.
120. Its date of composition is suggested as 'around 1954' (BFA 15, p. 489).
121. BFA 12, p. 308; *Poems*, p. 442.
122. BFA 27, p. 346.
123. Koopmann, 'Brechts "Buckower Elegien"', notes the echo of 'Heimkehr des Odysseus' (Odysseus' return home), but then foregrounds the personal element, making knowing references to the fact that the house seems to have been that lived in by Käthe Rülicke (pp. 115 and 118). On the question of symbolism in these poems, see Link, 'Klassik als List', *passim*. Though Link sees a larger political background to the *Elegies* than just the events of 17 June 1953 (p. 163), his general views on their context make a striking contrast to Koopmann's.
124. BFA 15, p. 262. The last line is echoed in a later poem, cf. BFA 15, p. 72.
125. BFA 15, p. 313; *Poems*, p. 442.
126. Brady, 'Der verfremdete Krieg', pp. 159–60.
127. BFA 12, p. 307. Several critics have attributed special status to this poem on the grounds that it was always intended to be the first poem in the *Buckow Elegies* group; the source for this view, which is presented with much more caution in BFA 15, p. 446, is an assertion by Käthe Rülicke-Weiler in 1986. It did, of course, stand first among the six printed in *Sinn und Form* in 1953.
128. *Poems*, p. 439.
129. I am grateful to my colleague Tony Phelan for this point.
130. Noted in *Bertolt Brechts Buckower Elegien, mit Kommentaren von Jan Knopf*, (Frankfurt am Main, 1986), p. 62.
131. Some commentators seem rather to wish to stress the realistic aspects of this poem, *see* Günter Häntzschel, 'Einfach kompliziert. Zu Brechts Lyrik', in *Hundert Jahre Brecht*, pp. 75–6.
132. In Jörg-Wilhelm Joost, Klaus-Detlef Müller and Michael Voges, *Bertolt Brecht. Epoche-Werk-Wirkung* (Munich, 1985), which discusses this poem alongside 'Paddling, talking', the hierarchy implied in the scene is brought out well, but it is suggested that the back-to-front image is accentuated by the fact that the boy is rowing backwards (presumably because we see the nun in the stern before we see the boy toiling in the bows) (pp. 330–1). The boat is indeed proceeding stern first, but in a normal manner; the nun is also facing backwards, the 'priest' is facing her.

133. Again recalling the word 'bequem' [comfortably] in 'Die Stimme des Oktobersturms' / 'The voice of the October storm' (BFA 15, p. 259; *Poems*, p. 432).

134. BFA 14, pp. 15–16.

135. The repeated word 'nebeneinander' [next to one another] which encapsulates that harmony carries a textual uncertainty with it. In his 1986 book on the *Buckow Elegies*, Knopf prints 'Neben einander' in line 3, and insists on that separation in his notes (see Knopf, *Bertolt Brechts Buckower Elegien*, pp. 123–4). In the new Brecht edition of 1988, Knopf the editor tells us that the second 'nebeneinander' (line 6) was, in all typescripts, 'neben einander' (BFA 12, p. 446). A misprint? A misreading? Either reading can be made to carry sense; the advantage of the variation is that we see togetherness and separateness expressed through identical letters.

136. BFA 23, pp. 416–17.

137. Whitaker, *Brecht's Poetry* (p. 263) quotes some of the piece in connection with 'Rudern, Gespräche' / 'Paddling, talking'. The old *Werkausgabe* (XX, p. 237) presents it under the somewhat misleading heading 'Zum 17. Juni 1953'.

138. Mennemeier, *Bertolt Brechts Lyrik* (p. 210), sees 'theory' and 'praxis' being unified here.

139. *Poems*, p. 443.

140. Knopf, *Bertolt Brechts Buckower Elegien*, p. 88.

141. BFA 19, p. 664.

142. Theodor W. Adorno and Max Horkheimer, *Dialectic of Enlightenment*, trans. John Cumming (London, 1997).

143. Ibid., p. 34.

144. Ibid., p. 35.

145. Ibid., p. 36.

146. Ibid., p. 34.

147. Knopf, *Bertolt Brechts Buckower Elegien*, p. 63.

148. *Dialectic of Enlightenment*, pp. 36–7.

149. BFA 27, p. 94; 29, p. 215; 29, p. 340.

150. BFA 15, p. 300; *Poems*, p. 451–2.

151. BFA 21.1, p. 139.

152. BFA 30, pp. 102–3.

153. BFA 23, p. 411.

9. 'May it seem to us our dearest . . .': Brecht's 'Children's Anthem'

1. Editors' Note: This is a roughly literal translation. The sentiment of the opening lines was originally 'Germany, to be esteemed above all things in the world', not 'Germany, superior to all other nations'. Hoffmann von Fallersleben wrote the song as a call for a united Germany, in the spirit of a liberal nationalism and against the autocratic rule of the many states and principalities which then made up the German 'cultural nation'. With the political unification of Germany in 1871 and above all in the context of twentieth-century right-wing nationalism, it took on a very different hue.

2. BFA 12, p. 303.

3. Compare the translation in *Poems*, p. 423.

4. Bertolt Brecht, *Gedichte. Ausgewählt von Autoren. Mit einem Geleitwort von Ernst Bloch* (Frankfurt am Main, 1975). 'Der Zweifler', BFA 14, pp. 376–7; *Poems*, pp. 270–1.

5. Peter Andert, 'Sehnsucht mit Brandgeruch', in *Wochenpost*, 34 (24 August), p. 15.

6. Friedrich Dieckmann, 'Deutsche Hymnen', in his *Glockenläuten und offene Fragen. Berichte und Diagnosen aus dem anderen Deutschland* (Frankfurt am Main, 1991), pp. 148–63 (pp. 156 ff).

7. Wilhelm Pieck, 'Notes on the German national anthem', in Heike Amos, *Auferstanden aus Ruinen . . . Die Nationalhymne der DDR 1949 bis 1990* (Berlin, 1997), pp. 191 ff.

8. Ernst Busch Archiv of the Akademie der Künste, Berlin. I am grateful to Peter Voigt for drawing this note to my attention.

9. Gerhard Seidel, *Bertolt Brecht – Arbeitsweise und Edition. Das literarische Werk als Prozeß* (Berlin, 1977), p. 185.

10. Bertolt Brecht Archiv (BBA), Berlin, 74/49. The typescript is reproduced in the catalogue to the Brecht exhibition of the Akademie der Künste: '. . . und mein Werk ist der Abgesang des Jahrtausends'. *1898 – Bertolt Brecht – 1998. 22 Versuche, eine Arbeit zu beschreiben*, compiled and annotated by Erdmut Wizisla (Berlin, 1998), p. 81.

11. BBA 1788/01.

12. *See* BFA 12, pp. 294 ff. None of the corrected proofs of the *Versuche*-Sonderheft *Carrar* (the textual basis) gives 'dieses'; in two cases 'dieses' was even corrected to 'dies'. In the *Hundert Gedichten/One Hundred Poems*, 'dieses' can be traced to an uncorrected printer's error which Elisabeth Hauptmann corrected in 1958 for the fifth edition.

13. Quoted from Eckart Spoo, 'Das Lied der Deutschen kommt ins Museum', *Frankfurter Rundschau*, 13 August 1991.

14. Friedrich Nietzsche, 'Götzen-Dämmerung', in: *Philosophie von Platon bis Nietzsche*, selected and introduced by Frank-Peter Hansen (Digitale Bibliothek vol.2) (Berlin: Directmedia, 1998), p. 68028.

15. Dieckmann (as note 6), p. 156.

16. Günter Hartung pointed out to me years ago that this relationship has scarcely been picked up in the secondary literature. One exception is the essay by Gerhard Müller, 'Lieder der Deutschen. Bemerkungen zum "Deutschlandlied", zur "Becher-Hymne" und zu Bertolt Brechts "Kinderhymne"', in *Der Sprachdienst* (Wiesbaden), 33 (1989), 5, pp. 137–45.

17. The former East German poet Wolf Biermann was thrown out of the country in 1976. This comment is on his *Seelengeld*, LP (EMI), 1986.

18. *Journal*, 10 November 1943. BFA 27, p. 181.

19. Dieckmann (note 6), p. 151.

20. *See* Dieckmann, op.cit.

21. Note from Peter Voigt, May 2000.

22. Quoted from Müller (note 16), p. 137.

23. Birgit Lermen, '"Daß ein gutes Deutschland blühe". Hoffmann von Fallerslebens "Lied der Deutschen" and Bertolt Brechts "Kinderhymne"', in

Gerd Langguth (ed.), *Autor, Macht, Staat. Literatur und Politik in Deutschland. Ein notwendiger Dialog* (Düsseldorf, 1994), pp. 86–109.

24. Iring Fetscher, 'Leidenschaftlich, aber kontrolliert', in Marcel Reich-Ranicki (ed.), *Frankfurter Anthologie*, vol.2, *Gedichte und Interpretationen* (Frankfurt am Main, 1977), pp. 160–2.

25. Biermann, op.cit.

26. *See* the questionnaire by the Hamburg weekly *Die Zeit*, 'Symbole für das neue Deutschland', 15 and 22 July 1990, and elsewhere.

27. *daß ein gutes deutschland blühe.* Single (GEMA), 1990.

28. Note by Ernst Busch on the back of a photograph (Ernst Busch Archiv, Akademie der Künste). Again, I am grateful to Peter Voigt for this tip.

29. Letter of 18 December 1999. In this letter, Schwaen also moderates the story attributed to him that Brecht had asked him to set the 'Children's Anthem' because 'he thought Eisler's song was too difficult for children' (Joachim Lucchesi and Ronald K. Schull, *Musik bei Brecht*, Berlin, 1988, p. 914). In fact, in a conversation with Wera and Klaus Küchenmeister, Brecht had 'regretted that his children's poems had been given settings which were too orchestral', and asked if Schwaen wouldn't like to write music for them. 'The remark was not particularly aimed at the "Children's Anthem".'

30. Heike Amos (*see* note 7), p. 167, quotes a ministerial official of the Federal Ministry of the Interior, according to whom the representatives of the two governments had indeed discussed the question, and agreed on the adoption of the FRG anthem. The files of the state treaties contain no record of this.

31. Amos, p. 169.

32. For the Heuss, *see* Spoo (note 12). Thanks for further information and advice are due to Günter Hartung, Helgard Rienäcker, Gerd Rienäcker, Kurt Schwaen and Helgrid Streidt.

10 'After Brecht': the reception of Brecht's poetry in English

1. The poems in this chapter are samples of a tradition of poetry inspired by Brecht. They are responses to and readings of Brecht which complement the work of critics and academics represented in this volume. Some of these poems – along with other poems by poets writing in English – are discussed by me here. The versions by Tom Paulin (along with that of Jamie McKendrick on p. 154) were commissioned for a special evening of celebrations for the Brecht centenary held in New College, Oxford in February 1998. The poem by Bernard O'Donoghue was also read on that evening. The poems are as follows: Derek Mahon, 'Brecht in Svendborg', *Selected Poems* (Oldcastle Heath, 2000); Tom Paulin, 'The Emigration of the Poets (after Brecht)', *The Wind Dog* (London, 1999), p. 71; Andy Croft, 'Desert Island Discs (after reading Brecht)', *Nowhere Special* (Hexham, 1996), p. 49; Bernard O'Donoghue, 'Neighbourhood Watch', *Gunpowder* (London, 1995), p. 45; Ken Smith, 'After Brecht', *the heart, the border* (Newcastle-upon-Tyne, 1990), p. 62; Michael Hamburger, 'Two Photographs', *Collected Poems 1991–1994* (London, 1995), pp. 175–6; Naomi Replansky, 'Housing Shortage', *The Dangerous World: New and Selected Poems* (Chicago, 1994), p. 14.

2. Günter Kunert, 'Versagen und Gedichte', 'Thirteen Poets Look at Brecht', in *Brecht Then and Now, Brecht Yearbook* 20, ed. John Willett (Madison, 1995), p. 32. References to this anthology will be given in brackets after references in the text.

3. Compare the now rather dated anthology of poems: Jürgen P. Wallmann (ed.), *Von den Nachgeborenen: Dichtungen auf Brecht* (Zürich, 1970). For a more recent response, see Jan Knopf's *Gelegentlich Poesie: Ein Essay über die Lyrik Bertolt Brechts* (Frankfurt am Main, 1996).

4. *See* my '"B. B.s spät gedenkend": Reading Brecht in the 1980s and 1990s', *Brecht 100<=>2000, Brecht Yearbook* 24, ed. John Rouse, Marc Silberman, Florian Vaßen (Wisconsin, 1999), pp. 111–29.

5. Compare Feinstein, *Loving Brecht* (London, 1992); John Fuegi, *The Life and Lies of Bertolt Brecht* (London, 1994).

6. Christopher Hampton, *Tales from Hollywood* (London, 1983) opened at the Donmar Warehouse in May 2001; *The Farewell: Brecht's last summer* [*Abschied*], directed by Jan Schütte, Germany 2000, was shown in the London film festival 2000 and went on general release in August 2001.

7. Darko Suvin, 'Marching Through the BB Mountain Range', in *Brecht Then and Now*, p.15. Compare Julian Preece, 'The Many Faces of B. B. in Fiction and Memoir: from Fleisser and Feuchtwanger to Canetti and Weiss', *Bertolt Brecht: Centenary Essays*, ed. Steve Giles and Rodney Livingstone, German Monitor 41 (Amsterdam – Atlanta GA, 1998), pp. 19–32.

8. Bertolt Brecht, *Poems 1913–1956*, ed. John Willett and Ralph Manheim with the cooperation of Erich Fried (London, 1976). The comments are printed on the back cover.

9. Compare John Willett, *Brecht in Context* (London, 1984), p. 23 and *Brecht Then and Now*, p. 3.

10. Tony Davies, 'Strength and clarity: Brecht, Auden and the "true, democratic style"', in *Brecht's Poetry of Political Exile*, ed. Ronald Speirs (Cambridge, 2000), p. 86.

11. Ibid.

12. Seamus Heaney, *The Haw Lantern* (London, 1987), from the sequence 'Clearances', pp. 24–32 (p. 28). Bernard O'Donoghue read this poem as part of his contribution to an evening of Brecht festivities in Oxford in 1998.

13. This is also the title of a book of essays: Heaney, *The Government of the Tongue* (London, 1988).

14. Adrian Henri, *AMERICA: A Confidential Report to Dr Bertolt Brecht on the Present Condition of the United States of America* (London, 1972).

15. Biermann's poem comes from his *Die Drahtharfe: Balladen, Gedichte, Lieder* (Berlin, 1965), p. 23.

16. Fredric Jameson, *Brecht and Method* (London, 1998), p. 1.

17. BFA 14, pp. 191–2; *Poems*, p. 218.

18. Jameson, p. 5; p. 6.

19. BFA 12, pp. 85–7; *Poems*, pp. 318–20.

20. *See* my 'Those born later read Brecht: The reception of Brecht's "An die Nachgeborenen"', in *Brecht's Poetry of Political Exile*, pp. 211–40.

21. Erich Fried discusses the Brecht poem 'An die Nachgeborenen', and includes his own poem 'Noch vor der Zeit', in Walter Hink (ed.), *Ausgewählte Gedichte Brechts*

mit Interpretationen (Frankfurt am Main, 2nd edition, 1979), pp. 94–7 (p. 94). The poem is not included in the volumes of Fried's poems which have been translated into English.

22. *Brecht Then and Now*, p. 38.

23. *See* Willett, *Brecht in Context*, pp. 21–72.

24. Ibid., p. 22.

25. Philip Thomson, *The Poetry of Brecht: Seven Studies* (Chapel Hill and London, 1989), p. 4. *See* Introduction for discussion of 'Empedocles' Shoe' and 'Visit to the banished poets'.

26. Brecht, 'Kurzer Bericht über 400 (vierhundert) junge Lyriker' / 'Short report on 400 young poets', BFA 21, p. 191.

27. Michael Hamburger, *After the Second Flood: Essays in Modern German Literature* (New York, 1986), p. 57.

28. Hugo Friedrich, *Die Struktur der modernen Lyrik: Von Baudelaire bis zur Gegenwart* (Hamburg, 1956).

29. Though there are other traditions, which have often been marginalised: from the proletarian tradition in English to Irish and Scottish verse. Compare Tom Paulin's introduction to his *Faber Book of Political Verse* (London, 1986). Paulin includes one poem by Brecht in the anthology: incidentally (curiously?) 'The God of War', p. 393.

30. Davies, p. 88.

31. Compare comments by Replansky, Croft and Henri, in *Brecht Then and Now*, p. 4, p. 12 and p. 37 respectively.

32. Walter Benjamin, *Understanding Brecht*, trans. Anna Bostock (London, 1973), p. 19; for the quotations *see Brecht Then and Now*, p. 33 and *After the Second Flood*, p. 59 respectively.

33. Ibid.

34. *See* Christopher Middleton's detailed examination of the syntactic patterning which he sees as characteristic of Brecht's verse, *Brecht Then and Now*, pp. 44–9. For close readings of some of these poems, *see* Ray Ockenden's piece in this volume.

35. *See* Introduction, p. 5.

36. Willett, *Brecht in Context*, p. 72 and Suvin, in *Brecht Then and Now*, p. 15.

37. Jameson, p. 2.

38. *See* illustration 9.

39. *The Dangerous World*, p. 25.

40. *Brecht Then and Now*, p. 4.

41. Ibid., p. 5.

42. *The Dangerous World*, p. 62.

43. Ibid., p. 6.

44. Ibid., p. 33.

45. Ibid., pp. 34–5.

46. Ibid., pp. 44–9.

47. Compare Middleton, *The Word Pavilion and Selected Poems* (Manchester, 2001) e.g. 'Ballad of the Putrefaction', pp. 299–301.

48. Michael Hamburger, *Collected Poems 1941–1994* (London, 1995). Compare the section 'Observations, Ironies, Unpleasantries', pp. 161–212, especially: 'The

Soul of Man under Capitalism', p.177, 'Two Photographs', p. 175, 'After a War', p. 182.

49. Ibid., p. 185.
50. BFA 12, p. 310; *Poems*, p. 440.
51. In very different mode one could also link Hamburger's fine 'Lines on Breughel's Icarus', *Collected Poems*, p. 31 with Brecht's 'Landscape with the fall of Icarus' (BFA 22.1, p. 270 and pp. 271–2), along with Auden's poem on the same theme and work by Hans Magnus Enzensberger, whom Hamburger has translated. Hamburger's little poem, 'Yew' (p. 354), uses the symbol of the tree reaching for the good soil in a way which causes anyone who knows Brecht to think of that poet's own use of the image of the tree especially in exile (see Introduction).
52. 'Verschollener Ruhm der Riesenstadt New York' (BFA 11, pp. 243–50), translated as 'Late lamented fame of the giant city of New York', *Poems*, pp. 167–74.
53. Compare *Brecht Then and Now*, p. 38.
54. Compare Mitchell, *Heart on the Left: Poems 1953–1984* (Newcastle upon Tyne, 1997), 'For my Son', p. 74 and 'Let me Tell You', p. 260.
55. Ibid., p. 258; p. 276; p. 277.
56. Ibid., pp. 48–50.
57. *Brecht Then and Now*, p. 40.
58. Ibid., p. 41.
59. *Poems*, p. 320.
60. Compare Tom Kuhn, '"Visit to a banished poet": Brecht's *Svendborg Poems* and the voices of exile', in *Brecht's Poetry of Political Exile*, pp. 47–65.
61. BFA 27, p. 80.
62. BFA 14, p. 388; *Poems*, p. 225.
63. BFA 12, pp. 35–6.
64. *Poems*, pp. 318–20.
65. The second part of the poem by Derek Mahon, 'Brecht in Svendborg' (*see* p. 223), begins at least as a translation of the poem before moving away from the original, but here I shall use the translation from *Poems* in my discussion.
66. Several of the songs in his *Ode to the Dodo* (London, 1981) seem to echo Brecht, e.g. 'Song of the Dead Soldier', p. 47, 'The Ass's Song', p. 9. The instructions in the preface to *New Numbers* (1969) have an ironic Brechtian cast – 'This book was written in order to change the world'; 'On the day of publication its price would buy 11 cut loaves, 3 yards of dripdry nylon, 5 rounds of M1 carbine ammunition, or a cheap critic' (p. 93). 'The Story of Two Gentlemen and the Gardener or How To Prove the Sun' (pp. 51–3) is a long narrative poem which takes up the gesture of the sage familiar from some of Brecht's exile poems. 'Criminal Incidents', p. 85, again echoes the spare, epigrammatic tone of the *Buckow Elegies*.
67. References in this text are to his *Selected Poems* (London, 1996), pp. 17–21.
68. *Poems*, p. 319.
69. *Selected Poems*, pp. 28–32.
70. BFA 12, p. 50.
71. Interestingly, Walter Benjamin reports that in his poem Brecht was thinking of an 'unhistorical epoch' which he saw as more likely than victory over Fascism.

Walter Benjamin, *Gesammelte Schriften*, ed. Rolf Tiedemann and Hermann Schweppenhäuser, vol.6 (Frankfurt am Main, 1985), p. 538.

72. Andy Croft, *Nowhere Special*, p. 52.

73. Ibid., p. 13.

74. Ibid., p. 12.

75. *Brecht Then and Now*, p. 14.

76. BFA 14, p. 439; *Poems*, pp. 304–5.

77. Derek Mahon, *Selected Poems* (London, 1993), pp. 130–1.

78. Craig Raine, 'Bad Language: Poetry, Swearing and Translation', *Thumbscrew*, 1 (Winter 1994–5), pp. 30–56 (p. 49).

79. BFA 12, p. 96; *Poems*, p. 304.

80. *Brecht Then and Now* p. 14.

SELECT BIBLIOGRAPHY

Brecht's poems and other writings

Berliner und Frankfurter Ausgabe der Werke, edited by Werner Hecht, Jan Knopf,
Werner Mittenzwei and Klaus-Detlef Müller (Berlin and Weimar: Aufbau, and
Frankfurt am Main: Suhrkamp, 1988–2000), abbreviated in references to BFA.
The poems are contained in volumes 11 to 15 inclusive.

Poems 1913–1956, edited by John Willett and Ralph Manheim, with the cooperation
of Erich Fried, the translations by many hands (London: Methuen, 1976).

Poems and Songs from the Plays, edited and mainly translated by John Willett
(London: Methuen, 1990).

Bad Time for Poetry, edited and introduced by John Willett (London: Methuen,
1995). Contains a selection from the above two volumes plus a couple of others.

War Primer, translated and edited by John Willett (London: Libris, 1998).

Manual of Piety/Die Hauspostille, translated by Eric Bentley, notes by Hugo Schmidt
(1966) (New York: Grove, 1991).

Selected Poems, translated and introduced by H. R. Hays (1947) (New York: Grove,
1959).

Both of these are parallel translations.

Collected Plays, vols 1–7, edited by John Willett, Ralph Manheim and Tom Kuhn
(London: Methuen, 1970–2001);

Brecht on Theatre, edited and translated by John Willett (London: Methuen, 1964).
Especially, in this context, for the essay 'On Rhymeless Verse with Irregular
Rhythms' (pp. 115–20).

There are further volumes of prose and of theoretical writings in the Methuen edition, and a further volume of Brecht's more personal poems and love poems, edited
by Michael Morley and Tom Kuhn, is in preparation.

A brief selection of books in English on Brecht and his poetry

Walter Benjamin, *Understanding Brecht* (London, 1973, 1983)

Keith A. Dickson, *Towards Utopia: A Study of Brecht* (Oxford: Clarendon, 1978)

Steve Giles and Rodney Livingstone (eds), *Bertolt Brecht: Centenary Essays*,
(Amsterdam and Atlanta GA, 1998)

Siegfried Mews (ed.), *A Bertolt Brecht Reference Companion* (Westport CT and
London, 1997)

Hanns Otto Münsterer, *The Young Brecht*, ed. Tom Kuhn and Karen Leeder

(London, 1992)

Ronald Speirs (ed.), *Brecht's Poetry of Political Exile* (Cambridge, 2000)

Peter Thomson and Glendyr Sacks (eds), *The Cambridge Companion to Brecht* (Cambridge, 1994)

Philip J. Thomson, *The Poetry of Bertolt Brecht: Seven Studies* (Chapel Hill, 1989)

Klaus Völker, *Bertolt Brecht: A Biography*, translated J. Nowell (London, 1979, originally Munich, 1976)

Peter Whitaker, *Brecht's Poetry: A Critical Study* (Oxford, 1985)

John Willett, *Brecht in Context* (London, 1984, revised 1998)

The *Brecht Yearbook* is a publication of the International Brecht Society (recent issues published by the University of Wisconsin Press) containing articles of a high standard on all aspects of Brecht's works; it is a good resource for those interested in recent scholarship.

For more specialist literature and criticism in German, please refer to the footnotes of the essays in this volume.

NOTES ON THE AUTHORS OF THE ESSAYS

Elizabeth Boa is Professor of German at the University of Nottingham. Her publications include *Kafka: Gender, Class, Race in the Letters and Fictions* (1996) and, with R. Palfreyman, *Heimat – A German Dream: Regional Loyalties and National Identity in German Culture 1890–1990* (2000), as well as numerous papers from a feminist standpoint on aspects of German literature from the eighteenth to twentieth centuries.

Hilda M. Brown is a Professor of German at Oxford University and Fellow and Tutor in German at St Hilda's College, Oxford. Her publications include *Leitmotiv and Drama: Wagner, Brecht and the Limits of 'Epic' Theatre* (1991); and *Heinrich von Kleist. The Ambiguity of Art and the Necessity of Form* (1998).

David Constantine has published half a dozen volumes of poetry, most recently *The Pelt of Wasps*, all with Bloodaxe books. He has translated works by Hölderlin, Goethe, Kleist and Brecht. He was Fellow in German at the Queen's College, Oxford from 1981 to 2000.

Tom Kuhn is a Lecturer at the University of Oxford and Fellow of St Hugh's College. He works primarily on Brecht and is co-editor, with John Willett, of the Methuen edition of Brecht's works. Recent work includes a translation of the play *Round Heads and Pointed Heads* (for volume 4 of the *Plays*), and a collection (with Steve Giles) of non-literary writings, *Brecht on Art and Politics*, due in 2002.

Karen Leeder is Lecturer in German at the University of Oxford and a Fellow and Tutor of New College, Oxford. She has published widely on modern German poetry, including Brecht, and has translated a number of young German poets. She is one of the general editors of the *Brecht Yearbook*.

David Midgley is a member of the German Department of Cambridge University and a Fellow of St John's College, Cambridge. He is the author of *Writing Weimar. Critical Realism in German Literature 1918–1933* (2000) and has published widely on the German literature of the twentieth century.

Hans-Harald Müller is Professor of German Literature at the University of Hamburg, and specialises in literature of the nineteenth and twentieth centuries; and the theory and history of literary scholarship.

Tom Kindt is part of a research team working on a project on narratology at the University of Hamburg.

Robert Habeck is a freelance writer and translator.

Ray Ockenden has been University Lecturer in German, Fellow of Wadham College and Lecturer at Balliol College since 1967; he has also taught at London University and in America. His lecturing and research interests range over eighteenth-century drama, nineteenth-century fiction and nineteenth- and twentieth-century poetry. He is currently working on Mörike, Storm and George.

Anthony Phelan is Lecturer in German at the University of Oxford and a Fellow and Tutor of Keble College. His publications include *The Weimar Dilemma: Intellectuals in the Weimar Republic* (1984) and *Rilke, 'Neue Gedichte': A Critical Guide* (1992).

Ronald Speirs is Professor of German at the University of Birmingham. He is the author of *Brecht's early plays* (1982) and *Bertolt Brecht* (1987), has edited *Brecht's Poetry of Political Exile* (2000) and has collaborated on the critical edition of the Brecht–Weill *Dreigroschenoper* (2000). He has also published on Kafka, Thomas Mann, Nietzsche and Max Weber.

Erdmut Wizisla has been the head of the Bertolt Brecht Archive in Berlin since 1993. Following on from a doctorate on Brecht and Walter Benjamin, he has published widely on aspects of German literature, including Brecht, Uwe Johnson and Heiner Müller, and was the curator of the exhibitions at the Berlin Akademie der Künste including the centenary exhibition 'Bertolt Brecht' (1998) and 'Helene Weigel' (2000).

INDEX OF BRECHT'S WORKS

All the poems quoted or mentioned in the book are included in this index, identified by their titles both in German and English or, where appropriate, by first lines.

D Poems

E Prose works

GENERAL INDEX